This comprehensive compendium of baking (more than 280 recipes!)
is from Dan Lepard, known for his much-loved food column in the
U.K.'s *Guardian* newspaper, and is the crossroad where cooking skills
and terrific recipes meet. It will guide you through the ins and outs of
baking, whether you are just starting out or already a solid hand in the
kitchen. Dan's impressive culinary expertise includes such delectable
treats as Bourbon Pecan Brownies; Swedish Almond Cake; Cardamom
Peanut Brittle; and Sugar-Crusted Pear Turnovers. From easy breads
to gluten-free essentials, from classic pavlovas to comforting pies, you
will discover new techniques and maybe even a trick or two to improve
the results as you bake, and you'll find that *Short & Sweet* is long on
baking inspiration.

SHORT & SWEET

SHORT & SWEET

THE BEST *of* HOME BAKING

DAN LEPARD

CHRONICLE BOOKS

SAN FRANCISCO

First published in the United States of America in 2013
by Chronicle Books LLC.

First published in Great Britain in 2011 by Fourth Estate,
an imprint of HaperCollins Publishers.

Text and photographs copyright © 2011 by Dan Lepard.
Some of the recipes included in this book have been previously
published in the *Guardian* or *Sainsbury's Magazine*.

Library of Congress Cataloging-in-Publication Data available.

ISBN 978-1-4521-1446-0

Manufactured in China

Typesetting by Happenstance Type-O-Rama

10 9 8 7 6 5 4 3 2 1

Chronicle Books LLC
680 Second Street
San Francisco, California 94107
www.chroniclebooks.com

To David, with respect and love

Acknowledgments

Louise Haines, always inspiring and remarkable. Antony Topping and David Whitehouse, for always wanting this book to be. Louise Tucker, Elizabeth Woabank, Ione Walder and everyone at 4th Estate. David Pearson, the brilliant designer, Cynthia Inions and Kim Morphew. Merope Mills, Bob Granleese, Matthew Fort, and *The Guardian*, the reason the baking column exists. Sarah Randell and Helena Lang at *Sainsbury's Magazine*, a big thank-you.

Contents

Preface

What I hope this book gives you are the blueprints for great baking at home, covering most sorts of cakes, pastries and breads that you'll want to make as well as adaptable base recipes that can turn seasonal ingredients and market finds into baking to be proud of.

With that in mind, I've combined my favorite recipes for this book alongside new ones, and added to them enough detail about kitchen science at work so that getting a really fine result will be much easier. You'll see the recipes still have simplicity and sweetness in their approach, but with the methods and techniques expanded just enough to be both extra clear and as distilled as possible.

In the past, friends and people I've cooked with have shared their baking ways and habits with me and, over time, those memories still guide me. Though I'm older now, and can also see how their personal tastes and biases got mixed with their strict advice, I still think after all that "you were right, that is a good way." So maybe in turn these recipes will become infused with your skills and style, and all the better for it.

So this book is where skills and recipes meet. Chapters begin with techniques and explanations that help to turn the mysteries of baking into something practical and achievable. Recipes follow with ideas and guides for, say, tweaking a recipe to get an entirely different result or ways to swap ingredients without knocking the legs from the science that binds it together.

If you're just starting out then this book will guide you, or if you're experienced in the kitchen it might introduce new ways and tricks with old favorites. Either way, I'm hoping this how-to manual will move your baking up a notch.

Bread

Bread

Being able to turn flour, water, salt and yeast into a loaf of bread is an alchemist's trick that has saved me from dashing to the supermarket so many times. Say I begin making dough at four in the afternoon. By seven that evening I can have great bread and in those three hours still have time to get on with the rest of my life. This is the joy in having some well-practiced recipes for homemade bread always at hand. So often, simple ingredients – like eggs, cheese or basic cuts of meat – can be stretched into a good meal by adding some homemade bread, and without having to leave the house. For me, the madness of driving to the shops and standing in lines is one part of life I'm happy to cut back on, and that makes room for something more enjoyable.

To make this happen, I've always got some basic items in my kitchen cupboard: a good white bread flour, some sort of bran-rich flour like whole-wheat or dark rye, a bag of gluten-free white flour mix and some semolina. Most of the time I use fine table salt, packets of dry instant yeast, a little oil in place of flour for kneading and that's about it. Then when we're done feasting, on slices of bread with a crisp, just-baked crust, a glass of wine and some grilled lamb, with soft oven-roasted tomatoes or onions, I think "This is the life. I honestly wouldn't swap it for the most exclusive restaurant meal in the world."

What I want you to get from this chapter is a sense of the ease with which good bread can be made. Exact measurements can appear daunting, but they help me share with you the steps it takes to make these breads. And when I'm in the kitchen, I follow my own recipes, to make sure they turn out just the way they did last time.

A gentle approach to dough making, hands-off rather than fiddling, will allow the flour and water to get on with the physical changes needed to turn from a sticky mass into a stretchy, resilient dough. Mix it, leave it for 10 minutes, knead very briefly at intervals, then leave it to rise. With practice you can add more water to the dough, and this will make the crumb extra soft. Forget about heavy-duty kneading, and knocking the dough back, that great bit of pointless punching that we were told was important but without a clear explanation why. These steps have changed my life and turned bread baking into this easy and relaxed part of my time in the kitchen.

Flour

Wheat flour is milled from a variety of wheats to produce a good soft crumb and crust. So that bag of simple-looking flour is actually a blend of different wheat grains, each adding a particular characteristic. Bread flour is not a "crisp" bread baking flour, nor a "lively" one that will have the yeast producing lots of bubbles. But it's the easiest flour to buy and for that reason I recommend it.

The bread flour we buy at the supermarket is roller-milled and ultra-fine, and this is great for making a smooth stretchy dough that's easy to shape and will withstand a few mistakes. It can tolerate overkneading, water that's a little too warm, a rising time that's longer than it should be. Also, bread made with it tends to keep soft and moist for a while compared to other white flours. But the downside is that the final texture of the loaf is not as delicate and tender as, say, French or Italian bread flour might produce, and the crust and crumb can be a little tough. As for "extra strong" flours, these have even more tolerance and are best when mixed with whole-wheat or rye, as you'll then get a more rounded and risen loaf.

Supermarket brand bread flour is very good, and spending more doesn't always mean you'll get better flour. To be honest, I go cheap when I buy bread flour, then spend a bit more on the other sorts like rye and whole-wheat. I buy organic flour when I can, but that's really my stab at being a responsible and health-conscious shopper rather than a step toward quality. I've baked tests with organic and nonorganic flour and couldn't see a difference, and if the grist (the selection of wheat varieties that are milled together to make the flour) used to make the organic flour isn't the best possible for bread making, then the nonorganic might be better.

The basic rule of thumb is: look at the label. If it says it's suitable for bread making, then it is. But don't worry too much about the protein content mentioned on the side of the bag. Also don't assume that you can't make good bread with a lower protein flour, while high protein flour will guarantee you a great loaf. In the past, bakers often couldn't pick and choose the flour they baked with, so they adapted recipes and techniques to suit what was available. Most supermarkets now offer a wider range of flours than ever before, and it may be helpful if you understand how they can affect your bread making.

For example, French or Italian bread-making flours will typically absorb less water than British bread flour, while (in that respect at least) Irish, Australian, American and Canadian flours will be similar to their British equivalent. I find that when I substitute a French or Italian white flour for bread flour, the amount of liquid in the recipe needs to be reduced by a fifth to a quarter (20 to 25 percent). If, after mixing everything together, the dough feels a little firm, you can always add a dash more water.

Changing your white flour to one from another country does produce a different result, even though the flour looks the same. Irish cream flour makes soda bread that tastes different, French flour produces a richer golden crust color, Italian flour is typically stretchier and bakes to a more brittle crispness. So if you get the chance, experiment with some of these flours and you'll change the texture and appearance of your bread.

Whole-wheat flour is milled from the whole grain minus the papery husk, and though it can be milled from any grain, the word typically refers to wheat flour. As bran and wheat germ make up part of the weight, the protein content is lower than in white flour, and you should minimize the mixing and rising of the dough, as it tends to be more fragile. Half a small vitamin C tablet, crushed between two spoons and added with the flour, will help to keep the dough stretchy, give it a more rounded shape as it bakes and reduce the crumbliness when you slice it. But even then, you may find that you prefer the taste and texture of a loaf that includes a proportion of bread flour, which will make the loaf lighter and softer, just as replacing a few tablespoons of the white flour in a white bread recipe with whole-wheat or another whole-grain flour will make the flavor much richer and more complex.

Rye flour is another essential in my kitchen. It adds a bright acidic tang to the bread and, like whole-wheat flour, makes a crumb that rises less but which has a reassuring density. I often add a spoonful each of whole wheat and rye to a white bread dough in place of some of the white flour, and this helps to give a flavor and crumb color reminiscent of bread from the best artisan bakeries.

"Granary" and malt-house flours are usually white flour blended with a little powdered malt: a simple sugar made by leaving grains to sprout, then drying and roasting them to a golden color. Though complex to mill, they're utterly natural and give a rich taste to the loaf. Do remember, if you're replacing the white flour in a recipe with malted flour, that the yeast will work even faster because of the malt, so keep the rising times shorter.

Spelt was a "prehistoric" grain, grown before the cultivation of common wheat, but the spelt flour you can buy today is more likely to be produced from a hybridized descendant of the original form. This improved its suitability for modern bread making, but removed many of the characteristics of the pure form. It has a sweet and nutty flavor and produces a moist, soft crumb. If you haven't baked with it before, start by replacing one-third of the bread flour in a bread recipe with spelt.

Yeast, salt and sugar

All the recipes here use instant yeast, the fine stuff that comes in a packet rather than the coarse granules they sell in small cans. I used to prefer using fresh yeast but it's not always the easiest thing to get hold of. If you want to use fresh yeast, then use the same volume (not weight!) as for dry: for example, one teaspoon of either.

Dry yeast needs moisture, and prefers just a little warmth at the outset, as it has a "coat" around the particles that needs to soften before the yeast can begin to ferment. But you don't need to add sugar to the yeast or the dough to get it working. The yeast in the packet is quite capable of using the starches and simple sugars in the flour to start fermentation, and while a tiny amount of sugar will speed the rising of the dough, too much will have the opposite effect. Better to add sweetly flavored bits like dried fruit or fragrant spices and oils to create the illusion of sweetness rather than lots of sugar if you want the dough to rise easily.

The temperature yeast needs is widely misunderstood. It's a hardy organism and once mixed into the dough, it will work slowly at 39°F (fridge temperature), then faster up to around 95°F (a very hot summer's day). So the higher the temperature, the shorter the time you leave the dough to rise for. I prefer to keep the dough cooler, and for a longer time, than other bakers might suggest: somewhere between 69 to 82°F. This way you get the best possible flavor and texture in a reasonable amount of time. In a warmer environment, the dough will be ready for baking sooner, but at the expense of flavor and quality.

You can make use of this time/temperature relationship. If you ever get interrupted and need to "pause" your bread making just after mixing the dough, you can place it in a covered bowl in the fridge and leave it, and the next day simply shape the dough and leave it to rise. Some people say they get an even better loaf this way.

When it comes to salt, I like sea salt flakes to scatter on the crust for a nice finish, and grind them finely to use in the dough if I have the time. Otherwise, I just use table salt in the mixture as it dissolves quickly. You can leave the salt out if you like, but you might find that the dough is a little sticky to shape, that it rises faster, and that the bread doesn't color as quickly. The bread might taste a little "flat," but serve it with something strongly flavored and you'll hardly know. Large amounts of salt can definitely knock the yeast out, but a fair amount — say 2 teaspoons for 4 cups flour — is fine and the yeast will ferment the dough quite happily.

Likewise with sugar, a small amount — up to say ¼ cup per 4 cups flour — will help the dough to rise more quickly and color in the oven, but more than that can stop the yeast from doing its job properly. Brown sugar and muscovado help to give a golden brown color to the crumb and are useful in making paler dough made with whole-wheat and white flour look more wholesome than it actually is, but again, you may find that higher amounts of sugar make the dough sweeter than you'd intended.

Liquids for the dough

Typically, water is used for making bread, but other liquids will give the dough different characteristics and flavors. The most common liquid is milk, which will help the crust color quickly and give the crumb a rich mellow flavor, but make it grow stale more quickly. Boiling and cooling milk, which destroys casein — a protein which would otherwise tighten the dough and reduce the amount it rises — is always a good idea. Replacing a fifth of the water or milk in a recipe with heavy cream will produce a crumb that is much softer and more delicate.

Soy milk is brilliant in baking, and has a slightly different effect than cow's milk. Typically loaves made with it rise higher and stay softer for longer after baking, so it's a magical ingredient. Replacing half the liquid with soy milk gives a good result.

Buttermilk, plain yogurt or whey is essential in soda bread as it aerates the dough by reacting with the baking soda, and it is also useful in yeasted bread baking if it replaces up to a quarter of the water, as it speeds up the maturation of the dough, giving a much softer crumb. Wine has a similar crumb-softening effect due to the acids it contains, and is best used to replace up to half the water. Fruit juices will soften the crumb too, but are intensely acidic and are best used when replacing one-third of the liquid. With all these acidic ingredients the dough will lose its strength much more quickly, so don't extend the rising time too much.

Beer will help to color the crumb and crust because of all the malt it contains, but the alcohol will slow the yeast down and make the rising time longer. If you replace only half the liquid with beer, this will keep this yeast-slowing action to a minimum.

One overlooked liquid you can add to a simple bread dough if you want to use it for buns or soft baps is beaten egg. Replacing ¼ cup of the liquid in a plain bread recipe with one beaten egg will make the crumb much softer and the crust darker and help to give a more rounded shape as the buns bake.

Butter, oil and lard

A little butter or oil added to a simple dough recipe helps the crumb take on a more delicate shortness, and helps the flavor taste richer and more complex. It also has the effect of stopping the crust from turning too brittle and hard during baking, so that the texture is a little more tender. The other thing it does is slightly slow the rise at first, so the dough appears sluggish. The fat coats the flour particles, slowing the yeast's access to the starches within the flour. One trick is to rub the butter or oil through only half the flour. That way, when the remaining flour, liquid and yeast are added, the rise will start more quickly, as the yeast will have flour particles untainted with fat to work on.

Another method is to work the softened butter or oil through the dough 10 minutes after it has first been mixed, using a vigorous beating action. This allows the yeast to start working before the fat is added, and this should keep the dough moving quickly. But only add up to 4 tablespoons of butter or oil if you want a good steady rise, as more than that can really slow the yeast, unless you leave the dough a long time. Brioche, for example, contains an extraordinary amount of butter, but as it's left overnight in the fridge the yeast gets a chance to multiply while the butter stays firm. Then at room temperature, the rising can really kick off.

Just a little on hard fats, like lard and cocoa butter. Though these two are rather hard on the arteries, they do make a loaf that is extra soft and moist. Cocoa butter needs to be melted first but can be added to the dough after mixing if beaten in well.

Kitchen temperature

You usually want to shape your dough as soon as bubbles start to appear within it. In summer that will happen quickly, as it's warm, but in winter it may seem to take forever. The recipes in this chapter were tested in "average" weather, but when the temperature gets hot and humid, or if a cold snap turns the kitchen ice cold, you need to either adjust the temperature of the ingredients and utensils, or alter the time you allow for the dough to rise.

In cold weather think about warming the mixing bowl with a splash of boiling water from the kettle, swirled around and wiped dry again. Increase the temperature of the water too and make it quite warm if the flour is very cold. In hot weather add an ice cube to the mixing liquid or, if you remember in time, place the bag of flour in the fridge overnight. The other way, as I've mentioned already, is to leave the dough to rise for longer after mixing if it's cold in the kitchen, or for less time if the weather is warm.

Making a loaf

Turning flour, yeast, salt and water into a loaf to be proud of only needs you to understand and follow a few basic steps. First, you need to mix the ingredients, and then give them one or more light kneads. Then, when the dough has had its first rise, and if possible a couple of folds, you need to shape it; and then, after a second rise, you need to bake it. But while none of these steps is technically difficult, your bread making will be greatly improved if you just take a few minutes to read and absorb the rest of this introduction.

The biggest change in modern home bread making is that we've noticed that dough simply left for 10 minutes after first mixing takes on a stretchy elastic quality as if it's been kneaded. And if we mix the dough with very little yeast and leave it for longer, or use the full amount of yeast and place it covered in the refrigerator overnight, then it turns out really well without any kneading.

Nothing has changed, it's still the same basic method that's been used for hundreds of years. It's just that we've noticed that it was "10 minutes" rather than "10 minutes of kneading" that was the key to good bread. I think secretly many home cooks and good bakers already knew this, as they rushed about with a dozen other jobs around the kitchen. Doris Grant, a remarkable home cook and author who, in the 1950s, was horrified by the state of factory bread in Britain, encouraged people to make their own bread. The simplicity of her method, she wrote, "is that it requires no kneading," and she believed it gave it a better flavor. By all means, if you get pleasure from kneading dough, carry on, but just remember that it's time rather than your pummelling effort that's creating most of the soft bounciness in your dough.

Don't worry about the dough being sticky at first; it should be, and this is natural when water is first added to dough and for about the first 30 minutes after. If you add more flour this will get rid of the stickiness but you'll end up with a heavy, poorly risen loaf with the flour out of proportion to the yeast and other ingredients. Remind yourself that sticky is a good thing for dough in its early stages.

Mixing and kneading the dough

You'll find this method referred to in most of the recipes in this chapter, and there's nothing more complicated to learn here than to have confidence in your bread making. This is an important technique for you to become familiar with.

First of all, mix the basic ingredients together so they form a round shaggy mass, making sure to dig right down to the bottom of the bowl to check no dry flour is lurking there. Scrape any bits of dough from your hands, cover the bowl with a clean tea towel and leave it for at least 10 minutes – or a little more if you're fitting this in between other tasks, as this gives the flour time to fully absorb the moisture.

Then rub a little oil over a 12-inch area of work surface, and a little more over your hands, just to stop the dough from sticking. Any light and fairly neutral oil such as sunflower will do; it doesn't have to be extra virgin olive oil. Turn the bowl over on the oiled surface and ease the dough out onto it without too much pulling and teasing (and if you quickly scrape down the inside of the bowl at this point and lightly oil it, you'll avoid the dough sticking to it later).

Take the edge of the dough farthest away from you with one hand and fold it toward you, to meet the edge of the dough nearest to you. Then with the heel of the other hand, push down lightly onto and into the dough and very slightly push and stretch the dough away from you by about 2 to 4 inches. Make your movements gentle, don't pound or tear the dough. Give the dough a clockwise quarter-turn, and once again fold the dough toward you, then push it gently away; and repeat this "turn, fold, and stretch" no more than eight to ten times. Then return the dough to the bowl, leave it to rest, and repeat this simple kneading probably twice more at intervals, depending on the exact instructions given in each recipe.

The trick is to do this as quickly as possible, lightly and evenly, without punishing the dough, repeating the same movements on each quarter-turn. Resist the temptation to add more flour – usually the dough will seem sticky or "wet" when you start kneading, but this will disappear in time. You'll see even after the first short knead that your dough has already become smoother. Then leave the dough to rise as suggested in the recipe.

Leaving the dough for its first rise before shaping

Once the dough has been mixed and lightly kneaded it needs to sit at room temperature (not too warm: 70 to 82°F), until the yeast has started to aerate the dough, and ideally until the dough has risen in volume by 50 percent, before you shape it. A long time ago we used to think that the strong yeasty odor caused by leaving the dough to rise then punching it down was a good thing, but today we look for the clean sweet aroma of the flour or a more complex wine-like acidity from a sourdough. And this change is more in keeping with modern artisan bakers in the rest of Europe and around the world, who typically try to hold on to the aeration in the dough, rather than punch the life out of it. Be gentle with the dough and you'll get the best loaf.

The blanket fold

During this first rise, one other trick that will transform your home bread making is actually an old technique first used by bakers probably in the early 1800s. If dough is made with more water so that it "flows" slightly when placed on the work surface, it can be made to sit more upright by giving it a series of "blanket" folds at intervals as the dough rises. This folding stretches and elongates the emerging air bubbles in the dough, creating a much more puffy interior and giving the dough a jelly-like wobble.

Simply pat the dough out gently into a rectangle, stretching it outward a little. Then fold one side inward, and over the central third, and then the other side inward as well, so that you are left with a tidy piece of dough, one-third its original width. It's that simple, and if you do it twice more at equally spaced intervals while the dough rises before it is shaped, you'll end up with a much lighter and more rounded loaf of bread after baking. Once you become more confident — and if the texture of the dough will permit — you can try a "double" blanket fold, bringing the sides in as described above and then giving the dough a clockwise quarter-turn before once again folding the outer thirds inward, to form a neat package.

Shaping

When the dough has completed its first rise, you can shape it. Don't leave the dough too long after you reach this point, unless the dough is kept at a cool temperature.

The way to see where you're up to is to take a blade, or small, very sharp knife, and make a quick clean cut into the dough. If you see lots of small holes, then shape the dough. But if you don't, leave the dough another 45 minutes before checking again. The main cause of heavy bread is dough that hasn't risen enough at this stage. It's vitally important to let the dough aerate slightly before you shape it, if you want the lightest possible loaf.

In most of the loaf recipes in this chapter, I've either suggested using a loaf pan, or given a simple instruction such as patting the dough out and rolling it up tightly before baking it "freestyle," but once again, as you grow in confidence you can experiment with more complicated shapes. I've also said to bake your loaves seam-side down, to get a more rounded and regular shape, but you can try the opposite, which will give you a much more random and rugged-looking tear along the top of your loaf.

Knowing when to bake the loaf

It's simply a matter of 50/50: let your dough rise in volume by half before you shape it, then after shaping, let it rise in volume by half again, before it goes into the oven. As soon as dough reaches that point, it's ready for baking. Dough should go into the oven while it's young, and still has some spring to it. You can leave it longer, sometimes until the dough has doubled in size, but then you risk pushing it too far, and the result will actually be a smaller, heavy loaf, with a yeasty taste and crumbly texture.

Press your finger gently into the dough and it should still bounce back a little and feel puffy, but if the dent stays, then it's risen too much. In that case, quickly bake it in the hottest oven you can for the first 20 minutes before dropping the heat until the bread is fully baked. But remember next time to bake the loaf earlier.

Before baking, it's usually a good idea to make a cut down the top of the loaf. There's a practical reason for this. Getting the dough into the oven while it still has some oomph means that it will spring upward as it bakes. But as the initial crust will form very quickly in the oven's heat, within 5 minutes and before the bulk of the loaf has really started rising, the cold dough underneath will be trapped and forced to find another way to burst out: usually around the rim of the pan, or around the base near the baking sheet. By slashing the top of the dough, an escape route forms, and the dough is more likely to break through at that point, rather than at the side – giving your loaf an extravagant tear down the center that always impresses the people who see it.

Adding steam

Another reason your loaf can burst out around the bottom or side, especially if the crust has a pale, almost dusty look to it, is if your oven is too dry and needs to be steamier. Heat the oven following the recipe instructions, with a small metal roasting pan on the lowest shelf, then put the loaf on a higher shelf before carefully pouring boiling water into the pan, making sure there is enough space around the loaf for the steam to circulate.

One home baker gave me a variation on this method to use if you are baking with the type of fan-assisted oven where the fan stops completely when you turn the oven off. Follow the steps given above, but once the loaf is in and you've poured boiling water into the pan, turn the oven off. Leave it for 10 minutes then, without opening the door, turn the oven back on again to at least 390°F (fan-assisted) and continue to bake until the crust is to your liking. But with either of these two techniques, do remember that when you open the oven door, there may be a rush of hot steamy air, so let this vent before you peer in too closely.

Crust, crumb and color:
how do I know if my loaf is done?

Forget all the bottom tapping, all loaves sound slightly hollow when first baked. There are three Cs to the perfectly baked loaf — crumb, crust and color — and each is modified in different ways. As a rough guide, the crumb inside a 1-pound loaf baked at 425°F will be set after 25 minutes (40 minutes for a 1¾-pound loaf).

At that point, the crust will still be very soft. The trick to getting a thicker crust is simple: adjust the baking time and temperature. For a thick firm crust, get the oven as hot as possible, bake the loaf for 20 minutes at this heat, then reduce the temperature to about 400°F and bake for about 45 minutes for a 1-pound loaf (70 minutes for a 1¾-pound loaf). This will dry the loaf out a bit, but produce a very firm crust. Some flours are better at producing crispy bread. Both Italian "00" flour and French white flour are good for crispness.

Once you've got the crust and crumb the way you want them, adjust the color by altering the oven temperature as described after the first 20 minutes. Keep it very hot if you want a dark, almost black loaf, or lower it for a golden crust.

Once your loaf is baked to perfection, take it out of the oven, turn it out of its pan (or take it off the baking sheet) and leave it to cool completely on a wire rack so that air can circulate around it. If you want a slightly softer crust, you can cover the loaf with a clean dry tea towel while it cools, and if you want to freeze it do so as soon as the loaf is completely cold.

Easy white bread

Don't imagine a bread machine is a must-have for stress-free baking. With a little effort and barely any kneading, you can conjure up an impressive crusty white loaf. If flavors are your thing, then toss in up to 7 ounces of cubed Cheddar, or a little crispy bacon or some well-drained pitted olives and a handful of chopped herbs and you'll have one of those "wow" breads you see in the best bakeries. If you're going to be at home for 3 or 4 hours, this recipe will take barely 20 minutes of your time, without you ever breaking a sweat.

3 cups bread flour, plus extra
  for shaping and dusting
1 teaspoon instant yeast

1 teaspoon fine salt
1¼ cups warm water
oil for kneading

Put the flour, yeast and salt in a bowl, pour in the warm water and stir everything together into a sticky shaggy mass. Scrape the dough from your hands, cover the bowl with a cloth and leave for 10 minutes. Lightly oil a 12-inch area of the work surface and your hands, and knead the dough (see pages 13 to 14), repeating twice more at 10-minute intervals. Return the dough to the bowl and leave it for 45 minutes. Wipe the work surface, dust it with flour then pat the dough into an oval. Roll it up tightly, give each end a pinch to keep it neat. Place the dough seam-side down on a floured baking sheet, cover with a cloth and leave until the dough has increased in size by a half – about 45 minutes. Heat the oven to 425°F. Flour the top of the dough, cut a slash down the middle and bake for 35 to 40 minutes.

Easy white rolls

For rolls, just divide the dough in pieces: 1 to 1¼ cups for dinner rolls; ⅓ to ¾ cup for hamburger buns or sandwich rolls. For round rolls or buns, simply shape the pieces into balls and place them seam-side down on a baking sheet lined with parchment paper; for longer, "finger" rolls, shape into balls, leave covered for 15 minutes for the dough to relax, then roll into a longer shape before placing on the paper-lined baking sheet.

Let them increase in size by half, and either lightly sift flour over the tops, or brush with beaten egg white and sprinkle with seeds (for example, linseed, sesame or poppy). Heat the oven with a pan of boiling water on the lowest shelf. For soft rolls, bake at 450°F for 15 to 20 minutes (dinner rolls) and 20 to 25 minutes (buns and sandwich rolls), then leave to cool on the baking sheet. For crusty rolls, use a longer time in a cooler oven, about 25 to 30 minutes (dinner rolls) and 35 to 40 minutes (buns and sandwich rolls) at 400°F.

Flash loaf

How do you make crusty bread in around two hours from mixing to cooling without it tasting a bit blah? With lots of yeast, some grated potato, whole-wheat flour and a dash of vinegar, that's how. Timing is essential, so stay with it.

This recipe is packed with tricks to mimic the desirable results a longer method would give. Vinegar (it doesn't have to be malt, though its rich nutty flavor suits this recipe) helps to soften the protein in the flour and very slightly mimics the effects that long fermentation would achieve. The acidity also helps the whole-wheat flour give the crumb a more complex flavor and color. Potato helps to counteract the drying effect you get when using a large quantity of yeast in a relatively small amount of flour. And the butter helps keep the crumb moist and soft, and blends the flavors together.

3 cups bread flour, plus
    extra for shaping and dusting
1 cup whole-wheat or rye flour
2 teaspoons fine salt
2 tablespoons butter, lard or fat
    from your Sunday roast
about 1 cup very warm water,
    86 to 100°F

1 large potato (about 6 ounces),
    washed, unpeeled and grated
2 tablespoons malt vinegar
1 tablespoon plus 2 teaspoons
    instant yeast
oil for kneading

Put the flours and salt in a large mixing bowl and rub in the butter. In another bowl stir the warm water, potato, vinegar and yeast together, then pour this

in with the flour. Mix it to a soft sticky dough, adding more water if the dough seems dry; then leave for 10 minutes. Lightly oil a 12-inch area of the work surface and your hands, and knead the dough (see pages 13 to 14), repeating once more after 10 minutes then resting the dough for 10 minutes more. Shape into a ball, place it seam-side down on a floured baking sheet, cover with a cloth and leave until risen in size by half – maybe as little as 20 to 30 minutes. Heat the oven to 425°F, place a small metal roasting pan on the lowest shelf and partially fill it with boiling water. Dust the loaf with flour, cut a deep cross in the center and bake on the shelf above for 40 to 50 minutes.

White farmhouse loaf

For everyday use, there's not much that can beat a well-made farmhouse loaf. The process here uses what old bakers used to call the half-sponge method, an easy way to improve the flavor and texture of a basic bread recipe. It was the way bread used to be made before additives, and motor cars, were heard of. Home cooks long before me have enthused about the great flavor you get from dough left to mature for hours rather than minutes, and this recipe allows half the flour to get the benefit of a long slow rise without tying you to the kitchen. So when you finally stir this mixture into the dough, it rises quickly and produces a loaf that keeps well, with a delicate moist texture.

FOR THE SPONGE	FOR THE DOUGH
1 cup warm water	1⅓ cups bread flour, plus extra
1 teaspoon instant yeast	for shaping and dusting
1⅓ cups bread flour	1 teaspoon fine salt
	2 tablespoons unsalted butter or lard,
	plus extra for greasing the pan
	oil for kneading

Make the sponge by pouring the warm water into a mixing bowl, stirring in the yeast and adding the 1⅓ cups flour. Stir it up well with a wooden spoon, cover the bowl and leave for 2 to 4 hours, or even overnight (so you can mix this in the morning before work and continue your bread making in the evening, or late on a Friday night when the house is quiet, for the next morning).

When you're ready to make the dough, put the other 1⅓ cups flour into a bowl, add the salt and rub the butter through until it vanishes, so there are no little lumps floating around. Pour in the yeast batter, mix the whole thing up into a big sticky clump of dough, then scrape the bits off your fingers. Cover the bowl with a tea towel and leave for 10 minutes. Knead the dough (see pages 13 to 14), repeating after 15 and 30 minutes, then cover and leave for another 30 minutes.

Butter and flour a loaf pan, about 7½ inches long. Lightly flour the work surface, roll the dough into a rectangle ¾ inch thick that measures (from left to right) slightly less than the length of the loaf pan; roll it up tightly and place seam-side down in the pan. Cover with a tea towel and leave until increased in size by half (1 to 1½ hours).

Heat the oven to at least 425°F, though if you can get it 75°F hotter, even better. Add some steam if you like (see page 16), dust flour over the dough with a small fine sieve or tea-strainer, quickly slash the loaf down the center about ½ inch deep with a sharp blade and bake for 20 minutes. Reduce the heat to 400°F and bake for another 20 to 25 minutes until the crust is the color you like.

FREEZING LOAVES

Whenever I don't have time to bake every day, I make two loaves by doubling the quantity of dough, and as soon as my loaves are completely cooled after baking, I simply cut them in half, pop them into ziplock bags and freeze them until needed. They defrost in 1 to 2 hours at room temperature and need no further baking, though you can give them 12 to 15 minutes in a hot oven once defrosted, if you want an extra crisp crust.

Sour cream sandwich bread

For those days when all you want is a high-risen loaf, with a beautifully soft tender crumb and a crisp golden crust, which toasts like a dream. Try to find a traditional loaf pan with crisp, sharp corners, for that almost industrial look.

¾ cup cold water
½ cup boiling water
½ cup sour cream, cold from
   the fridge
2 teaspoons fine salt
2 teaspoons super-fine sugar

2½ teaspoons instant yeast
4⅓ cups bread flour, plus
   extra for dusting
oil for kneading and butter
   for the pan

Mix the cold and boiling water together in a large bowl, stir in the sour cream, salt, sugar and yeast, then mix in the flour until it forms a rough ball. Cover and leave it for 10 minutes, then lightly oil your hands and a 12-inch area of the work surface. Knead the dough (see pages 13 to 14), repeating this twice more at 10-minute intervals, then return the dough to the bowl and leave it for an hour. Butter the base and sides of a loaf pan, about 7½ inches long, and line the base with parchment paper. Pat the dough out until about ¾ inch thick, roll it up tightly like a scroll and squish it seam-side down into the pan. Leave to rise until increased in size by half to three-quarters. Heat the oven to 400°F, dust the top of the loaf with flour and bake for about 45 minutes.

THAT TENDER CRUST

The fat content in the cream is what gives the crust its tenderness, so don't be tempted by any low-fat substitutes. But make sure you give this loaf plenty of headroom when you come to bake it, as it has more "oven spring" than most.

Whole milk and clotted cream loaf

The perfect loaf to make those delicate oblong apéritif sandwiches, the sort you see in Paris carefully wrapped in wax paper to keep the bread soft and moist, with the crusts banished so a sliver of filling peeks out. Or a bread pudding groggy with Armagnac and prunes. Or just toasted in the morning with a little dark and bittersweet marmalade.

The proportions are virtually the same as the white farmhouse loaf, but the method and ingredients are slightly different. Boil the milk and let it cool before using it as this will make the crumb extra light and fluffy.

FOR THE SPONGE
1 cup whole milk
¼ cup clotted cream
1 teaspoon instant yeast
1⅓ cups bread flour

FOR THE DOUGH
1 tablespoon molasses
1½ cups bread flour, plus
   extra for shaping and dusting
1 teaspoon fine salt
a little butter for greasing the
   pan, and oil for kneading

To make the sponge, by pour the milk and cream into a saucepan, bring to a boil, then remove from the heat. Pour into a jug and leave until tepid. A skin will form on the surface but don't worry about it. Top off with warm water to make 1¼ cups. Pour into a bowl and add the yeast and the 1⅓ cups flour, stir it together, cover the bowl and leave for 2 to 4 hours until the mixture froths up and collapses a little in the center.

To make the dough, add the molasses to the sponge and beat well. Add the 1½ cups flour and the salt and mix to a sticky dough. Knead the dough (see pages 13 to 14), repeating after 15 and 30 minutes, then cover and leave for another 30 minutes. Butter and flour a loaf pan, about 7½ inches long. Lightly flour the work surface, roll the dough out into a rectangle, roll up tightly and place seam-side down in the pan. Cover with a tea towel and leave until increased in size by half.

Heat the oven to at least 425°F, though if you can get it 75°F hotter, even better. Steam the oven if you like (see page 16), dust flour over the dough with a small fine sieve or tea-strainer, slash the loaf down the middle with a sharp blade and bake for 20 minutes. Reduce the heat to 400°F and bake for another 20 to 25 minutes until the crust is the color you like.

Double cheese and chive loaf

This recipe also uses the half-sponge method, with the flavor coming from fresh chives, strong Cheddar (but economize a little, no need for the vintage stuff here) and freshly grated Parmesan. Once again, you can mix the sponge in the morning before work, or late on a Friday night when the house is quiet, and continue your bread making when you come home or on a Saturday morning.

FOR THE SPONGE
1 cup warm water
1 teaspoon instant yeast
1⅓ cups bread flour

FOR THE DOUGH
1⅓ cups bread flour, plus
    extra for shaping and dusting
1 teaspoon fine salt
2 tablespoons unsalted butter,
    plus extra for greasing the pan
⅓ cup grated Parmesan
8 ounces Cheddar, cut into
    ½-inch dice
a small bunch of fresh chives,
    snipped into ½-inch lengths
oil for kneading

To make the sponge, pour the warm water into a mixing bowl, stir in the yeast and add the 1⅓ cups flour. Stir it together, cover the bowl and leave for 2 to 4 hours, or even overnight.

To make the dough, put the 1⅓ cups flour into a bowl, add the salt and rub the butter through until it vanishes, so there are no little lumps floating around. Add the Parmesan, Cheddar and chives. Pour in the yeast batter, mix the whole lot up into a big sticky clump of dough, then scrape the bits off your fingers. Cover the bowl with a tea towel and leave for 10 minutes. Knead the dough (see pages 13 to 14), repeating after 15 and 30 minutes, then cover and leave for another 30 minutes.

Butter and flour a loaf pan, about 7½ inches long. Lightly flour the work surface, roll the dough into a rectangle ¾ inch thick that measures (from left to right) slightly less than the length of the pan; roll it up tightly and place seam-side down in the pan. Cover with a tea towel and leave until increased in size by half.

Heat the oven to at least 425°F, though if you can get it 75°F hotter even better. Steam the oven if you like (see page 16), dust flour over the dough with a small fine sieve or tea-strainer, slash the loaf down the center about ½ inch deep with a sharp blade or sharp serrated knife, and bake for 20 minutes. Reduce the heat to 400°F and bake for another 20 to 25 minutes until the crust is the color you like.

Gluten-free white bread

Making this loaf is rather simple, and less work than your typical wheat bread. It has a crisp golden crust and a moist crumb, which slices without crumbling. Getting a gluten-free loaf to look and taste like one made from wheat involves an alchemist's kit of ingredients. The newest helper is psyllium husk, a fiber that acts a little like gluten and helps to give the dough a stretchy resilient quality. It's a bit pricey but keeps well in the cupboard if you buy a big tub. Look for a supplier on the Internet, or try your local health food store.

4 teaspoons soy flour
¼ cup potato starch
2½ cups cornstarch
2 tablespoons psyllium
   husk powder
2 teaspoons instant yeast
1 teaspoon non-iodized
   fine salt

1 tablespoon super-fine sugar
2 teaspoons vinegar
1 tablespoon sunflower oil, plus
   extra for shaping and brushing
2 tablespoons low-fat plain yogurt
1⅓ cups warm water
2 tablespoons milk

Put the dry ingredients into a bowl, whisk the liquids separately then mix everything really well for about a minute into a soft dough. Leave for an hour, then lightly oil the work surface and your hands. Either line a loaf pan, 7½ inches long or similar, with parchment paper, shape the dough into a baton and place it in the pan, seam-side down, or line a baking sheet with parchment paper and shape the dough into rolls, placing them about 1½ inches apart. Leave, covered, for another hour and a half or until almost doubled in size. Gluten-free dough doesn't have any "oven spring," so can be left to bulk up more than a conventional white loaf, and baking in a very hot oven helps to create a better result.

Heat the oven to 475°F, brush the top of the dough with oil and bake for 25 minutes (for rolls) or 50 minutes (for a large pan loaf). Remove from the oven and from the loaf pan (or baking sheet, for rolls) and leave to cool on a wire rack, covered with a cloth to retain softness.

CORNSTARCH, CORN FLOUR OR CORNMEAL?

What is known as "cornstarch" in the United States is a white, very finely milled product, sometimes called "corn flour" in other countries. It's cheap, and is more often used as a thickening agent in sauces and liquids, though it has its uses in baking. However, the flour made by milling corn — which would be called cornmeal, or polenta — is also sometimes called "corn flour" in other places. It is usually yellow, and grittier in appearance and a lot more expensive than white cornstarch. And, just to take this back to the recipe, it's the white tasteless cornstarch powder that you want here, almost because it is white and tasteless, as its neutral flavor will help give the bread a plain "white bread" flavor. Also, the cornstarch will bind better than the grittier texture of coarser ground corn. By all means add a little of the yellow stuff if you like, but if you use it in place of the starch, the result will be crumbly after baking and lack that white wheat bread texture.

Whole-wheat

The best time to tempt someone who's wary about whole-wheat bread is the instant the loaf is cool after baking, while the crumb is still fresh, moist and slightly sweet from all the bran it contains. Slice it that very moment, spread a little salted butter on it, and simply serve. Every time I've done this I've won doubters over, because no matter what finesse a working baker can add to a white loaf, a whole-wheat loaf is almost without exception better for being baked at home.

If you're not regularly eating whole-wheat bread, made with flour milled from 100 percent of the grain, then you need to start right away. Increasing the amount of whole-grain cereal you eat means that more of the phytochemicals — nutrients that protect cells from age-related DNA damage — found in the bran that encloses the seed will be in your diet.

Getting whole-wheat bread light and easy to slice is tricky. White flour is only made from the parts of the grain that are rich in gluten. Whole-wheat flour also contains a large proportion of bran and the outer layers of the grain, and this means that the gluten-rich part is a smaller portion compared to white flour. So dough made with whole-wheat flour acts as if it has less stretch and resilience and this can make a loaf feel heavy and crumbly once baked. The bran is also very good at soaking up moisture and this will make the crumb feel slightly sticky.

So there are a few tricks that will make sure the dough still has enough spring to rise well during baking, and hold together better when cold and sliced. Avoid the dough rising too much, and don't leave it too late to get it into the oven. One reliable helper is half a small plain vitamin C tablet, crushed and mixed in with the flour. This will make sure that the whole-wheat dough becomes as stretchy and resilient as possible, and it will help to make your bread lighter and easier to slice. It's one of the few additives allowed in organic baking by the strict U.K. Soil Association, and even the protective French baking laws approve of a little being added to help the bread.

I've taken a broad-brush approach to whole-wheat here, with most of these recipes containing just a proportion of whole-wheat flour, often backed up with oats, seeds or sprouted grains, to encourage you to introduce this ingredient into your diet, and because the inclusion of bread flour should ensure success. But if you still find you're having problems with lightness and crumb quality, you can always experiment with substituting one of the "extra strong" white flours now on the market for some of the white bread flour in the recipe.

Whole-wheat loaf

The idea behind this recipe was to make it quick and easy, rather than the definitive whole-wheat loaf, so do tweak it once you're used to making it. But bear in mind that whole-wheat contains far less gluten, as a percentage of the flour weight, than white flour due to the presence of bran, wheat germ, etc., so don't go too far in reducing the yeast or lengthening the rise.

1¼ cups warm water
2 teaspoons instant yeast
1 tablespoon brown sugar,
    any kind
half a 500-mg plain vitamin C
    tablet, crushed to a powder

3½ cups whole-wheat flour,
    plus extra for shaping and
    dusting
1 teaspoon fine sea salt
4 tablespoons unsalted butter,
    melted, plus extra for the pan
oil for kneading

Pour the warm water into a mixing bowl, then add the yeast and sugar. Stir well then add the vitamin C, flour and salt and stir well. Pour in the melted butter and mix the whole lot together to work the fat through the dough. Cover the bowl with a cloth and leave for 10 minutes.

Knead the dough (see pages 13 to 14), repeating after 15 and 30 minutes, then cover and leave for 15 minutes. Butter and flour a loaf pan, about 7½ inches long. Lightly flour the work surface, roll the dough into a rectangle, roll up tightly and place seam-side down in the pan. Cover with a tea towel and leave until increased in size by half.

Heat the oven to at least 425°F, though if you can get it 75°F hotter, even better. Steam the oven if you like (see page 16), dust flour over the dough with a small fine sieve or tea-strainer, cut the loaf down the middle with a sharp blade and bake for 20 minutes. Reduce the heat to 400°F and bake for another 20 to 25 minutes until the crust is the color you like.

Spelt and ale loaf

Once you've mastered the easy whole-wheat loaf, you might like to try this variation, which uses flour made from spelt, a grain that has seen a massive increase in popularity over the last few years. The malt in the ale makes the dough work very quickly so bake it as soon as it's increased in size by 50 percent, as the spelt dough will collapse if left too long.

1¼ cups dark ale or porter
2 teaspoons instant yeast
half a 500-mg plain vitamin C
    tablet, crushed to a powder
3½ cups spelt flour, plus extra
    for shaping and dusting

1 teaspoon fine sea salt
2 tablespoons unsalted butter,
    melted, plus extra for the pan
oil for kneading

Bring the ale to a boil in a saucepan, watching that it doesn't boil over, and simmer for a minute or two to drive off some of the alcohol, which could slow down or even stop the yeast. Pour this back into the measuring cup, leave until just warm, then top off with warm water to make 1¼ cups again. Pour the liquid into a mixing bowl then add the yeast. Stir well, then add the vitamin C, spelt flour and salt and stir well. Pour in the melted butter and mix the lot together evenly. Cover the bowl with a cloth and leave for 10 minutes.

Knead the dough (see pages 13 to 14), repeating after 15 and 30 minutes, then cover and leave for 15 minutes. Line a baking sheet with parchment paper and lightly flour the work surface. Roll the dough into a rectangle, then roll it up tightly and place it seam-side down on the baking sheet. Cover with a tea towel and leave until increased in size by half.

Heat the oven to 425°F. Steam the oven if you like (see page 16), dust flour over the dough with a small fine sieve or tea-strainer, cut the loaf down the middle with a sharp blade and bake for 20 minutes. Reduce the heat to 400°F and bake for another 20 to 25 minutes until the crust is the color you like.

SHORT & SWEET

Simple walnut loaf

This will get applause rather than prizes as it relies on a big walnut flavor rather than complex baking techniques. Still, you end up with a moist purple crumb studded with big chunks of walnuts, encased in a tender crust.

2 cups bread flour, plus extra for shaping and dusting
⅓ cup whole-wheat flour
1 teaspoon fine sea salt
2 teaspoons instant yeast
½ cup red wine
⅓ cup water
1 tablespoon olive oil
1 tablespoon honey
1⅓ cups coarsely chopped walnuts
oil for kneading

Mix the flours, salt and yeast together in a bowl. In a blender, whiz the wine, water, oil, honey and ½ cup of the walnuts until smooth, then pour this into the flour. Add the remaining walnuts and stir briskly to make a soft, sticky dough. Cover and leave for 10 minutes. Knead the dough on a lightly oiled work surface (see pages 13 to 14), then return to the bowl. Cover and leave another 10 minutes. Repeat the light knead once only, replace the dough in the bowl, and leave it for 30 to 45 minutes or until increased in size by half.

Line a baking sheet with parchment paper, lightly flour the work surface and roll the dough to roughly 6 by 8 inches. Roll the shorter side up to form a tight sausage and plonk this seam-side down on the baking sheet. Cover then leave for an hour until increased in size by half. Heat the oven to 400°F. Lightly dust flour over the dough with a small fine sieve or tea-strainer and make rapid crisscross cuts with a small, very sharp knife or blade. Bake for 40 minutes, then leave to cool on a rack.

Soy and flaxseed loaf

If you can overcome any reluctance you have about handling a really sticky dough, you'll love this one. This easy sandwich bread will stay extra soft and moist for days after baking, thanks to the soy milk, and has the added boost of omega-3 oil together with lots of extra protein and oat fiber.

⅔ cup rolled oats
⅓ cup golden flaxseed
⅜ cup boiling water
1½ cups lukewarm soy milk
1½ teaspoons instant yeast

2½ cups bread flour,
   plus extra for shaping
⅓ cup whole-wheat or rye flour
1½ teaspoons fine salt
oil for kneading

Place the rolled oats and flaxseed in a large mixing bowl, stir in the boiling water and leave for 10 minutes to soften. Add the soy milk and yeast and mix well. Add the two flours and salt, then stir everything together into a big soft and sticky dough. Cover and leave for 10 minutes, then knead the dough (see pages 13 to 14), repeating after 10 and 20 minutes, then leave, covered, for 45 minutes.

Line a baking sheet with parchment paper. Using a little flour, pat the dough into a rectangle. Roll it up tightly, then roll a little more, pressing just on the ends so the dough forms a fat "lemon" shape. Place this seam-side down on the baking sheet, cover with a cloth and leave until risen in size by half. Heat the oven to 425°F, slash the top and bake for about 45 minutes. Remove the loaf from the oven, and transfer to a wire rack to cool.

Sprouted grain seed bread

One early no-knead loaf was Doris Grant's recipe from the 1940s, and here I've supercharged it with sprouted grains (see "Sprouted Grains" below), orange juice and toasted seeds. Leave it a day before slicing if you can.

¾ cup warm water
2 teaspoons instant yeast
1 teaspoon honey
1 teaspoon blackstrap molasses
3 tablespoons orange juice
1 cup sunflower seeds, toasted
½ cup sprouted grains

2 tablespoons sunflower oil
2⅔ cups bread flour,
   plus extra for shaping
¾ cup rye or whole-wheat flour
1½ teaspoons fine salt

Stir the water and yeast till dissolved in a large mixing bowl. Stir in the honey and molasses then add the juice and seeds, sprouted grains and sunflower oil. Add the flours and salt then mix thoroughly, adding a little more water if the dough seems dry. Cover and leave for 45 minutes.

Line a loaf pan, 7½ inches long or similar, with parchment paper. Flour the work surface, then pat the dough out to about the length of your pan and three times the width. Roll the dough up tightly and place it seam-side down in the pan. Punch it down to firm it, then cover with a cloth and leave for about an hour until risen only by about a quarter to a third. Heat the oven to 425°F, brush the top of the loaf with water, bake for 20 minutes, then drop the temperature to 400°F and bake for another 30 minutes. Remove from the pan and cool on a rack.

SPROUTED GRAINS

Though you can often find sprouted grains at the supermarket or health food store, they're very easy to make at home as you just soak, drain and rinse grains — like barley and wheat, but also whole lentils and beans like aduki, chickpeas etc. — in water, keeping them barely damp until they germinate and produce small ¾ inch shoots. That's the basics. I rinse them daily, and with wheat and barley I soak them, drain them, then leave them on moistened paper kitchen towels for 3 to 4 days.

Other people know much more about this than I, so type "sprouted grains" into an Internet search engine for a more detailed explanation.

Multigrain and honey loaf

The simple "porridge" of honey, oats and seeds added to the dough gives a chewy sweetness to the crumb and helps it to stay moist for days. Having said that, my favorite way to eat it is hungrily: thickly sliced and toasted in the morning, butter and honey or homemade marmalade a must.

FOR THE SPONGE
1 cup warm water
1 teaspoon instant yeast
1⅓ cups bread flour

FOR THE "PORRIDGE"
⅔ cup rolled oats
3 tablespoons honey
⅓ cup flaxseed
⅓ cup sunflower seeds
½ cup boiling water

FOR THE DOUGH
¾ cup bread flour,
    plus extra for shaping
    and dusting
¾ cup whole-wheat flour
1 teaspoon fine salt
2 tablespoons unsalted butter
    or lard, plus extra for greasing
    the pan
oil for kneading

To make the sponge, pour the warm water into a mixing bowl and stir in the yeast. Add 1⅓ cups flour, stir it up well, cover the bowl and leave for 2 to 4 hours, or even overnight.

To make the "porridge," put the oats, honey, flaxseed and sunflower seeds in another bowl. Pour in the boiling water, stir well and leave to get cold.

To make the dough, beat the oat porridge into the yeast sponge very well, then put both the dough flours into a mixing bowl. Add the salt and rub the butter through until it vanishes, so there are no little lumps floating around. Pour in the yeast batter, mix the whole lot up into a big sticky clump of dough, then scrape the bits off your fingers. Cover the bowl with a tea towel and leave for 10 minutes. Knead the dough (see pages 13 to 14), repeating after 15 and 30 minutes. Then cover and leave for another 30 minutes.

Butter and flour a loaf pan, about 7½ inches long. Lightly flour the work surface, roll the dough into a rectangle ¾ inch thick that on the short side measures slightly less than the length of the pan; roll it up tightly and place seam-side down in the pan. Cover with a tea towel and leave until increased in size by half.

Heat the oven to at least 425°F, though if you can get it 75°F hotter, even better. Steam the oven if you like (see page 16), dust flour over the dough with a small fine sieve or tea-strainer, slash the loaf down the center about ⅜ inch deep with a sharp blade and bake for 20 minutes. Reduce the heat to 400°F and bake for another 20 to 25 minutes until the crust is the color you like.

The two-day loaf

This recipe was written to fit the routine of a working week, as it relies on the longer fermentation of the sponge while you're at work to provide enough yeast cells to give the crumb good aeration during that final long, slow rise in the fridge. This pushes the dough toward the point of collapse, but the lower temperature helps to keep it firm enough to bake. It's more difficult to achieve during the summer months, as you need a cool place for the sponge to work its magic.

FOR THE SPONGE
1½ cups warm water
1 tablespoon low-fat plain yogurt
¼ teaspoon instant yeast
1¼ cups bread flour, plus extra
   for dusting
1¼ cups whole-wheat,
   spelt or rye flour

FOR THE DOUGH
1 tablespoon brown sugar
2¼ cups bread flour
2 teaspoons fine salt
oil for kneading

To make the sponge, start at about 8 a.m. on day one by combining the warm water, yogurt and yeast in a mixing bowl. Stir until dissolved, then add both flours and mix to a smooth batter. Cover and leave out, in a cool kitchen, until 7 p.m. or after.

To make the dough, stir the brown sugar into the sponge, add the 2¼ cups flour and the salt and stir to a sticky soft mass. Leave the dough for 15 minutes. Lightly oil your hands and the work surface and knead the dough for about 10 seconds (see pages 13 to 14), repeating this light kneading after 15, 30 and 45 minutes. Shape the dough into a ball and place it in a bowl lined with a heavily floured linen tea towel. Leave in the fridge at 39 to 43°F, covered with a cloth or plastic wrap, for 24 hours, then take out and bake when risen by at least half its original size (see "Use Your Loaf" below). Get the oven to 450°F, turn or ease the dough carefully onto a floured baking sheet, so that you do not lose its shape or knock too much of the air out of it. Slash the top, bake for 25 minutes then lower the oven temperature to 400°F and bake for another 20 minutes.

USE YOUR LOAF

In warmer weather, you might reduce the yeast even more. You'll know you need to reduce it when the loaf gets too puffy at the end of its 24-hour rise. By increasing the water when you feel more confident with soft sticky dough, you'll get a more open texture in the loaf.

If the bread has risen by half or more during its time in the fridge, just bake from chilled. In this event, be really careful when you turn the dough out from the bowl onto the baking sheet. Think of it like a big fragile puffy bubble that needs delicate handling to keep it from deflating. Get your oven ready, tip the dough quickly and gently onto a well-floured baking sheet, try slashing it with a razor blade (without slashing your fingers or hand in the process, be very careful), then get it in the oven. For the first 15 minutes try keeping the oven temperature as hot as it will go, even if this raises the temperature to 500°F. This initial burst of heat will help, as the dough will be quite tired at the end of the 24-hour rise.

Black bread

Utterly soft and moist, but with a blackish crumb that suggests it has some sturdy character to it. Sandwiches look so cool when made with this bread, as the color of the filling looks much more vibrant. The molasses is there to give the flavor of the bread a distinctive "dark" accent, but if you prefer something lighter, you can use honey.

1⅓ cups cold water
1½ cups rye, spelt
    or whole-wheat flour
2 teaspoons instant yeast
1 teaspoon muscovado sugar
2 tablespoons cocoa powder
2 tablespoons instant coffee
    granules
¼ cup blackstrap molasses

1 tablespoon fennel, caraway and/
    or cumin seeds
4 tablespoons unsalted butter
5 ounces starchy root vegetable,
    like carrot, coarsely grated
3¼ cups bread flour
2 teaspoons fine sea salt
oil for kneading and for
    the baking sheet
sesame seeds to finish

Whisk 1 cup of the cold water and ½ cup of the rye flour in a large saucepan, bring to a boil then spoon into a bowl and leave for 30 minutes, until lukewarm. Stir in the yeast and sugar and leave, covered, at room temperature for 45 minutes. Heat the remaining ⅓ cup water with the cocoa, coffee, molasses, fennel seeds and butter until melted. Leave until lukewarm then stir with the grated vegetable into the yeast mixture. Add the remaining rye flour, the bread flour and salt and stir to a soft sticky mass. Rub 1 tablespoon oil on the work surface and your hands, then knead the dough (see pages 13 to 14), repeating twice at 10-minute intervals. Shape into a ball, oil a baking sheet and place the dough on it seam-side down. Brush the top of the loaf with water then sprinkle sesame seeds thickly over it, and slip the baking sheet inside a grocery bag, lightly oiling the side that touches the dough so it doesn't stick. Leave until increased in size by half. Heat the oven to 425°F, uncover the dough and cut a deep X into the top with a serrated knife. Bake for 20 minutes, drop the heat to 350°F, and bake for 15 to 20 minutes more.

Black pepper rye

A very moist and soft light rye bread with a crisp crust and a kick of pepper; just the ticket for soft cheese and smoked salmon sandwiches.

1⅓ cups regular black coffee, warm or cold

1½ cups rye flour

2 teaspoons crushed black pepper

2 teaspoons anise, fennel or caraway seeds

1 teaspoon instant yeast

1⅓ cups bread flour, plus extra for shaping

1½ teaspoons fine salt

oil for kneading

beaten egg and poppy seeds to finish

Put the coffee in a saucepan with ¾ cup of the rye flour and the pepper and anise seeds, whisk well, and heat until thick and just reaching boiling. Immediately remove from the heat, spoon into a mixing bowl and leave until just warm. Add the yeast, mix well, add the remaining rye flour and the bread flour and salt and mix to a smooth dough. Cover, leave for 10 minutes, then knead the dough for 10 seconds on a lightly oiled work surface (see pages 13 to 14). Cover, repeating the kneading twice more at 10-minute intervals, then leave for 30 minutes.

Line a baking sheet with parchment. Using a little flour, pat the dough out into an 8-inch square then roll up tightly. Place the dough seam-side down on the baking sheet, cover with a cloth and leave until risen by half, probably around 45 minutes. Heat the oven to 450°F. Egg wash the top of the dough, cut six diagonal slashes across it, sprinkle with poppy seeds and bake for 40 minutes.

Deli bread

This is Saturday-night, Sunday-morning bread, only the slightest bit rye but perfect as the base for a corned beef sandwich, the sort you'd buy from an old-fashioned Eastern European–style deli. This kind of bread should "firm" when it's stored but retain a sticky moistness to the crumb, and the potato holds that moisture and improves the keeping quality (if you're going to make it often, then a box of instant mashed potato in the back of the cupboard where no one can see it may be useful). Chilling the dough overnight helps to develop a stronger flavor in the crumb: not really sour, but not too yeasty either, and the long, slow rise gives more emphasis to the onion and caraway as well.

2 teaspoons instant yeast
¾ cup warm water
2½ cups bread flour, plus
   extra for dusting
1 medium onion, thinly sliced
¼ cup sunflower oil

about ¼ cup mashed potato
¾ cup rye flour
1½ teaspoons fine salt
2½ teaspoons caraway seeds
oil for kneading and for preparing
   the pan

Mix the yeast with ¼ cup of the warm water and 2 teaspoons of the bread flour, stir well and leave for 30 minutes. Place the onion and oil in a pan and cook on a low heat for 15 to 20 minutes, stirring well. As soon as it's golden, pour into a bowl and cool. Combine the onion and oil, potato and remaining water with the yeasty mixture, then pour this into a bowl with the rest of the bread flour and the remaining dry ingredients. Mix to a dough and leave, covered, for 10 minutes. Finally, knead the dough once for 10 seconds (see pages 13 to 14), return to the bowl, cover and refrigerate overnight for about 12 hours.

The next morning, knead the dough lightly again and flatten on a lightly floured surface into a rectangle about 8 by 6 inches, then roll it up tightly like a scroll. Oil and flour a loaf pan, about 7½ inches long or similar, and drop the dough seam-side down into the pan. Cover and leave for 2 to 3 hours or until increased in size by half. Heat the oven to 425°F. Flour the top of the dough and cut a slash down the center. Bake for 35 minutes, then lower the heat to 350°F and bake another 10 minutes. Remove from the pan and leave to cool on a wire rack.

Malt vinegar rye

This makes a dark, very dense disk of sweetly sour rye bread, the sort you'd happily slice thinly and eat with smoked salmon, cold butter and dill sauce. Leave the loaf for a day once cooled, wrapped in oiled paper, and the hard crust will soften and make slicing easier.

1¾ cups warm water	2½ tablespoons honey or
1 tablespoon instant yeast	blackstrap molasses
6½ cups rye flour, plus	⅓ cup malt vinegar
extra for shaping	2 tablespoons sunflower oil
	1 tablespoon fine salt

Pour the water into a mixing bowl, sprinkle in the yeast with 2 cups of the flour, stir well and leave to bubble for 30 minutes.

Beat in the honey, vinegar, oil and salt. Stir in the remaining flour and beat to a smooth, thick, paste-like dough. The texture will seem a little odd at first as the rye flour lacks any of the spring you expect with wheat flour. Line a baking sheet with parchment paper and, using more rye flour, pat the dough out on the tray to a disk about 2 inches thick. Cover loosely with a cloth and leave at room temperature until the center has risen by about a third (usually 1 to 2 hours).

Heat the oven to 400°F and bake the loaf for about 50 minutes until cracked on top and a rich brown color.

Seeded rye bread

A hefty mix of spices, say 1 tablespoon each of whole coriander, caraway and anise or fennel seeds stirred into the dough with the last of the flour, along with the finely grated zest of an orange or lemon, gives each slice a curious flavor that goes rather well with shavings of smoked salmon and a blob of soft cream cheese.

Oatmeal soda bread

This is the original quick and easy no-knead bread to serve alongside ice-cold oysters and stout or a glass of ale. For a change I've made this with the coarse oatmeal you get in cans. More expensive, I know, but it gives the bread the best chewy texture and would have been traditional before rolled oats were widely available. For this recipe, I make a sort of porridge and beat the other ingredients through it. It's baked in a pan, as the mixture is a bit sloppy. In Ireland, I've only ever seen soda bread as a slab and to me that's much easier to cut and use.

⅔ cup coarse or
    steel-cut oatmeal
1 cup water
2 tablespoons butter
    or meat drippings,
    plus extra for the pan

⅓ cup low-fat plain yogurt
¾ cup cold milk
1½ tablespoons brown sugar
2½ cups whole-wheat or spelt flour
1½ teaspoons baking soda
¾ teaspoon fine salt

Place the oatmeal and water in a saucepan. Bring to a boil, then remove from the heat, stick the lid on and leave for an hour, adding the butter toward the end. Whisk in the yogurt, milk and sugar until smooth and free of lumps. Butter an 8-inch square cake pan, line the bottom with a square of parchment paper, and heat the oven to 400°F. Stir the flour, baking soda and salt into the oatmeal mixture until smooth. Spoon the batter into the pan, cover the top with foil, and bake for 15 minutes. Remove the foil and bake for another 30 minutes until the crust is a good rich brown.

Seaweed, onion and toasted oatmeal soda bread

Lovely served cold and buttered with fish or shellfish. Place the oatmeal on a baking sheet and bake in the oven until a rich dark brown. Then proceed with the recipe as directed, adding 3 to 4 tablespoons finely chopped dried seaweed (dulse or nori or laver) and 1 small finely chopped and fried onion to the batter.

Breakfast soda breads

My original idea here was to encourage B&Bs to improve their breakfasts by replacing that grim, tepid "sliced white" toast with individual soda breads, using a stored dry mix that enabled them to bake exactly what they needed in a matter of minutes. If you have access to local, coarse stone-milled whole-wheat flour, it would be perfect here. You can mix in toasted seeds, honey or a little melted butter to make use of other local ingredients.

FOR THE DRY MIX

4¼ cups whole-wheat flour
3½ teaspoons baking powder
¾ teaspoon fine salt

2½ tablespoons light
   brown sugar

FOR EACH INDIVIDUAL BREAD

about ¾ cup dry mix (4½ cups for 6)
¼ cup cold whole milk
   (1½ cups for 6)

rolled oats or toasted pumpkin
   seeds to finish

2 tablespoons low-fat plain yogurt
   (¾ cup for 6)

To make the dry mix, sift the ingredients together so that they are evenly mixed. This mixture will keep happily for months, so once you've tried and tweaked it, you can mix a bigger batch.

Heat the oven to 400°F.

To make individual breads, weigh out and combine the appropriate quantities of dry mix, milk and yogurt for the number of soda breads you want to make. The mixture should be of a consistency that you can just about stir with a spoon. Place a square of parchment paper in a bowl on your scale and spoon approximately 7 ounces of the mixture into the center, then lift by the corners and drop into the pocket of a muffin pan, gently pressing it down if necessary. Repeat as required. Sprinkle a few rolled oats or toasted pumpkin seeds over the tops and bake for 25 to 30 minutes or until puffed and brown. Serve warm.

North-South cornbread

The Southerners in America like their cornbread made with white cornmeal and lots of it, without any sweetness, whereas in the northern states they like it yellow and fluffy with a little sugar. The small amount of flour used here moderates the chewiness and gives a lighter texture, but with yellow cornmeal and some sugar to add sweetness and a golden color. Bacon fat is the traditional thing to stir into the mix and rub around the pan, a "must" if you have it, but butter and oil are easier to get hold of. Sliced thinly it's the perfect accompaniment for hot spicy pork ribs and a bowl of fresh homemade coleslaw.

oil for the pan, or bacon fat if
   you have it
1⅓ cups polenta or coarse
   yellow cornmeal
¾ cup bread flour
1 teaspoon fine salt

1 teaspoon baking soda
¼ cup super-fine sugar
1⅔ cups low-fat plain yogurt
2 eggs
2 tablespoons melted butter
   or more bacon fat

Get a round ovenproof skillet or baking dish about 8 inches in diameter and pour a few tablespoons of oil into it, rubbing a little up the sides to stop the mixture from sticking. Place the skillet in the oven and heat it to 400°F.

Spoon the polenta, flour, salt, baking soda and sugar into a bowl and mix them together. In another bowl, beat the yogurt with the eggs and melted butter. When the skillet is hot, remove it from the oven and place it on the stove top.

Beat the yogurt mixture evenly through the dry ingredients, and quickly spoon the mixture into the hot skillet. Smooth the top gently, then place it back in the oven and bake for 20 to 25 minutes until it starts to pull away from the sides of the pan. The top won't have colored much but the bottom should be a deep golden brown. Remove from the oven then leave to cool slightly before turning out onto a serving plate.

Earlier in this chapter, I talked about using cornstarch, as opposed to cornmeal. But now I need you to make sure that for cornbread recipes, you use cornmeal (or polenta meal), the coarse yellow grainy stuff, not fine white cornstarch! You can make the cornbread lighter by replacing some of the polenta with more bread flour, and of course leave out the sugar if you prefer less sweetness.

Sesame chili cornbread

Old recipes for cornbread often don't use any wheat flour but instead make a cornmeal porridge, then beat in extra cornmeal and baking powder. I based this one on a recipe from Jessup Whitehead's *American Pastry Cook* from 1891, and the result is soft and a little squishy, almost like a pudding and not like the "cakey" cornbread common today. Chili and sesame add a bright spiced flavor that's good if you serve a scoop of it warm with roast chicken and buttered kale.

¼ cup sesame seeds, plus extra for the top
1 to 2 teaspoons red chili flakes, more or less as you prefer
¼ cup sesame oil
2⅔ cups cornmeal or polenta
2 cups water

1 tablespoon super-fine sugar
½ cup (1 stick) unsalted butter, plus extra for the pan or skillet
1⅔ cups cold milk
2 eggs, whisked
1 teaspoon fine salt
2 teaspoons baking powder

Fry the sesame seeds and red chili flakes in the oil in a saucepan until lightly toasted, then spoon in two-thirds of the cornmeal with the water and sugar, and whisk well until thick and hot. Remove from the heat, cut the butter up small and beat it in until melted. Whisk in the milk a little at a time, beating until smooth, finally beating in the eggs and salt.

Meanwhile, place a deep, 8-inch, round ovenproof skillet or baking dish in a 400°F oven. When the skillet is hot, butter it lightly, then beat the remaining cornmeal and the baking powder into the mixture. Spoon it into the hot pan and sprinkle more sesame seeds over the top. Return to the oven and bake for 30 to 40 minutes or until puffed and golden. Either serve scoops of it hot from the pan, or allow to cool before slicing.

Carrot and cumin burger buns

Grated carrot and cornstarch keep these buns bouncy, soft and moist, helped by a hot oven and a short baking time.

MAKES 5 OR 6

½ cup cold milk

½ cup boiling water

1 egg

2 teaspoons instant yeast

1½ cups grated carrot

1 medium onion, finely chopped

4 cups bread flour, plus
   extra for shaping

½ cup cornstarch

2 teaspoons fine salt

2 to 3 teaspoons each ground
   cumin and paprika

4 tablespoons unsalted butter,
   cut into small dice

oil for kneading

poppy or sesame seeds to finish

Pour the milk into a bowl and add the boiling water. Beat in the egg then stir in the yeast, carrot and onion. Into a large mixing bowl measure the flour, cornstarch, salt, spices and butter. Rub the butter in until the lumps have vanished. Add the carrot mixture and stir well together, adding a little more water if the dough seems dry. Leave for 10 minutes then knead the dough (see pages 13 to 14), repeating after 10 and 20 minutes. Leave the dough, covered, for 45 minutes, then divide into five or six equal pieces. Shape into balls and leave to rise on a baking sheet lined with parchment paper until risen by a half (mine took about 30 minutes). Heat the oven to 425°F, brush the buns with water and sprinkle with seeds, then bake for 25 minutes.

Red onion and green olive rolls

The key to this recipe is a curious method bakers once used to keep bread moist. Cooked starch, as simple as flour boiled in water, was found to help keep the crumb extra soft. Perfect for cold roast lamb sandwiches. The vinegar is added to bring back the color of the red onions, which otherwise tend to turn a purplish-blue!

MAKES 9

4 tablespoons unsalted butter
1 medium red onion, roughly
    chopped
4 cups bread flour,
    plus extra for rolling
1½ cups cold water
1 tablespoon red wine vinegar

¾ cup pitted green olives,
    drained, dried off and
    roughly chopped
2 teaspoons instant yeast
2 teaspoons fine salt
polenta or cornmeal
oil for kneading

Melt the butter in a saucepan, add the onion and get it sizzling. Stick the lid on, drop the heat and cook gently for 10 minutes until the onion is soft. Remove from the heat, beat in ⅓ cup of the flour, then add the water and vinegar and whisk. Bring to a boil, whisking furiously, then spoon the mixture into a large mixing bowl, stir in the olives and leave until just warm. Beat in the yeast, add the remaining flour and the salt, and mix to a smooth dough. Cover and leave for 10 minutes, then knead the dough on a lightly oiled work surface (see pages 13 to 14) for about 10 seconds. Return to the bowl and cover. Repeat the kneading twice at 10-minute intervals, then leave, covered, for 30 minutes.

Roll the dough on a floured surface to about 8 inches by 10 inches, brush with water and sprinkle with polenta. Cut into nine pieces, lay these spaced apart on one or two baking sheets lined with parchment paper, cover and leave for 1½ hours. Heat the oven to 425°F and bake for 20 to 25 minutes.

Tapenade dinner rolls

A single anchovy and a dozen capers will enhance the flavor of the tapenade, or you can just buy a jar of it ready-made. For plain white or garlic butter rolls, replace the tapenade with softened butter or garlic butter, then proceed with the recipe as directed.

MAKES 8 to 10

4 cups bread flour, plus
   extra for rolling
2 teaspoons instant yeast
2 teaspoons fine salt
1¼ cups warm water
1 garlic clove, mashed
¼ cup olive oil, plus more for
   kneading, and for the
   tapenade

½ cup pitted black or green olives
1 teaspoon chopped fresh thyme
1 anchovy and 12 capers, chopped,
   or some finely grated
   lemon zest (optional)

Mix the flour, yeast, salt, warm water, garlic and 3½ tablespoons olive oil, then cover and leave for 10 minutes. Oil a patch of work surface and your hands, and give the dough a 10-second knead (see pages 13 to 14). Return the dough to the bowl, repeat the light kneading twice more after 10 and 20 minutes, then leave the dough, covered, for 45 minutes.

Purée the olives and thyme with enough olive oil to make a soft paste, for a basic tapenade. Include the anchovy and capers, or some lemon zest, if you like. Roll the dough out to a 30-by-10-inch rectangle, and cut it into three 10-inch squares. Spread the tapenade evenly over two pieces and stack them neatly on top of each other, then place the plain square on top. With a sharp knife, cut into 2-by-5-inch fingers. Press the length of a pencil firmly across the center of each finger so it butterflies, then press each "V" into the oiled pocket of a muffin tray. Leave for 45 minutes. Heat the oven to 425°F and bake for about 20 minutes.

Soft white baps

Squishy-soft baps, or yeast rolls, are heading toward extinction in crusty baguette–favoring Britain. Here's your chance to help the cause and give a sausage a proper home.

MAKES 9

FOR THE SPONGE
1½ tablespoons cornstarch
4 cups bread flour
2 teaspoons instant yeast
1¾ cups warm water

FOR THE DOUGH
¼ cup water
⅓ cup milk
5 tablespoons unsalted butter,
    cut into small cubes
2 tablespoons cornstarch
2¼ cups bread flour, plus
    extra for shaping and
    dusting
¼ cup super-fine sugar
2½ teaspoons fine salt
oil for kneading

To make the sponge, in a large bowl sift the cornstarch and bread flour together. Add the yeast, pour in the warm water and stir to a soft dough. Cover the bowl and leave to rise for 2½ to 3 hours.

Next, to make the dough, bring the water and milk to a boil, then remove from the heat, add the butter and set aside until just warm. Pour the liquid into a measuring cup and top off with water to make ¾ cup. Toss the cornstarch and flour together, add the sugar and salt and mix well. Beat the buttery liquid into the yeast sponge until combined, then add the dry ingredients and mix to an even dough. Knead the dough (see pages 13 to 14), repeating after 15 and 30 minutes, then leave the dough, covered, for 15 minutes. Divide into nine 6-ounce pieces, shape on a floured surface into balls, and place on a parchment-lined baking sheet, flour the tops, cover and leave to rise for 45 to 60 minutes, until increased in size by a half. Heat the oven to 425°F and bake for 25 minutes. Leave until cold before removing from the baking sheet.

Simple bagels

Think of this as a starting point on your road to bagel excellence. Halving the yeast and letting the bagels rise slowly would produce an even chewier texture; reducing the water has the same effect, while increasing the water makes them fluffier.

MAKES 10

4 cups bread flour

1 teaspoon instant yeast

2 teaspoons fine salt

1 tablespoon super-fine sugar

1¼ cups warm water

1 tablespoon white wine vinegar

oil for kneading, and for
   the baking sheet

¼ cup brown sugar or malt extract

seeds or coarse salt flakes for
   the tops

Combine the flour, yeast, salt and super-fine sugar in a bowl and add the warm water and vinegar. Stir together to a firm dough, cover the bowl and leave for 10 minutes. Knead the dough for 10 seconds on a lightly oiled work surface (see pages 13 to 14) before returning it to the bowl and covering with a cloth. Repeat this light kneading twice more at 10-minute intervals before again returning the dough to the bowl, covering it and leaving for an hour. Divide the dough into 10 pieces. Shape each piece into a smooth ball, cover with a cloth and leave for 20 minutes. Then shape your bagel; the easiest but least authentic way is to stick one finger through the center and stretch the dough outward with your other fingers.

Heat the oven to 425°F. In a large pot, heat 2 quarts of water to boiling. Add the brown sugar or malt extract and drop the bagels in, one or two at a time. Leave for 30 to 60 seconds, then flip them over and repeat on the other side. Place on an oiled baking sheet, sprinkle seeds or salt on top, and bake for 20 to 25 minutes.

Alehouse rolls

These rolls stay really moist inside because of the cooked oats and butter. They taste a little bit like "granary" bread with a slight nutty flavor and a gentle sweetness from both the malt in the ale and the honey, so make them big for an amazing cheese and pickle sandwich or small to serve warm with dinner.

MAKES 5

1 cup rolled oats
1¾ cups ale or stout
2 tablespoons unsalted butter
1 tablespoon honey
3½ cups bread flour,
    plus extra for shaping
    and dusting

¾ cup whole-wheat, rye or spelt
    flour
2 teaspoons instant yeast
2 teaspoons fine salt
oil for kneading and oats
    (optional) for finishing

Heat the oven to 400°F. Place the oats on a baking sheet in the oven for about 25 minutes or until they turn a rich golden brown. Pour the ale into a saucepan and add the oats, then bring to a boil over medium heat. Remove the pan from the heat, add the butter and honey, pop the lid on and leave it about 30 minutes till it's barely warm.

Mix the bread flour and whole-wheat flour, the yeast and salt together in a large bowl. Pour in the warm oat and ale mixture and stir everything together with your fingers, adding a little cold water if necessary to make a soft dough. Cover the bowl and leave for 10 minutes. Lightly oil the work surface and your hands, scoop the dough out of the bowl and gently knead it for 10 seconds (see pages 13 to 14). Scoop the dough back into the bowl, cover, then repeat the light knead twice more at 10-minute intervals.

Leave the dough for 30 minutes, ideally somewhere it won't get chilled, then divide it into pieces. For huge sandwich rolls weigh about five 8-ounce pieces. (For dinner rolls weigh about a dozen 4-ounce pieces.) Shape each piece of dough into a ball on a lightly floured surface. To protect the bottoms of the rolls from scorching due to the honey and the malt in the ale, line a baking

SHORT & SWEET

sheet with parchment paper. If you want a coating of oats on the rolls, lay a sheet of wet paper towel on one dinner plate and spoon rolled oats onto another, then roll each dough ball first across the wet paper and then through the oats. Sit each roll on the baking sheet spaced 1½ to 2 inches apart, cover the baking sheet loosely with a grocery bag and leave for about an hour until risen in height by a half.

Heat the oven to 400°F. Bake the rolls for 20 minutes, then reduce the heat to 350°F and bake until a good golden brown. Leave to cool on a wire rack covered loosely with a dry tea towel.

BAKING FROM FROZEN

To make life a bit more relaxed I make these ahead but only lightly bake them, perhaps 20 minutes in the oven. Then I leave them on the baking sheet to cool and freeze them in a ziplock bag. Then just before dinner, or whenever I need them, they get baked once more from frozen in a preheated oven at 400°F for 10 to 12 minutes.

Cider vinegar muffins

What Americans call an "English muffin" the British population just used to call, well, a muffin. But since those little packaged cakes invaded supermarket shelves and stole the name, Britain's little plain bread muffin has become neglected in its homeland. American bakers have raised the quality of their English muffins to something close to perfection. Crisp on the outside, sour and holey inside, and chewy when toasted and slathered with butter. Make these and you'll see what the English have been missing all these years. In this recipe, the dough gets mixed and lightly kneaded the night before and is left in the refrigerator overnight to rise slowly. You can even leave it until the following evening if that works better for you.

MAKES 5 OR 6

4 tablespoons unsalted butter
½ cup warm water
¼ cup cider vinegar
⅓ cup low-fat plain yogurt
1 egg
1 teaspoon fine salt

3 cups bread flour, plus
    extra for dusting
2 teaspoons instant yeast
oil for kneading and for
    the bowl

The night before, melt the butter in a saucepan, then remove from the heat and beat in the warm water with the vinegar, yogurt, egg and salt until smooth. Measure the flour and yeast into a bowl, tip the butter and vinegar mixture in and stir to a thick batter. Cover the bowl and leave for 10 minutes. Lightly oil the work surface and knead the dough once for 10 to 15 seconds (see pages 13 to 14). Scrape the bowl clean of odd scraps of dough, wipe the inside with a little oil, place the dough back in the bowl, cover with a plate or plastic wrap, and place the bowl in the refrigerator overnight.

The following morning (or evening), lightly oil a small baking sheet and turn the bowl over on it, easing the dough out gently. Pat the dough out a little and give it a blanket fold (see page 14) then leave, covered, to rest for 1 to 2 hours until it warms and begins to rise again.

Line a small baking sheet with a tea towel and sprinkle the surface liberally with flour. Then gently roll the dough out until about ¾ inch thick, while trying not to knock too much of the gas from it. Cut the dough into disks using a 5-inch biscuit cutter (yes, that large, as they'll pull inward as they cook), or take a sharp knife and cut the dough into eight or nine squares. Carefully lay the dough pieces on the floured cloth and, when finished, dust the tops with more flour and cover with a tea towel. Leave for 1½ to 2 hours or until risen in height by at least a half.

Heat the oven to 350°F. Get a large heavy-bottomed frying pan with a snug-fitting lid if possible and place over medium heat until the surface is hot but not scorching. Uncover the muffins and flip them onto your hand one at a time with the cloth, then slide them into the pan. You should be able to fit three or four in at a time. Cover the pan with the lid to create a bit of steam, to help them rise, and cook for 2 to 3 minutes. Then check to see that they're not burning. If the bottom is a good brown color, take a spatula and flip them over. Cook on the other side for 3 to 4 minutes. When done move to a baking sheet in the oven and bake another 10 minutes or so until

cooked through. Cook the remaining dough in the same way, and cool on a wire rack, covered with a cloth to keep them soft.

Crispy bacon muffins

Fry or grill 9 ounces smoked bacon until crisp. Finely chop it and add in with the flour, then continue with the recipe as directed.

FLATBREADS

Corn oil flour tortillas

These very tender flatbreads, cooked simply in a frying pan on the stove top, are what I often turn to if there's cold leftover roast meat in the fridge and I just fancy a sandwich for dinner. You know, with slices of ripe tomato, perhaps some slippery roasted red peppers from a jar and the last few lettuce leaves.

MAKES 5 OR 6
2¼ cups all-purpose flour
1 teaspoon baking powder
½ teaspoon fine salt
⅓ cup cold milk or water

⅓ cup boiling water
2 tablespoons corn or sunflower oil, plus extra for kneading

Spoon the flour, baking powder and salt into a bowl. Pour the cold milk, boiling water and oil into another bowl, stir them together, then tip this in with the flour and quickly work to a smooth dough. Cover the bowl and leave for 10 minutes. Lightly knead the dough (see pages 13 to 14), then return it to the bowl and leave an hour or two at room temperature. During this time the dough will soften and become pliable enough to roll thinly.

Divide the dough into five or six pieces about 3 ounces each. Roll each into a disk about 4 to 6 inches in diameter and place these to one side, fanned out on a plate with a dusting of flour underneath and between them to stop them from sticking together. Get a wide, heavy frying pan hot over a high heat, then one at a time, in the same order that you rolled them out before, roll each tortilla even thinner with more flour, until about 8 inches in diameter. As each one is finished, slip it onto your hand, then slide it into the hot dry pan. When it puffs up in random pockets across its surface, use a spatula to flip it over. Cook the other side lightly, then transfer it to a dinner plate and cover with a clean dry tea towel. Repeat with the remaining disks of dough, one at a time, and stack the cooked ones on top of each other on the plate.

STORING TORTILLAS

These freeze very well, just kept in a stack in a ziplock bag. Sometimes they stick together a little when defrosted, and if you need them to be pristine you could lay sheets of parchment paper between them. Reheat from frozen in a dry frying pan.

Frying pan naan

The best naan starts with a very soft dough shaped with lots of flour. A torn edge can soak up the sauce from a slow-cooked rogan josh with ease. You can make them just with a frying pan or wok; if they sit in a hot oven for a few minutes after frying, this will set the crumb and trap the air within.

MAKES 4 OR 6

½ cup cold milk

½ cup low-fat plain yogurt

¼ cup boiling water

1 teaspoon instant yeast

2¼ cups all-purpose flour,
   plus extra for shaping

⅓ cup whole-wheat flour

½ teaspoon baking soda

¾ teaspoon fine salt

1 teaspoon sugar

garlic oil made with 1 crushed garlic
   clove stirred with a little oil

black onion or cumin seeds
   (optional)

Stir the milk, yogurt and boiling water together in a large mixing bowl until smooth, then stir in the yeast. Add both flours, baking soda, salt and sugar and mix to a soft sticky dough. Cover the bowl, leave for half an hour. Lightly knead the dough once (see pages 13 to 14), return it to the bowl and leave for an hour. Lightly flour the work surface, place the dough on it, pat it down into a circle, then flour the top and cut it into four or six wedges. Quarters make huge

thick naan, best if you're very hungry. Roll each of the wedges out into triangles ½ to ¾ inch thick, using extra flour to stop them from sticking. Put a large frying pan over medium heat on the stove top and, if you like, heat the oven to 400°F. Once the pan is hot, take the first dough triangle and stretch it as you lower it onto the pan. Brush the top with garlic oil, pressing the brush in here and there to dimple the naan, sprinkle with onion seeds, if you wish, and cook until puffed and the bottom is light brown. With a spatula, flip the naan over, cook lightly on the other side, then keep warm, or leave to dry slightly in a hot oven, while you cook the remaining dough. They freeze well.

Superwraps

Those curious little seeds called quinoa (pronounced keen-wah) will add a hefty oomph of complex protein to the kind of bread now known as a "wrap." Traditional British flatbreads, from Lancashire oatcakes to barley bannocks, were often made from coarsely milled grain, cooked or soaked. If you wish, you can just substitute finely ground grains of barley, rye, millet or oats in place of quinoa.

MAKES ABOUT 10

½ cup quinoa

¾ cup water, plus about ½ cup extra to make the dough

1¼ cups bread flour, plus extra for rolling

1¼ cups whole-wheat, spelt or rye flour

1½ teaspoons fine salt

½ teaspoon baking powder

¼ cup sunflower oil, plus extra for cooking

Cook the quinoa in a dry frying pan over low heat to a nutty brown. Put it into a pan with the ¾ cup water, put the lid on tight and leave over a gentle heat for 10 to 15 minutes until the water is absorbed and the grain cooked, before spreading out on a dinner plate to cool. Sift both flours, the salt and baking powder together in a bowl, rub in the oil, then toss the quinoa through evenly. Add the ½ cup water and squeeze into a dough. Cover and leave for 30 minutes, then divide into 3-ounce balls. Roll each ball out thinly on a floured surface. Get the frying pan hot. Drop one flatbread into the pan, drizzle the upper surface with a little oil, cook until the bread blisters slightly, flip over and cook the other side. Cover on a plate and repeat with the others.

Lentil-stuffed flatbreads

I made these during a day spent with Caribbean food writer Franka Philip — this is our version of the excellent Trinidadian dhal puri roti. A bit of work, but so good to eat freshly made; they should be almost paper-thin. By aging the mixture overnight, it becomes far more elastic than if it's mixed and immediately used — an important characteristic with a thin, filled flatbread.

2⅔ cups bread flour, plus
   extra for shaping
1 teaspoon baking soda
1 teaspoon fine salt
¼ cup sunflower oil
½ cup milk
½ cup water

¾ cup red lentils
1 garlic clove, flattened under
   the blade of a heavy knife
1 teaspoon turmeric
2 teaspoons ground coriander
3 teaspoons ground cumin

The night before, mix the flour, baking soda and ½ teaspoon of the salt, add the oil and milk and water, stir well, then cover the bowl and leave overnight at room temperature. Next day, boil the lentils in water with the garlic for 8 to 10 minutes, then leave to drain in a sieve. Wring out any excess water from the cooked lentils using cheesecloth. Pluck out the garlic, pour the lentils into a bowl, stir in the spices and the remaining ½ teaspoon salt, and leave until cold. Cut the dough into 2-ounce pieces. Using lots of flour, pat out each piece in the palm of your hand, squeeze a spoonful of the lentil dhal into a ball and wrap the dough around it, dabbing the edges with water and pinching them to seal them. Tap the dough out firmly using more flour, then roll as thinly as you can. Get a heavy 10-inch frying pan quite hot, then lay the flatbread on it and cook for about 1 minute on each side. Then roll and cook the remaining pieces in the same way.

Herb and garlic roti

Adding flavors to a simple Indian-style flatbread can create a surprisingly good accompaniment to a selection of Italian cured meats, roasted peppers, olives and soft cheese.

1¼ cups warm water
1½ teaspoons instant yeast
1 tablespoon low-fat plain yogurt
a few handfuls of chopped, fresh, mild herbs
1½ cups whole-wheat flour

2½ cups bread flour, plus extra for rolling and shaping
1½ teaspoons fine salt
3 garlic cloves, mashed
4 tablespoons unsalted butter
finely grated zest of 1 lemon
olive oil to finish

In a bowl mix the water, yeast, yogurt and herbs. Add both flours and the salt and combine to a soft sticky dough. Leave, covered, for 3 to 4 hours at room temperature, or overnight in the refrigerator. Fry the garlic and butter in a pan until the garlic toasts very slightly. Pour into a cup with the lemon zest and leave for 5 minutes. Flour the work surface, roll the dough out to about 16 inches by 20 inches. Brush all the garlic-lemon butter over the surface of the dough, then roll the dough up tightly into a cylinder. Heat a large frying pan until scorching hot. Slice the dough into ¾-inch sections, then thump each piece flat using the heel of your hand on a floured surface. Roll it very thin with a rolling pin, then place this immediately on the dry hot pan. Drizzle 1 teaspoon of oil over the surface, and when bubbles puff up in the dough, flip it over and cook the other side. Keep the roti warm on a plate under a cloth while you cook the rest.

HERBS

The best herbs to use here are things like thyme, oregano or basil, rather than anything harder or more astringent such as rosemary.

Perfect plain pita

Freshly made and baked, homemade pita reminds me how stale and tough the shop ones are. Don't even get me started on long-life pita. Homemade ones frozen and reheated still taste better to me. Here, I've used a combination of all-purpose flour and bread flour, and this seems to produce a good soft result without being too chewy. Pita needs very little yeast, as the rolling and the very hot oven create the lift. So if your oven doesn't get hot enough, you'll have to make them at a friend's house.

MAKES ABOUT 8 OR 9

2¼ cups bread flour	1 teaspoon fine salt
1½ cups all-purpose flour	2 tablespoons sunflower oil,
1 teaspoon instant yeast	plus extra for kneading
1 tablespoon super-fine sugar	1⅓ cups warm water

Measure the two flours, yeast, sugar and salt into a mixing bowl, then add the oil and water and mix to a soft sticky dough. Cover, and leave the dough for 10 minutes, then rub another 1 tablespoon of oil onto the work surface to cover an area about the size of a dinner plate. Place the dough on the oiled surface and knead it lightly just for 10 seconds until smooth (see pages 13 to 14). Return the dough to the bowl, cover again and repeat the light kneading twice more at 10-minute intervals. Then leave the dough for 30 minutes.

Heat the oven to at least 475°F. Place a clean baking sheet in the oven and leave it for 20 minutes to get very hot. Meanwhile, on a lightly floured surface, divide the dough into roughly 4-ounce pieces. Shape each piece into a ball and leave, covered, for 15 minutes to rest. Roll each ball out into an oval roughly ¼ inch thick, and leave to rest for 2 minutes.

Quickly lift the baking sheet out of the oven, shut the door, lay one or two pita on it and return the baking sheet to the oven. Bake for 3 to 5 minutes or until risen and barely colored. Immediately remove with tongs and leave to cool under a cloth, to keep the pitas soft and moist, while you finish baking the remaining dough.

Garlic, dried thyme and lemon pita

Slice and fry several cloves of garlic in 2 tablespoons sunflower oil, leave to cool, then use this to replace the plain sunflower oil in the recipe. Add 2 teaspoons dried thyme (not fresh), ground to a powder, and the finely grated zest of a lemon to the dough, then follow the remaining steps as directed.

Olive oil and potato flatbread

This is a focaccia-style dough, which makes a great base for everything from pizzas to bread rolls. Adding grated potato keeps the crumb a bit softer after baking but, I'll warn you, the dough here is much stickier than you may be used to. If you rely on a coating of olive oil on both the work surface and your hands, it will help you along. The recipe combines a long rise with stretching and folding, to open up the texture of the dough and give you lots of big bubbles in the crumb.

1½ cups "oo" flour	1 large potato (about 6 ounces), peeled
1½ cups bread flour	1 cup warm water
1 teaspoon fine sea salt	olive oil
1 teaspoon instant yeast	sea salt flakes for finishing

Put the "oo" flour, bread flour, salt and yeast into a large bowl and stir it together with your fingers. Grate the potato into the warm water, then mix this with the dry ingredients until you have an incredibly soft and sticky dough, adding more water if the dough seems dry. Cover the bowl with a tea towel and leave it for 10 minutes.

   Pour 1 tablespoon of oil over the dough and a little more onto your hand. Rub the top of the dough to spread the oil, and push down around the edges with your fingers to loosen the dough so it moves freely, coated in oil. Now, while rotating the bowl, pull the dough up out of the bowl by about a hand's width, then let it drop back down. Do this six to eight times to stretch the dough, then cover the bowl again and leave. Repeat this stretching after

10 and 20 minutes using just enough additional oil to stop your hands from sticking, then cover the bowl and leave for 30 minutes.

Oil a large dinner plate well. Using a plastic scraper, lift the dough out of the bowl in one swift movement and plonk it on the plate. Give the dough a blanket fold (see page 14), then stick the plate and dough inside a grocery bag and leave for 30 minutes. Repeat the blanket fold, then cover the plate and leave for another 30 minutes. Try to keep the dough in a neat-looking rectangle each time.

Heat the oven to 425°F. Oil a 12-inch-square rimmed baking sheet (or similar) and place the dough in the center of it. Give the dough another blanket fold to get it looking neat, then flip it over so the seam is underneath. Cover once more with the grocery bag, cutting it open with scissors to get an easier fit and oiling the side that touches the dough so it doesn't stick.

Leave the dough for about 30 minutes, or until you notice it looks puffier. To bake, simply take off the bag, pour a little more oil over the dough, press firmly right down through the dough with your fingertips to "dimple" the top well, sprinkle a little sea salt over the top and pop it in the oven. Bake for 20 minutes, then reduce the heat to 400°F and bake for another 10 to 15 minutes until the loaf is a light golden brown.

Leek rarebit flatbread

Slice three medium-sized leeks into thin rings and simmer in a pan of water until tender. Drain well and press with a cloth to remove some water. Then, just before your bread is ready to be baked, beat together ½ cup flour, ½ cup dark ale, 1 tablespoon Colman's dry mustard powder and ½ teaspoon fine salt until smooth. Add 1¼ cups grated Cheddar, stir the mixture through the leeks, then carefully spread over the top of the dough just before it goes into the oven.

Nothing signifies a breakfast loaf quite like the sight of dried fruit bursting through the crust, ready to be sliced, toasted, spread with butter and eaten while still hot. Forget croissants; a heartier slice or small bun of fruit bread is for me the ultimate lazy morning pleasure.

There are a couple of things to watch with fruited, sweet and spiced dough. The dried fruit draws moisture from the dough as it rises, so if you're adding lots of fruit to the mixture you might want to keep the dough extra soft and moist so the crumb doesn't end up dry. Sugars and spices slow down the rising time of yeast dough, so the sweeter and spicier the dough the more yeast and warmth you need to get it to rise. Sugar also makes the crust brown very quickly, and as dried fruit often pop through the crust during baking, watch the temperature for the last 20 minutes and reduce it if it starts to burn.

Layering spices through a fruit bread is one of the best ways of boosting the flavor while still keeping the dough light and quick rising. Rolling the dough flat, dusting it with spices and rolling it up tightly creates a spiced swirl through the crumb when baked. This gives each slice an intense flavor while still allowing the yeast to bubble in the dough without hindrance, keeping the crumb delicate and soft.

Cinnamon and raisin loaf

Here the half-sponge method is used to make an easy fruited bread.

FOR THE SPONGE
1 cup warm water
1 teaspoon instant yeast
1⅓ cups bread flour
1½ cups raisins

FOR THE DOUGH
1⅓ cups bread flour, plus extra
    for shaping and dusting
1 teaspoon fine salt
2 tablespoons unsalted butter or lard,
    plus extra for greasing the pan
¼ cup light brown sugar
2 teaspoons ground cinnamon
oil for kneading

To make the sponge, pour the warm water into a mixing bowl and stir in the yeast. Add the 1⅓ cups flour, stir it well, then fold in the raisins. Cover the bowl and leave for 2 to 4 hours, or even overnight (so you can mix this in the morning and return to it after work, or late on a Friday night for baking on a Saturday morning).

When you're ready to make your dough, put the 1⅓ cups flour into a bowl, add the salt and rub the butter through until it vanishes, so there are no little lumps floating around. Add the sugar and cinnamon and stir. Pour in the yeast batter, mix the whole lot up into a big sticky lump of dough, then scrape the bits off your fingers. Cover the bowl with a tea towel and leave for 10 minutes. Knead the dough (see pages 13 to 14), repeating twice at 10-minute intervals, then cover and leave for another 30 minutes.

Butter and flour a loaf pan, 7½ inches long or similar, then lightly flour the work surface, roll the dough into a rectangle ¾ inch thick that measures slightly less than the length of the pan across the short end, roll it up tightly and place seam-side down in the pan. Cover the pan with a tea towel and leave until increased in size by half, about 1 to 1½ hours.

Heat the oven to at least 425°F, though if you can get it 75°F hotter, even better. Steam the oven if you like (see page 16), dust flour over the dough with a small fine sieve or tea-strainer, slash the loaf down the center about ½ inch deep with a razor blade or sharp knife, and bake for 20 minutes. Reduce the heat to 400°F and bake for another 20 to 25 minutes until the crust is the color you like.

Winter apple loaf

When colder weather arrives and the nights start drawing in, I begin to think about log fires, real ale and hot roast pork sandwiches, and this is the bread for it. Toast the seeds at 400°F for 10 minutes to give them a nutty flavor.

1 small dessert apple
1 small onion, finely chopped
⅓ cup cider or ale
¾ cup warm water
2 teaspoons instant yeast
½ cup sunflower seeds, toasted

½ cup pumpkin seeds, toasted
2 cups malted-grain flour
1⅓ cups bread flour
1½ teaspoons fine sea salt
oil for kneading

Grate the apple into a bowl, with the peel but without the core and seeds, then add the raw onion. Stir in the cider, warm water and yeast. Add the toasted seeds, the two flours and salt, then mix well, adding more water if the dough seems dry. Leave for 10 minutes, then lightly oil the work surface, knead the dough just once for 10 seconds (see page 13), then return it to the bowl and leave for 45 minutes. Shape the dough into a ball, then sit it on a baking sheet lined with parchment paper, so the seam side is hidden underneath the loaf. Cover with a cloth and leave for about an hour to rise. Heat the oven to 425°F, cut a cross in the top of the loaf and bake for 20 minutes. Reduce the heat to 350°F and bake for another 20 minutes.

Apricot and wheat germ loaf

I read that scientists working in Jordan discovered that adding a small amount of mashed-up dates to ordinary white dough produced a bigger loaf that lasted longer. A tip well suited to this moist apricot bread.

¾ cup boiling water
⅓ cup chopped pitted dates
½ cup low-fat plain yogurt
1½ teaspoons instant yeast
1 cup chopped dried apricots
¾ teaspoon ground cinnamon
1 tablespoon honey

2 tablespoons wheat germ
2⅔ cups bread flour, plus
    extra for shaping and dusting
1 teaspoon fine salt
oil for kneading
sesame seeds

Pour the boiling water on the dates and leave until just warm, then place in a blender with the yogurt and whiz it at high speed until smooth, or press through a fine sieve with the back of a spoon. Pour into a bowl, stir in the yeast, apricots, cinnamon, honey and wheat germ, then add the flour and salt and work to a sticky dough. Cover and leave for 10 minutes, then knead on a lightly oiled work surface for about 10 seconds (see pages 13 to 14). Return to the bowl, cover, repeat the kneading twice at 10-minute intervals, then leave, covered, for 30 minutes. Roll the dough out into a rectangle on a lightly floured work surface, then roll it up tightly and place seam-side down on a floured baking sheet. Brush with water and sprinkle generously with sesame seeds. Leave for 30 to 45 minutes or until increased in size by half, cut a slash along the top and bake at 425°F for 15 minutes. For a darker crust, bake about 20 minutes more at 400°F, or for a paler crust, bake at 350°F for another 20 to 25 minutes.

Banana maple pecan buns

Soft, dark and moist, an alternative to hot cross buns at Easter.

MAKES 12

FOR THE SPONGE
1 cup milk
2 teaspoons instant yeast
2 cups bread flour

FOR THE DOUGH
about 1 cup ripe mashed banana
4 tablespoons unsalted butter, melted
2 tablespoons maple syrup or honey
1 cup roughly chopped pecans
1 cup raisins
2 cups bread flour,
    plus extra for shaping
1½ teaspoons each ground
    cinnamon and ginger
1 tablespoon cocoa
¼ cup muscovado sugar
¾ teaspoon fine salt
oil for kneading
beaten egg for brushing

To make the sponge, boil the milk, then return it to the measuring cup, topping off with water to make sure you still have 1 cup. Leave until just warm, then stir with the yeast and the 2 cups flour in a mixing bowl. Cover and leave to bubble for 2 to 3 hours.

When ready to make the dough, add to the sponge the banana, butter, maple syrup, pecans and raisins. Sift the of 2 cups flour, the spices, cocoa, sugar and salt together. Stir this into the mixing bowl and work everything together into a sticky dough. Leave for 10 minutes, lightly oil the work surface and gently knead the dough for 10 seconds (see pages 13 to 14). Return to the bowl, cover and repeat the light kneading twice more at 10-minute intervals, then leave the dough to rest for 30 minutes. Divide into 12 equal pieces; shape into balls with a little flour, then place touching on a baking sheet lined with parchment paper. Slip the baking sheet inside a grocery bag, tuck the end in to keep it warm and leave until risen by half. Heat the oven to 400°F. Brush the buns with beaten egg, then bake for 20 to 25 minutes.

Spiced stout buns

Another Easter bun, but with a dark spicy richness.

MAKES ABOUT 20

1⅓ cups stout or dark ale

1½ teaspoon each ground ginger, cinnamon and mace

1½ teaspoon instant yeast

6½ cups bread flour, plus extra for shaping and piping

2 cups raisins

1 cup hot black tea

1 cup mixed candied citrus peel or finely chopped dried apricots

1 egg

4 tablespoons melted butter

¼ cup super-fine sugar, plus 1 tablespoon

1½ teaspoons salt

oil for kneading

cold water for piping and boiling water for glazing

The night before, mix the stout, spices, yeast and 2½ cups of the flour in a large bowl, and put the raisins, tea and mixed peel in another bowl. Next day, beat the egg and butter with the soaked fruit, then stir this mixture into the spiced stout batter. Mix in the remaining flour, the sugar and salt and leave for 10 minutes. Lightly oil your hands and a 12-inch patch of work surface, and knead the dough for 10 seconds (see pages 13 to 14), repeating this twice at 10-minute intervals. Leave it for an hour.

Line a baking sheet with parchment paper, divide the dough into 4-ounce pieces, shape them into balls with a little flour and place, touching, on the baking sheet. Leave until increased in size by about half. Heat the oven to 400°F, mix a little flour with water to make a paste and pipe a cross onto each ball of dough; then bake for 25 minutes. Mix the 1 tablespoon super-fine sugar with a little boiling water, and brush this over the tops while still hot.

Rather than pipe an individual cross onto each unbaked bun, I find it easier to pipe a line of paste along each row from left to right, then toward me at right angles to these lines, to form a piped cross shape on each bun.

Sticky toffee apple buns

Pecan-studded cinnamon dough twisted around golden apple pieces in rum syrup.

MAKES 9

3½ cups bread flour

3 teaspoons instant yeast

¼ cup warm water

1½ teaspoons fine salt

1½ teaspoons ground cinnamon

¼ cup brown sugar, any sort

9 tablespoons unsalted butter, softened

⅔ cup milk, scalded then left until just warm

1⅓ cup low-fat plain yogurt

1 egg

1¼ cups chopped pecans

oil for kneading

¾ cup super-fine sugar

¼ cup cold water

5 large dessert apples, peeled, cored and diced

2 tablespoons dark rum

Mix ⅓ cup of the flour in a cup with the yeast and warm water, and leave for 15 minutes to bubble. Put the remaining flour, salt, cinnamon and brown sugar in a bowl and rub in the butter. Whisk the yeast mixture into the milk with the yogurt and egg, then add with the pecans to the flour. Mix together, then leave for 30 minutes. Knead the dough once on a lightly oiled work surface for 10 seconds (see pages 13 to 14), cover and leave for 1 to 2 hours or until risen by half.

Gently heat the super-fine sugar in a frying pan with the cold water until the sugar dissolves, then boil hard until it turns to a dark reddish caramel. Remove from the heat and carefully add the apples and rum, watching as it may splutter fiercely; then return to the heat and cook until the caramel is a thick syrup and the apples tender. Drain the apples and cool, saving the syrup.

Line a deep 12-inch square pan with parchment paper. Roll the dough out to about a 12-inch square, spoon the drained apples over the top and roll up tightly. Cut into nine slices and place three by three in the pan. Leave, covered, until risen by a half, about 1½ hours. Heat the oven to 400°F, then bake for 30 minutes. Spoon the syrup over the top and leave in the pan until just warm.

Lemon and almond buns

These buns are made with a lemon-flavored butter dough that bakes like brioche around a gooey core of marzipan. Stollen for the sultana-shy.

MAKES 9

3 cups bread flour
1½ teaspoons fine salt
finely grated zest of 2 lemons
2 teaspoons instant yeast
3 tablespoons super-fine sugar
7 tablespoons unsalted butter,
  plus extra for the pan

1 cup milk
1 egg
oil for kneading
12 ounces marzipan (see page 340)
melted butter, toasted almond
  slivers and confectioners' sugar
  to finish

Start the night before. Toss the flour, salt, lemon zest, yeast and sugar together in a bowl. Barely melt the butter and beat with the milk and egg. Pour this into the dry ingredients and squish everything together into a soft and sticky dough. Mix it evenly then scrape any remaining dough from your fingers, cover the bowl tightly and leave in the refrigerator till the following morning.

Lightly oil the work surface, knead the dough once (see pages 13 to 14), then roll out to about 28 by 4 inches. Form the marzipan into a 28-inch stick, place along the center of the dough, then fold the dough over to seal. Allow it to relax for 10 minutes. Cut into nine pieces and place three by three, without turning them on end, in a deep 12-inch square pan lined with buttered foil. Leave to rise for about 1 to 1½ hours till risen by half. Heat the oven to 400°F and bake for 35 minutes until golden. Leave to cool, then brush with melted butter and dredge with almonds and confectioners' sugar.

Top tea cakes

This simple dough can be used for many bun recipes, even for little balls of dough deep-fried and dusted in confectioners' sugar as a New Year's Eve treat. But the tea cake, toasted and buttered, is my favorite. A hard fat in the dough keeps the tea cakes softer than butter would. White chocolate is called for in place of traditional or hard-to-find beef dripping, as its cocoa fat content stays as hard as dripping at room temperature. Now who would have thought beef fat and white chocolate had something in common?

MAKES 9

1½ tablespoons instant yeast
½ cup warm water
4⅔ cups bread flour
⅔ cup milk
1 tablespoon corn syrup
2 tablespoons super-fine sugar
2 ounces white chocolate, roughly chopped
1 cup currants

1 cup chopped mixed candied citrus peel
½ teaspoon each ground ginger, nutmeg and cinnamon
1 teaspoon fine salt
3 eggs
oil for kneading, butter for the baking sheets and beaten eggs for glazing

Dissolve the yeast in the warm water with 3 tablespoons of the flour. Stir this together well, then leave for 15 minutes to bubble. Meanwhile, heat the milk until boiling, then remove from the heat and add the corn syrup, sugar, white chocolate, currants, peel, spices and salt. Stir well and leave to cool. Beat the eggs and stir these into the milk mixture. Place the remaining flour in a bowl, stir the yeast mixture with the milk mixture, then tip this into the flour and stir well until evenly combined. Cover the bowl, leave for 10 minutes, then knead the dough (see pages 13 to 14), repeating after 15 and 30 minutes. Cover and leave for another 30 minutes.

Divide the dough into nine pieces and shape into balls. Butter two baking sheets, roll the balls flat so they sit about ¾ inch high and lay them on the baking sheets about 1½ inches apart. Place the baking sheets inside grocery bags and leave until increased in height by half (about 1 to 1½ hours). Heat the oven to 425°F. Brush the tops of the dough with beaten egg and bake for 12 to 15 minutes or until risen and golden. Don't bake for too long as you want them to stay soft. Leave to cool on a wire rack, covered with a clean tea towel.

TWEAKING THOSE TEA CAKES

You can change this tea cake recipe by varying what you add to the dough: marmalade instead of candied peel, crystallized ginger instead of the spices, candied cherries and other fruit such as mango in place of the currants, or by adding some slivered nuts. But master the basic recipe first, so that you know the consistency of the dough you're aiming for, and be prepared to adjust the amount of flour to allow for changes you may have made to the moisture content. One favorite of mine follows, to get you started.

"Panettone" tea cakes

This recipe marries some of the flavors of Italian panettone to the dough and convenient dimensions of a British tea cake.

MAKES 9

1½ tablespoons instant yeast
½ cup warm water
4⅔ cups bread flour
¼ cup milk
3 ounces white chocolate, roughly chopped
1 tablespoon corn syrup
2 tablespoons super-fine sugar
11 ounces mixed dried fruit
1 teaspoon fine salt
3 eggs, plus 3 egg yolks

finely grated zest of 1 orange and 1 lemon
1 tablespoon honey
1 tablespoon each vanilla extract, orange flower water and rose water
oil for kneading, butter for the baking sheets and beaten egg for glazing
sugar cubes

Dissolve the yeast in the warm water with 3 tablespoons of the flour. Stir this together well, then leave for 15 minutes to bubble. Meanwhile, heat the milk

BREAD

until boiling, then remove from the heat, add the white chocolate and leave to melt. Stir in the corn syrup, sugar, dried fruit and salt, stir well and leave to cool. Beat the eggs and yolks with the zest, honey and liquid flavorings and stir these into the milk mixture. Place the remaining flour in a bowl, stir the yeast mixture with the milk mixture, then pour this into the flour and stir well until evenly combined. Cover the bowl, leave for 10 minutes, then knead the dough (see pages 13 to 14), repeating after 15 and 30 minutes. Cover and leave for another 30 minutes.

Divide the dough into nine pieces and shape into balls. Butter two baking sheets, roll the balls flat so they sit about ¾ inch high and lay them on the baking sheet about 1½ inches apart. Place the baking sheets inside grocery bags and leave until increased in height by half (about 1 to 1½ hours). Heat the oven to 425°F. Brush the tops of the dough with beaten egg. Smash up some sugar cubes and sprinkle on each bun, then bake for 12 to 15 minutes. Don't bake for too long as you want them to stay soft. Leave to cool on a wire rack, covered with a clean tea towel.

Brioche

A classic recipe for making the French bread that permits you to consume a large amount of butter in an elegant fashion. The dough keeps in the refrigerator for a few days so it can be mixed ahead of time. Perfect for any dinner party conversation that would benefit from you saying, "We make our own brioche as you can't buy anything decent." Listen, there's a style war raging out there and you need to throw in every culinary grenade you can lay your hands on.

The butter isn't mixed in until the dough has been made and though this makes the whole thing a right pain in the bum it also gets the best result. Just get down and dirty and mix it on the work surface. It's easy, but messy, so make sure you've got a sink full of warm soapy water ready to wash your hands in at the end. And take the phone off the hook.

MAKES 2

¼ cup milk

2 teaspoons instant yeast

3 cups bread flour

5 eggs, plus 3 yolks

¼ cup super-fine sugar

1½ teaspoons fine salt

1 cup (2 sticks) unsalted butter,
softened, plus extra for the pans

At least one day before you want to bake the dough, heat the milk in a pan until boiling, then pour into a measuring cup and leave until just warm. Top off with warm water to bring it back to ¼ cup (some liquid will have evaporated), then stir in the yeast. Add 2 tablespoons of flour to the yeast mixture. Stir well, cover the measuring cup with a saucer and leave for 30 minutes. (This step helps get the yeast revved up to take on the butter-rich dough.) Once the yeast is active, beat 4 of the eggs and the yolks, sugar and salt together in a mixing bowl, then pour in the yeast mixture. Add the remaining flour and stir until it forms a rough dough. Cover the bowl and leave for 30 minutes; no kneading, no nothing.

Scrape the dough onto a clean work surface and have a scraper ready. This is the time when you need to be left alone. Cut the butter into small pieces and mix it into the dough with your hands. Then start working the butter into the dough, as if you're energetically playing a sticky accordion, rubbing the butter into the dough as you stretch it back and forth. Do this as fast as you can, scraping the dough off the work surface as you go. Use the scraper to push the dough back together should it start to spread too far. Once all of the butter has disappeared, and the dough feels elastic and very soft, scrape it back into the bowl, cover and chill overnight. At this point the dough can be kept for another 2 days before using.

To bake, simply butter two loaf pans, 7 inches long or similar, divide the dough in half and shape each piece into a cylinder. Place them in the pans, seam-side down, cover with a cloth and leave for 2 to 3 hours until increased in size by at least half. Heat the oven to 425°F. Beat the remaining egg, brush on the tops of the loaves and bake for 15 minutes. Then reduce the heat to 350°F and bake for about 20 minutes more, or until a rich golden brown all over.

Snips across the top made with a large pair of scissors encourage the dough to tear at those points when it bakes, rather than along the side. Scissor snips are more typical on a brioche loaf than a razor cut.

Chocolate chip brioche

To make chocolate chip brioche, stir in 9 ounces chocolate, chopped into ¼-inch bits, just before you finish kneading the dough, then proceed with the recipe as directed.

Stollen

The adopted Christmas favorite in Britain. Once buttered, sugared and wrapped in waxed paper it's best stored for at least a few days before eating, so that the crumb becomes slightly firmer. My inspiration for this recipe was Erich Weber's *250 Konditorei-Spezialitäten, und wie sie entstehen* from 1934.

3 cups bread flour, plus
    extra for shaping
⅓ cup super-fine sugar
¾ teaspoon fine salt
1 teaspoon each ground
    cardamom, nutmeg and
    cinnamon
½ cup ground almonds
2 teaspoons instant yeast
8 ounces mixed dried fruit

⅔ cup milk
9 tablespoons unsalted butter
1 egg, plus 2 yolks
2 tablespoons dark rum
finely grated zest of 1 lemon
oil for kneading
8 ounces marzipan (see page 340)
melted butter and confectioners'
    sugar to finish

Combine 2⅔ cups of the flour with the sugar, salt, spices, almonds, yeast and fruit in a large mixing bowl. Whisk the milk and remaining ⅓ cup flour together in a pan and bring just to a boil. Spoon the resulting paste into another bowl.

Use the pan to barely melt the butter; then when it has cooled a little, beat this into the milk mixture with the egg, yolks, rum and zest. Stir this into the flour and mix to a very soft and sticky dough. Leave for 10 minutes, then lightly knead the dough (see page 13), return to the bowl and leave for about 2 hours. Knead the dough once more then roll out on a lightly floured work surface into an oval measuring about 10 by 8 inches. Roll the marzipan out to a 10-inch stick, lay it in the middle of the dough, and then fold the dough over and press it down around the bump of the marzipan to seal it. Lay the dough on a baking sheet lined with parchment paper, cover with a cloth and leave until increased in size by half. Heat the oven to 400°F. Bake the stollen for 35 minutes, then remove from the oven and leave to cool. When warm, brush all over lavishly with melted butter to seal it. Leave to cool, dust with a thick layer of confectioners' sugar, and wrap snugly in wax paper to store.

STOLLEN MOMENTS

You can soak the dried fruit in boiling water for 10 minutes to make it plumper, but do make sure that you then drain it well and pat it dry, or you'll make the dough too wet. Be careful only to bake the stollen until the crumb is set, as this will ensure it stays soft and moist inside.

Poppy-seed walnut strudel

Allow about five hours for this sweet yeasted dough epic, and make sure you add the ingredients as specified, reserving parts until needed!

1 cup milk

1 teaspoon instant yeast

2⅔ cups bread flour,
    plus more for shaping

⅓ cup poppy seeds

5 tablespoons unsalted butter,
    softened

½ teaspoon each ground cloves
    and cinnamon

1¼ cups finely ground walnuts

⅓ cup dark brown sugar

1 tablespoon honey

1 small pinch of ground cardamom

1 egg, plus 1 yolk

1 tablespoon dark rum

1 big pinch of finely grated
    lemon zest

¾ teaspoon fine salt

SHORT & SWEET

Bring ¾ cup of the milk to a boil, pour into a mixing bowl and leave until just warm. Stir in the yeast and 1⅓ cups of the flour and leave for an hour.

In a saucepan, make the filling by gently heating the poppy seeds, 2 tablespoons of the butter, the cloves and cinnamon with the remaining milk until boiling, then spoon this into a bowl and beat in the walnuts, sugar, honey and cardamom. Beat the whole egg in a cup; stir three-quarters of it into the filling and reserve the rest.

When the yeast mixture has had an hour to ferment, beat in the egg yolk, rum and zest. Rub the remaining 3 tablespoons butter through the remaining 1⅓ cups flour with the salt, then add the yeast mixture and work to a sticky dough. Leave the dough, covered, for 30 minutes, then knead just once for 10 seconds (see pages 13 to 14) and leave again for 30 minutes. Roll the dough out to a 14-inch square on a lightly floured work surface and spread with the poppy-seed filling. Roll up tightly, lay the log on a baking sheet lined with parchment paper and leave, covered, for about 1 hour until increased in size by half. Heat the oven to 350°F. Brush with the remaining beaten egg and bake for about 40 minutes.

I didn't want to let this chapter pass without saying something about sourdough bread making. Even if the process is more "slow and steady" than "short and sweet," my hope is that, as you become more confident in your baking, you might become interested in trying something new, something that can push your baking up another notch.

So here's something to try. Take a small handful of rye flour and mix it with some warm water into a soft dough that you can form into a ball. Place this in a bowl, cover it with more rye flour and leave at room temperature for four or five days. What you'll see happen is that the crust of flour over the dough ball starts to crack as the natural yeast and bacteria found in the flour start to aerate the dough. If you then take the ball, mash it to a soupy consistency with water in a very clean jar, adding more flour to get it to a soft paste, then leave it another day, lightly covered, you will – in the most basic way – have created your first leaven (or sourdough "starter").

At first the mixture has very little acidity and aeration, but if you encourage the microorganisms' competition for nutrients, then in a week or so it should be bubbling well and have taken on a distinct sour aroma. Each day, stir the mixture, then discard most of it and replenish it with equal quantities of fresh flour and water. Don't cover the jar too tightly, it may need – quite literally – to be able to let off a little pressure. Adding a little acidity when you first mix your sourdough leaven soup, like a scant 1 teaspoon of yogurt, will make the mixture slightly sour and should stop bad-smelling bugs taking hold. Occasionally they still do, as there's a "potluck" element to what organisms you get in your leaven to begin with, in which case it's better to start again with a clean jar. But usually it's enough to keep discarding and refreshing the mixture, and, like with regular exercise for us, it will gradually get stronger (and more acidic) over time. Once you've got it into a sturdy state where it can double in volume in six to eight hours, you're ready to bake.

Of course going from this to a great naturally leavened loaf is a little complex but here's the basic recipe: a mixture of three-quarters bread flour to a quarter whole-wheat or rye is easiest; all white can get a bit sticky and more whole-wheat can make the loaf too heavy.

Take 2¼ cups bread flour and ¾ cup whole-wheat flour, and add to it 1½ cups leaven from your jar, with about 1 cup warm water and 1½ teaspoons salt, and mix this into a smooth soft dough, adding more water if the dough seems dry. Knead the dough (see pages 13 to 14) then leave it to rise by half. Be prepared for this first rise to take anywhere from 2 to 4 hours, longer if it's very cold in your kitchen. Then shape the dough and bake it when it has risen by half again; but be patient, this rise takes much longer than a loaf made with instant yeast.

You can even use leaven in place of commercial yeast in some of the recipes in this chapter. As long as you refresh your leaven each day with the appropriate amounts of flour and water (e.g. ¾ cup flour and ½ cup water), the basic rule when adapting a recipe is then to omit the instant yeast and reduce both the flour and the water in the recipe by ¾ cup and ⅓ cup, adding instead 1 cup of leaven. But measure your water and add it to the dough gradually, to allow for any variations in the consistency of your leaven.

So, to turn the easy white loaf (see page 19) into a bread with a much more complex acidic flavor, reduce the bread flour to 2½ cups, omit the yeast, keep the salt the same and add 1 cup leaven to the flour and salt. Measure out your water but only use about 1 cup — enough to mix everything to a soft dough. Then follow the recipe, but allow much longer for the first and final rise. The key thing is to shape the dough when it has risen by half, then bake it when it has risen by half again.

Do experiment with other simple bread recipes in the chapter, but bear in mind, it gets more complex when the recipes contain lots of fat, sugar or spices as these can stop the leaven in its tracks, or when the "sponge" method is used — the calculations can get a bit complicated. Start simply, and accept that you're learning a complex and fascinating set of new baking skills, and in time your naturally leavened loaves will improve with practice. And you'll find that the difference in the baked loaf is really noticeable. The flavor will be more strongly acidic, the crumb texture will be slightly waxy and darker, and the aeration will be a little more irregular and interesting.

But there ain't no shortcuts here, I'm afraid. You can't mimic making a leaven sourdough starter from scratch by mixing flour and water with a little instant yeast and leaving it in a jar for a week — the result will be a loaf that smells unpleasantly of yeast. The beautiful flavor and texture that a naturally leavened bread displays can only be achieved by taking the long route.

The convenience of a bread machine has changed the way many think about home bread making, and you have to give a nod to the genius who worked out how to combine the mixing, kneading and baking into one neat box, which sits on the kitchen work surface. The advantage is in simplicity and a little time saving, as you do need to be around when the bread is ready. Bread machines make sandwich bread very well, and sometimes better than your own oven, as the machine traps the steam inside to produce a crumb that is extra moist, light and soft. Other bread styles that aren't baked in the unit aren't really worth the machine's involvement, and are arguably easier by hand.

I firmly believe, after using different machines and recipes, that the best plan is to work with the manufacturer's recipe book that came with the machine, as different brands and models have subtly different programs that work to different times, temperatures and methods. If you have a machine, you'll also have a good idea of what works with it and what you'd like to change, and recipe books often can't cater to that. So what might be more helpful are some ideas for gently changing your own machine's recipes, in order to get an even better loaf.

To get the texture that you feel is perfect in your bread, you have to alter the ingredients, as times and temperatures are usually predetermined by the manufacturer. In some ways this makes life easier as there is less to worry about. What you need to focus on are the amounts of flour, water and yeast; the rest are much less important.

Adding more or less water will dramatically change the type of loaf you get. More water will make the dough lighter and softer, less will pull the texture in more tightly and make the loaf slightly heavier. If your loaf develops a crack around the top during baking or, when made with mostly bread flour, feels heavy, then add a few tablespoons more water and see if the problem lessens. Some ingredients, like rolled oats, cornmeal or dried fruit, will steal water from the dough so always allow a little extra if you're using them. A recipe that has a high proportion of whole-wheat flour will collapse back upon itself if you use too much water, so it's better to replace some whole-wheat with bread flour if you want to add more water.

The proportion of white bread flour in the recipe can be varied in a similar way, to improve the texture of the loaf. Often for simplicity the manufacturer will suggest, say, 50/50 whole-wheat flour and bread flour for a light whole-wheat texture, and this should make a nice soft-textured loaf. But increasing the proportion of bread flour and reducing the whole-wheat will lighten the loaf and help it rise more, just as half a crushed vitamin C tablet, added with the flour, will help to get a better rise from your loaf.

Most of the time I use slightly less yeast than the manufacturers suggest, say three-quarters of a teaspoon rather than a full one, as this usually produces a crumb that is more moist and free of any yeasty aroma. If you increase the water in the dough, the yeast will work faster, so slightly less is needed. And if there is a large amount of fat, or strong spices like ground ginger, then slightly more yeast is needed to get a light loaf.

When it comes to creating your own recipes, or adapting one from this book, the same rules apply. If you want to add grated vegetable or fruit to a loaf, or cooked vegetables like soft onions, remember that this will effectively add more liquid to the dough so you will need to reduce the water. Yogurt, soft cheese, honey and syrups, oils and melted butter all count as liquids to some degree, so if you're adding them to a plain bread machine recipe, you'll need less water to mix the dough. The reverse applies to adding oats or other "absorbing" ingredients: add a little extra water to the recipe or pour a little boiling water on the addition so it completely soaks in, and this will stop the ingredient making the dough too dry.

Cakes

Cakes

I truly believe that life is improved by cake. Cake soothes and charms all but the stoniest of attitudes, and brings a shine to the eyes of even the grumpiest children. And from the happiest to the saddest of life's experiences, icing and a soft crumb give us something sweet to cut and eat quietly when we've run out of words.

To be fair, all the best-tasting cakes made from scratch take a little effort. But as life goes that's not one of the biggest challenges you'll face. As cakes involve a little kitchen chemistry, it's usually best to stick with a recipe rather than trying to wing it, as the ratios of ingredients are much more important than in, say, a casserole where a little extra meat or wine will be perfectly acceptable. Be accurate with measurements and temperatures, have everything set up and ready in advance, and every cake recipe will be much easier.

In a cake recipe, the ingredients are less interchangeable than they might be in a cookie or brownie, because you're trying to hold this mixture of ingredients suspended in a light fragile crumb. In a raisin oatmeal cookie, it doesn't matter if the fruit sinks; no one will know. A chocolate brownie can have slightly too much sugar and butter, causing it to fall back upon itself and become moist and heavy, but is all the better for it. But in a cake, the aim is for airiness and delicacy, so measuring carefully and mixing thoughtfully become more important.

But I have those days when a cake needs a little extra help after baking, when it's a little too heavy, or sinks slightly in the middle when I'd wanted it to dome gently. That's when I dig into my bag of tricks, to give it a last-minute makeover. Dry cakes can be sliced horizontally and brushed with a light sugar syrup to make them moist, and some grand pastry chefs do this to all their cakes. Sunken cakes can be trimmed flat and the crumbs frozen, to be mixed through a crumble topping or hidden in the base of a trifle later on.

What matters most is that this cake, once dolled up and proudly displayed on a plate, gives you a sense of pride and satisfaction. You're the one who spent time carefully choosing and measuring the ingredients, even if the pace at times has been frantic. And when guests say, "You're a great baker," don't shrug it off. It's true. All the proof they need is in the glorious slice of cake they've just eaten.

What flour?

The mainstay of home cake baking is all-purpose flour, milled from soft grades of wheat. Don't look on the bag for a more detailed description of what it is for: unlike bread flour, it's not milled for a particular purpose. It may be of good quality or be rather poor, since for pastry, biscuits and cookies and some cakes its use is more for binding than for holding aeration or delicate structure, and so the quality of the flour will often be hidden in the final result. I tend to spend a bit more on all-purpose flour and go for a brand name that might at least fear the wrath of angry home bakers if the quality isn't good enough.

Adding flour that has a coarseness to it, like whole-wheat, spelt or rye, works best on cakes where there is already more texture in the crumb. So if ground almonds or hazelnuts are in the ingredients, or if the baked texture is quite firm or crisp, these flours work well. Sometimes the bran can add a slight bitterness, so think about mixing in something that will steer this toward a more positive association. Finely grated orange zest and almond extract have bitter elements that can be mixed with whole-wheat flour in this way. Rye flour has an acidity that works well with chocolate or apple. Remember with all bran-rich flours that they absorb more liquid, so add a little milk or water to the cake mixture to compensate.

Leavening agents

I usually use all-purpose flour and add in the leavening agent, as some cake mixtures require more or less according to how acid or alkaline the other ingredients are. Bananas will be quite acidic when they're green, but when very ripe they turn alkaline, usually needing more baking powder to stop cakes made with them from turning out heavy. You can replace the all-purpose flour and baking powder with self-rising flour, but some recipes might still need a little extra leavening agent to work well. You'll have to experiment.

I also keep small canisters of baking soda, which reacts to release gas bubbles when mixed with milk or yogurt and cream of tartar, an acidic powder that assists this reaction. When one part baking soda is freshly combined with two parts cream of tartar, the result is similar to using commercial baking powder but much more powerful, so less of this combination is needed if you're using it to replace baking powder. There are a few reasons for this. The first is that cream of tartar is, to be honest, both more expensive and more powerful than the cheaper agents often used in baking powder. Another is that when the two are combined, they start to react very slightly and degrade, and become less powerful as they sit on the shelf. This also means that even your baking powder should be bought in small quantities and discarded every 6 to 9 months if you want the best result.

Gluten-free baking powder

Baking powder often has an inert starch added to absorb moisture during storage, and this starch can be wheat-based, so if you're planning any gluten-free baking, do make sure that the leavening agent you're using is free from any unwanted ingredients.

Sugars and syrups

Super-fine sugar is usually best in cake making when you want the sugar to dissolve quickly and don't want brown speckles on a pale crumb. But if the crumb is slightly coarse and darker colored, then granulated sugar is fine. Light brown sugar is usually interchangeable with granulated but will give you a darker crumb, whereas extra dark molasses or muscovado sugar will make the sweetness less intense and introduce a new background flavor that reminds me of Guinness.

Honey and syrups aren't easy substitutes for the sugar in cakes as they add moisture as well, stressing the flour and pushing the mixture toward collapse. Do experiment but you'll need to reduce any other liquid in the recipe for the best result.

Butter and fats

Butter and other fats give cakes their rich texture and make the crumb more crumbly and delicate than, say, a loaf of bread. I use unsalted butter simply to help control how much salt I'm eating, but salted butter will work equally well in any recipe. Butter straight from the refrigerator or freezer is too firm to use for cake making. The simple trick is to cut it into small pieces and heat it in a pan or microwave until roughly one-third has melted. Spoon this into a mixing bowl, leave for 5 minutes and then add the sugar and beat well.

Hard vegetable fats sold for baking are the modern equivalent of using pork lard and will hold more aeration in the crumb and produce a slightly higher rise and a more stable cake. They can be used in place of butter but give the best combination of flavor and texture when used to replace just part of the butter in the recipe.

Keep some sunflower oil in the cupboard for baking, to use either in a carrot cake or to replace a small proportion of the butter in a recipe for an extra soft texture. You can replace a fifth of the butter in a cake recipe with oil and this will make the crumb fine and soft, and keep it moist for longer.

Eggs

Animal welfare issues aside, cakes made with factory-farmed chicken's eggs will still bake well-risen cakes, but sometimes the flavor is thin or, at worst, depending on how the poor caged birds are fed, decidedly fishy. So there is some benefit to the flavor of the cake in taking the moral high ground. But curiously, freshness is less desirable. You don't want eggs to be off, but if the whites are a little thin and sit softly rather than firmly when the egg is cracked, the cake mixture will be lighter and emulsify better. Room-temperature eggs will whisk much lighter than ice-cold ones so, if you remember, leave them out of the fridge overnight or warm them slightly for a few minutes in a bowl of warm water.

Liquids in the mix

Be really careful about adding extra liquid to cake mixtures, as they can collapse or develop a heavy thick layer at the base of the cake. Better always to look for drier ways to add flavor. Use orange zest rather than orange juice, for example, or a few drops of orange extract. The other way to add flavor is to make a syrup with the juice by stirring in some super-fine sugar, which will dissolve without heating, and spoon this over the cake after baking.

Sifting ingredients

If you don't have time to sift your flour and other ingredients before mixing them into the cake batter, it will probably work out just fine. The cake texture might be a little coarse with random pockets of air throughout but if you're relaxed about that, then go ahead. I nearly always sift just to make sure it's the best it can be.

Adding flour, and knowing when to stop

When flour is added to a cake mixture that is high in moisture, it can give you a slightly heavy crumb if overbeaten. Occasionally you find a recipe where flour is beaten with butter first (see Blueberry Crème Fraîche Cupcakes, page 191) and this restricts the gluten by coating the flour particles with fat so that moisture can't be absorbed that easily before baking. But the general rule is to only mix flour into other ingredients until barely combined, no more. The usual way to do this is by folding the flour through with a rubber spatula.

Electric or hand mixing?

To make the lightest cakes, you need to alternate between an electric mixer — either handheld or a stand — and gentle hand mixing. Yes, our grandmothers (and some grandfathers) would mix their cakes with little more than a hand whisk and determination, but given that even with a machine you need to cream butter and sugar for at least 3 minutes until light and fluffy, only the bravest would follow in their footsteps. Very old cookbooks would sometimes insist that eggs be whisked for 30 minutes by hand. Today, the simple way is to buy an electric mixer and make good use of it. Handheld electric mixers do a fine job, but if you're rushing around the house then a stand mixer might be a more useful option.

Creaming, beating, whisking, folding and stirring

"Cream" means to beat the butter and sugar — or eggs and sugar — until the texture of the sugar vanishes and the mixture is airier and a few shades paler in color, and this is easier if the bowl and ingredients aren't too cold or too hot. Once you get to this point, stop mixing; you can destroy the texture if you overdo it. It's not a great sin if you stop before the sugar is fully dissolved, but you'll get a lighter, finer texture if you really cream the mixture well.

"Beat" means to work all the ingredients together vigorously. The two important things to check are that the ingredients are soft enough to mix and that you continue until you have a smooth, even mixture. You can beat with a whisk attachment on a mixer, but by hand with a bowl and a wooden spoon is often easier, particularly when you're adding small amounts late in the method.

"Whisk" means beating the ingredients together but specifically to incorporate more air, using a much lighter action than beating. You can't do this with a wooden spoon, and an electric mixer will simply make a better, faster job of it.

"Fold" means to gently combine using a moderate cutting action right through the center of the cake mixture. Not too slowly as this can cause lumps to form, not too quickly, roughly or for too long as this risks losing any delicacy in the texture. Best to stop when the mixture is barely combined rather than risk overdoing it.

"Stir" means almost the same as fold but you don't need to be as careful. Just make sure to get the spoon or spatula down to the bottom of the bowl or pan so that every ingredient is mixed evenly.

Combining light and heavy mixtures

Whisked egg whites beaten to a froth that softly holds its shape are sometimes folded through a cake mixture to make the cake even lighter. The whisked egg whites contain millions of tiny air bubbles, which expand when the mixture is heated in the oven and this adds to aeration of the cake. There are two schools of thought on how best to fold the delicate egg whites through the heavy cake mixture: in stages, or all at once.

To do it in stages, take a third of the egg whites and fold them quickly and gently through the cake mixture to loosen it, then add the remaining egg whites and fold this through quickly, but stop just as the last traces of white are vanishing. The other way is to add all of the beaten egg whites and quickly and gently fold them through the mixture. The key to both methods is to be fast, light with your movements, and stop as soon as you see only the slightest trace of white remaining.

Into the pan

Before you start any recipe, get the pan ready. You'll get the best result if you can spoon the mixture into the pan as soon as it's mixed. But once you've done this you can often leave the filled pan for 5 to 10 minutes while you heat the oven since even if the mixture rises, it won't be disturbed. But do take care to gently transfer it to the oven. If the cake mixture is thick, then smooth the top lightly before you bake it. It doesn't need to be perfectly flat.

I use the same parchment paper, which has a coating that stops the paper from sticking to the crust of the cake, for almost all my baking, just to keep the shopping easier, and for most baking this nonstick surface is ideal. My mother used to cut up old brown paper bags and rub them with oil to make them nonstick, or use them without oil if, say, on a fruitcake, the sticking wasn't a problem.

You can use cake pans that are different from the ones suggested in the recipes, but do remember to adjust the baking times. The general rule is that the thinner the layer of mixture that sits in the pan, the shorter the baking time needs to be. So if you're using a pan with a larger surface area (and therefore less depth), the baking time will need to be less.

Baking

Heavy cake mixtures can sit in the pan at room temperature for a few hours before baking without major problems. But you still need to treat the pan as something slightly fragile, and not knock it around; the leavening agents will have started to work and you don't want to deflate the mixture. Cakes with a very light texture are best baked as soon as possible after mixing, as preserving every bit of aeration is more important here. So I usually put the oven on to heat up as soon as I start my mixing.

Most cakes are baked at 350°F or lower. If you want a very even rise to the top of the cake, you can cover the pan with a sheet of foil before baking and carefully remove it halfway through baking. This traps steam close to the top of the cake as it rises, making it slightly paler and preventing it from setting before the cake has fully risen.

It's usually best to position a rack in the oven so the cake sits in the center or top third of the space, where the heat is best. It can happen that a cake starts to color too quickly, particularly with fruit cakes. If it does, cover the top with a little foil, lower the temperature a little then continue to bake until done.

Try not to peep at the cake by opening the oven door during baking. If you must, make it brief and just open it an inch or so and peek in. I've never had a problem doing that but remember that you want to keep the heat in at all costs. Fruit cakes are much less fragile than butter or sponge cakes, and less likely to suffer from opening the door.

Sometimes you need to open the oven door during baking. On a soft cake mixture in a loaf pan (not a heavily fruited one), to get a perfect crack down the center like you see on those beautiful French pound cakes, open the oven door after 10 minutes' baking and very carefully run an oiled knife down through the center of the crust. Close the door carefully and continue.

Ideally you want to remove the cake as soon as the crumb is barely set, not later, as residual heat from the cake and the tin will continue to cook the crumb for 5 to 10 minutes after it has been removed from the oven. So if you get a fine wooden skewer, like a bamboo skewer or toothpick, and poke this into the center of the cake, it should have a few tiny moist crumbs stuck to it when you pull it out. If it's bone dry, then it should have come out earlier. Oops.

Judging the time it takes is a bit of an art, and I've under- and over-baked enough cakes to know that there's a degree of luck in getting it just right. Some things make the cake take longer to bake than the recipe suggests. A colder batter, especially a cold fruitcake mixture, takes longer to bake than a warm one, and could add 10 to 15 minutes to the bake time.

When things go wrong

If a cake sinks in the middle, the most likely reason is that the proportions of butter and sugar are too high for the amount of egg and flour in the recipe, and to solve it next time add a little more egg (or egg white) and flour to the recipe. It's very unlikely that a cake will sink because you've opened the oven door too early or shut it too forcefully. The ratios can be wrong for all sorts of reasons: your measurements might be off, it could be the recipe, or the characteristics of the particular batch of butter, eggs and flour you have might be different.

Butter can vary in fat content according to the price of milk, and sometimes butter contains more or less liquid to keep the price constant. Eggs will contain more or less liquid simply because eggs are unique, even though they're sold to us on the premise that they're as identical as nuts and bolts. Flour can hold more or less fat and sugar if the protein characteristics vary, and as all-purpose flour milling does not have a formula in the way that bread flour does, it can vary considerably. So lots of reasons for a fallen cake, but rectified by adding more flour and egg to the recipe next time. The rogue element here is liquid. If there is extra liquid in the recipe, reduce that as well, as that will stress the flour even further and might cause the cake to sink.

Dry cakes can be caused for a similar reason: maybe the butter, sugar or eggs were insufficient for the amount of flour used. Rectify this next time by slightly increasing the butter, sugar and egg (or egg yolk). If you need to keep it healthful, then add a grated apple or pear and this will make the crumb extra moist.

But if you're stuck with a cake that, for whatever reason, has sunk in the middle, or turned out dry, or burnt around the edges, don't despair. If you can't disguise it by trimming and icing, you need to take more drastic action. Fill a sunken center with whipped cream or berries, or cut the cake in half horizontally, put a bulging layer of fruit and thick custard in the middle, and turn the top half upside down before replacing it. If all else fails, cut out that fallen center and ice the whole cake as a ring, and nobody need ever know. Or if it's just that the crumb seems dry, slice the cake into layers, make holes with a cocktail stick, and brush the surfaces with Fresh Cake Syrup (page 339).

Easy carrot cake

This is a great standard recipe to keep handy, perfect for tweaking with other ingredients. If it's too hot in the house, keep the cake chilled in the refrigerator after icing.

1⅓ cups all-purpose flour
2 teaspoons baking powder
1 teaspoon ground cinnamon
½ teaspoon ground cloves
½ teaspoon ground nutmeg
1 cup light brown sugar

⅔ cup sunflower oil
3 eggs
1¾ cups grated carrot
⅔ cup chopped walnuts or pecans
Simple Lemon Cream Cheese
    Frosting (page 330)

Heat the oven to 350°F and line the bottoms of two 8-inch round cake pans with parchment paper. Sift the flour, baking powder and spices together into a bowl. In a large bowl, mix the brown sugar with the oil and beat with the eggs until smooth. Stir the carrot and chopped nuts into this mixture, then fold in the sifted dry ingredients. Divide evenly between the two pans and bake for about 25 minutes until a skewer inserted comes out with just a few tiny moist crumbs stuck to it. Cool in the pans. Sandwich the cake layers together with a third of the frosting, and spread the remainder over the top and sides.

SCALING UP

I made a bigger version of this cake for a friend's birthday party a while back, and the easiest way to scale up the cake is to increase the "cake" ingredients by 50 percent and bake three, rather than two, 8-inch layers.

You may like more or less frosting, so you need to use your judgment on how to handle that part of the finished cake, but do bear in mind that compared to a two-layer cake, you won't need anything like a 50 percent increase in the quantity of icing for a three-layer version. I'd suggest increasing it by maybe 25 percent.

Carrot, orange and pistachio cake

This is just a little more difficult than the easy carrot cake – a big American-style layer cake with Arabic bits. Imagine Pamela Anderson as a platinum-blonde Scheherazade. I don't know if it counts as a healthful cake but it has a few points to recommend it to the health police. Like carrots. Carrots are good for you. Tahini, excellent for the liver and skin. Pistachios, all that nutty protein and those plant sterols that reduce cholesterol. All that sugar and cream cheese? Okay, it slips quite a bit there. Maybe just one wee slice then.

⅓ cup tahini
½ cup sunflower oil
3 tablespoons pomegranate
   syrup or blackstrap molasses
finely grated zest of 3 oranges
1 cup light brown sugar
3 eggs, 2 of them separated
1¾ cups grated carrot
¾ cup chopped pistachios

½ cup orange juice
1⅓ cups all-purpose flour
2½ teaspoons baking powder
2 teaspoons ground cinnamon
½ teaspoon ground cloves
½ teaspoon ground nutmeg
Simple Lemon Cream Cheese
   Frosting (page 330)

Line three 8-inch round cake pans with a disk of parchment paper. In a large mixing bowl whisk together the tahini, oil, syrup, orange zest and brown sugar until smooth. Beat in one whole egg plus two yolks (reserving the whites) until combined, then stir in the grated carrot, pistachios and juice. Sift the flour, baking powder and spices together, then stir them through the mixture. Whisk the two egg whites until white and fluffy, then carefully fold through the mixture.

    Divide the mixture evenly between the three pans and bake at 350°F for 25 to 30 minutes or until a toothpick inserted comes out with just a few tiny moist crumbs stuck to it. Remove from the oven, leave to cool in the pans, then layer with the frosting.

Cherry beet cake

A ruddy beet-tinted crumb dotted with sour cherries under a streusel top, just the cake for a winter's afternoon spent listening to Tchaikovsky. Making cakes with vegetables used to be a necessary economy, while today we use it as a way to improve the "keeping" quality of the cake and add a range of flavors we'd forgotten about.

FOR THE CAKE
½ cup grated raw or cooked beets
5 ounces dried sour cherries
1 teaspoon almond extract
2 teaspoons mixed spice (cinnamon, nutmeg, ginger and cloves)
1 teaspoon red wine vinegar
9 tablespoons unsalted butter, softened
⅔ cup super-fine sugar
2 eggs
½ cup ground almonds
1¼ cups all-purpose flour
1 teaspoon baking powder

FOR THE STREUSEL TOPPING
¾ cup all-purpose flour
2 tablespoons unsalted butter, softened
2 tablespoons super-fine sugar
½ teaspoon ground cinnamon
1 teaspoon cold water

cherry jam, whipped cream and confectioners' sugar to serve

To make the cake, line the bottoms of two 7-inch round cake pans with disks of parchment paper. Combine the beets, cherries, almond extract, mixed spice and vinegar in a bowl and leave to infuse. In another bowl, beat the butter and sugar together until soft and smooth, then add the eggs one at a time and beat again until smooth. Beat in the ground almonds and the beet mixture, then sift the flour with the baking powder and fold this in. Divide the mixture evenly between the pans and smooth the tops.

To make the streusel topping, rub the flour, butter, sugar and cinnamon together with the water till it crumbles, then sprinkle this over the top of just one cake.

Heat the oven to 350°F and bake both layers for 35 minutes, then give the streusel-topped pan 5 to 10 minutes more before leaving to cool. Sandwich together with swirls of cherry jam and whipped cream and dust with confectioners' sugar.

Almond and apricot cake

The Potting Shed at Drake's Alpines Inshriach Nursery, deep in the Cairngorms National Park, got my vote as one of the top tearooms in Britain with classy cakes like this. Gunn Borrowman bakes with perfect balance and good taste, while outside the windows red squirrels and wild birds snack at their own feeding stations. Utter bliss.

5 eggs, separated
1 cup super-fine sugar
2 teaspoons vanilla extract
2⅓ cups ground almonds
about 9 ounces fresh ripe apricots
    or other stone fruit

2½ cups heavy cream
8 ounces Homemade Marzipan
    (page 340)
cornstarch for rolling

Line a 9½-inch springform cake pan with parchment paper. Heat the oven to 350°F. Beat the egg yolks with half the sugar and all the vanilla till thick and pale. In a separate bowl, with utterly clean whisks, beat the egg whites with the remaining sugar to a soft meringue. Mix the ground almonds with the yolks, fold in the meringue lightly but evenly, then spoon into the pan. Smooth the top and bake for 40 to 45 minutes or until firm. Leave to cool, then split the cake into two layers.

Meanwhile, pit and roughly chop the apricots, and cook in a saucepan over a low heat with a little water until tender. Increase the heat slightly and cook until the moisture has evaporated and the fruit is thick, then leave until cold. Whip the cream until it holds firm peaks, then both fill and top the cake with thick layers of apricots and cream. Roll out the marzipan until about ½ inch thick on the work surface, dusting with a little cornstarch. Then put the paste between sheets of parchment paper and roll even thinner, until about ¼ inch thick. Peel off one sheet of paper and drape the marzipan over the cake, tucking it in snugly, then carefully peel off the other sheet of paper. Last of all, trim the edges neatly and serve.

If you need to save time or simply don't want to make your own almond paste, you can buy ready-to-use marzipan, but make sure you get the good stuff — minimum 36 percent almonds.

Apple, walnut and custard cake

Very moist with a pudding-like texture, the crumb has nuggets of thick vanilla custard and cooked apple hidden through it. Perfect as a simple afternoon cake or warm as an easy pudding. Add a pinch or two of mixed spice to the apples to give the flavor an extra lift.

FOR THE CUSTARD
¾ cup milk
2 teaspoons vanilla extract
¼ cup light brown sugar
2 tablespoons cornstarch
1 egg

FOR THE APPLE AND
WALNUT FILLING
¼ cup light brown sugar
3 to 4 dessert apples, peeled,
  cored and quartered
⅓ cup brandy
⅓ cup water
⅔ cup chopped walnuts

FOR THE CAKE
½ cup light brown sugar
5 tablespoons unsalted butter,
  softened
2 eggs
⅓ cup all-purpose flour
1½ teaspoons baking powder

crème fraîche and maple syrup
  to serve

To make the custard, whisk all the milk, vanilla, brown sugar, cornstarch and egg together in a saucepan till smooth, then bring to a boil, continuing to whisk all the time until thick. Spoon the custard into a lightly buttered bowl, then chill until very firm.

To make the filling, place the brown sugar, apples, brandy, water and walnuts in a frying pan and cook over a high heat until the liquid evaporates, then leave to cool.

To make the cake, beat the sugar with the butter until light and smooth, then beat in the eggs one at a time until evenly mixed through. Stir in the flour and baking powder. Line the bottom of a deep 8-inch cake pan with parchment paper. Chop the custard roughly then fold through the cake mixture without combining. Scrape the mixture into the pan, then place spoonfuls of the apples and walnuts on top and swirl slightly through with a teaspoon. Bake at 350°F for about 50 minutes. Serve warm with crème fraîche and maple syrup.

Butterscotch banana cake

My mate Jason Warwick, a talented baker in Sydney, taught me his way to boost the flavor and color of a banana cake, by bubbling all that soft banana flesh with a rich caramel: perfect for this sweet loaf. The cake takes on a sunburned bronze hue and has a strong banana toffee flavor. Great with a few handfuls of chopped blonde walnuts, tossed in and stirred through when you spoon the mixture into the baking pan. You can also make this into cupcakes; just reduce the cooking time to 20 to 25 minutes.

FOR THE BUTTERSCOTCH
BANANAS
¾ cup super-fine sugar
¼ cup water
1⅓ cups chopped banana
  (¾-inch pieces)
1 tablespoon unsalted butter
2 teaspoons vanilla extract

FOR THE CAKE
½ cup super-fine sugar
¾ cup sunflower oil
3 eggs
¼ cup plain yogurt
1¼ cups all-purpose flour
¾ cup spelt, rye or
  whole-wheat flour
2 teaspoons mixed spice
  (cinnamon, nutmeg,
  ginger and cloves)
2 teaspoons baking powder
½ teaspoon baking soda

To make the butterscotch bananas, tip the super-fine sugar into a frying pan with the water, bring to a boil then cook over a high heat until the sugar turns to a rich reddish-golden caramel. Add the banana pieces, butter and vanilla, reduce the heat to a gentle simmer and cook until the bananas break up in the caramel. Spoon onto a plate and leave to cool.

To make the cake, line an 8-inch square cake pan with parchment paper. Beat the sugar with the oil and eggs until thick and slightly aerated, then beat in the cooled bananas and the yogurt. Sift both flours, the spice mix, baking powder and baking soda together two or three times (adding the bran back in), then fold this through the banana mixture. Spoon the mixture into the prepared pan, heat the oven to 350°F and bake for about 50 minutes or until a skewer inserted comes out with just a few tiny moist crumbs stuck to it.

KEEP IT LIGHT

Don't be stingy with the baking powder; ripe bananas are very alkaline and this is often the cause of a heavy, dense cake.

Cinnamon cake with blackberries

This is one of the lightest cakes you'll make with whole-wheat flour, but it depends on both beating the eggs to a thick froth and adding a little baking powder. The cake freezes well unfilled so you could bake in advance and wait till the berries look just right.

4 eggs, at room temperature	2 teaspoons ground cinnamon
1 cup super-fine sugar	½ cup cold milk
2½ tablespoons corn syrup	1¼ cups heavy cream
1¼ cups whole-wheat flour	1 pint blackberries, or
½ teaspoon baking powder	blackberry jam
	confectioners' sugar

Line the bottom and sides of a deep 8-inch round cake pan with parchment paper, and heat the oven to 350°F. Beat the eggs with the sugar and syrup using the whisk attachment on an electric mixer, until pale and thick and the

mixture falls like thick ribbons when the beaters are lifted from the bowl. Sift the whole-wheat flour, baking powder and cinnamon once, adding back any bran that the sieve collects. Add the milk to the beaten eggs and whisk, then add the flour and whisk once more until just smooth. Pour the mixture into the cake pan and bake in the center of the oven for 35 minutes, covering the top of the cake with foil for the last 10 minutes if you need to stop it from burning. When a skewer inserted comes out with just a few tiny moist crumbs stuck to it, remove from the oven and leave to cool. Whip the cream lightly, halve the blackberries, then slice the cake into two layers and fill with cream and fruit. Reassemble the cake and dust lightly with confectioners' sugar.

Ginger cake

David thought of the name when I was puzzled after making different versions. "Rutabagas make it sweeter, turnips give it a peppery taste, and the parsnip version tasted almost hazelnutty – call it a ginger cake," he said. Absolutely. This is even better topped with a simple lemon water icing (see page 335 and photo on 130).

2 eggs
½ cup dark brown sugar
¼ cup blackstrap molasses
⅔ cup sunflower oil
5 ounces rutabaga, turnip or
  parsnip, coarsely grated
4 nuggets crystallized ginger,
  roughly chopped

1⅓ cups whole-wheat flour
2 teaspoons baking powder
1 teaspoon baking soda
2 teaspoons ground ginger

Line an 8-inch round cake pan – either springform or with a removable bottom – with parchment paper. Heat the oven to 350°F. Separate one of the eggs, then beat one whole egg plus one yolk with the sugar for 5 minutes, until thick and foamy, saving the remaining egg white until later. Add the molasses and oil and beat again until smooth. Stir in the grated rutabaga and chopped ginger. Mix the flour, baking powder, baking soda and ground ginger together, then stir this through the mixture. Finally whisk the remaining

egg white until it holds soft peaks, then fold this through the batter gently and evenly. Turn the batter into the pan and bake for 40 to 45 minutes, or until a skewer inserted comes out with just a few tiny moist crumbs stuck to it. Remove from the pan when cool.

Lemon butter cake

Condensed milk is one of those often-overlooked ingredients that cake makers should have in their pantry. Here it helps this lemon cake stay moist without tasting overly sweetened.

FOR THE CAKE
2 eggs, separated
⅔ cup super-fine sugar
½ cup (1 stick) unsalted butter,
    melted
½ cup condensed milk
½ cup lemon juice
finely grated zest of 2 large
    lemons
2¼ cups all-purpose flour
2 teaspoons baking powder

FOR THE ICING
finely grated zest of 1 large lemon,
    plus 2 tablespoons
    lemon juice
1 cup confectioners' sugar

To make the cake, line the bottom and sides of a 7½-inch long loaf pan or similar with parchment paper. Beat the egg whites to a froth using an electric mixer, then slowly add 2 tablespoons of the super-fine sugar and continue beating to form a soft meringue. In a separate large bowl, beat both egg yolks with the remaining sugar, melted butter, condensed milk, lemon juice and lemon zest until smooth and the sugar is dissolved. Sift the flour and baking powder together and beat this into the egg yolk mixture until smooth, then fold the meringue through quickly and evenly. Tip this into the loaf pan and smooth the top. Bake at 350°F for 40 to 50 minutes or until a skewer inserted comes out with just a few tiny moist crumbs stuck to it.

To make the icing, beat the lemon zest and lemon juice with the confectioners' sugar (adding a tiny bit of water to soften it if necessary), and slather this over the top of the cooled cake.

Orange cassata cake

This is the "Sophia Loren" of cakes: four layers of orange sponge cake filled with a simplified Sicilian cassata mixture and drizzled with a light orange icing. The sponge alone is a good standby recipe for the lunch box as well.

FOR THE CAKE
9 tablespoons unsalted butter,
    softened
⅔ cup super-fine sugar
3 eggs
finely grated zest of 3 oranges
1½ cups all-purpose flour
2½ teaspoons baking powder
¼ cup cornstarch
⅔ cup confectioners' sugar
⅓ cup cold milk

FOR THE RICOTTA FILLING
1 pound ricotta
1 cup confectioners' sugar
2 ounces dark chocolate, finely
    chopped
2 teaspoons vanilla extract
⅓ cup candied citrus peel,
    very finely chopped

FOR THE ICING
3 to 4 tablespoons orange juice
1¼ cups confectioners' sugar

To make the cake, line the bottoms of two 7-inch round cake pans with disks of parchment paper. Cream the butter, super-fine sugar, eggs and orange zest until light and fluffy. Sift the flour, baking powder, cornstarch and confectioners' sugar together. Fold this alternately with the milk into the butter mixture, then divide between the pans and smooth the tops. Heat the oven to 350°F and bake for 25 to 30 minutes or until a skewer inserted comes out with just a few tiny moist crumbs stuck to it, then leave to cool.

To make the filling, beat the ricotta with the confectioners' sugar, chocolate, vanilla and candied peel till combined. Cut each cake horizontally into two equal-sized layers, spread a third of the filling on three of the cut layers and stack them on top of each other, finishing with the remaining cake top.

To make the icing, gradually add the orange juice to the confectioners' sugar and beat until a smooth and spreadable consistency is reached and let this drizzle over the top and sides of the cake.

Someone asked me if this cake could be prepared in advance for a special occasion. If you'd like to do that, simply remove the cakes from the pans as soon as they are cool, and wrap them, uncut, in plastic wrap. Freeze for up to 3 weeks, then when required, thaw, cut and fill. You can make the filling a couple of days ahead and store it covered in the fridge, and the only thing that needs to be made at the last moment is the orange juice and confectioners' sugar drizzle.

Orange macaroon cake

Combining two or more ingredients with the same basic flavor can produce a dazzling effect. This works not just with oranges but with lemon cakes and others. Here, the zest and liqueur in the cake combine with the zest and juice in the icing to emphasise the taste of oranges.

FOR THE CAKE
finely grated zest of 2 large oranges
1¾ cup (1½ sticks) unsalted butter, softened
¾ cup super-fine sugar
3 eggs
½ cup shredded coconut
1¼ cups all-purpose flour
2 teaspoons baking powder
⅓ cup orange liqueur, like Cointreau or Grand Marnier

FOR THE ICING
finely grated zest of 1 large orange, plus 2 tablespoons orange juice
1¼ cups confectioners' sugar

To make the cake, line the bottoms of two 7-inch round cake pans with disks of parchment paper and heat the oven to 350°F. Put the orange zest into a bowl with the butter and sugar and beat until light and creamy. Beat in the eggs, one at a time, then beat in the coconut. Sift the flour and baking powder together, beat half into the butter mixture followed by the orange liqueur, then fold through the remaining flour. Divide between the pans and bake for 25 to 30 minutes. Leave the cakes to cool in the pans, then remove and peel the paper off the bottom. To make the icing, beat the orange zest and orange juice with the confectioners' sugar until spreadable. Top each cake, stack one on the other and serve.

Most oranges are sprayed with pesticides and herbicides, so if you want chemical-free zest, use organic and unwaxed. This will mean that they attract mold quicker so don't keep them hanging around.

Pear upside-down cake

Pears in red wine sit at the bottom of the pan but, once flipped, form a burgundy top to a simple butter cake. You need to use rock-hard pears; ripe fruit simply won't work. If you like, cook extra pears in wine syrup and use these to decorate the cake after baking.

½ cup (1 stick) unsalted butter, softened, plus more for the pan	2 eggs
	2 tablespoons light honey, like acacia
2 to 3 large firm pears, about 11 ounces	⅔ cup plain yogurt
⅔ cup muscovado sugar, plus more for the pan	1⅓ cups all-purpose flour
	2 teaspoons baking powder
1 cup red wine	

Start with a deep 7-inch round cake pan, then take a large sheet of thick aluminum foil, double the circumference and rub it generously with butter. Carefully press this into the pan butter-side up, using your fingers, so that the foil lines the bottom and runs up the sides, and set the pan on a baking sheet. Peel the pears, halve them lengthwise, spoon out the core and slice them from the bottom almost to the top, so they stay joined at the stem end, and fan them over the lined bottom of the pan with a little extra sugar.

Heat the wine in a saucepan and boil until it has reduced to a thin syrup. Remove from the heat and pour this over the pears. Beat the butter, sugar,

eggs and honey until pale and fluffy. Add the yogurt, flour and baking powder and beat until smooth. Spoon the cake batter over the pears and smooth the surface. Heat the oven to 350°F and bake for 45 to 50 minutes or until a skewer inserted comes out with just a few tiny moist crumbs stuck to it. Leave to cool in the pan for 10 minutes, then invert onto a plate and carefully remove the foil while still warm.

Rye apple cake

This is a simple cake, both to make and in the soft flavors that surround the chunks of sharp cinnamon-coated apple. If you haven't used rye flour in cake making, this is an ideal introduction and I think you'll be pleased with the result.

1 medium apple, 4 to 5 ounces	2 tablespoons corn syrup
1 teaspoon ground cinnamon	½ cup muscovado sugar
½ cup sliced almonds	⅓ cup milk
1½ cups rye flour	2 eggs
2 teaspoons baking powder	Demerara or brown
5 tablespoons unsalted butter	sugar to finish

Line a 7-inch long loaf pan or similar with parchment paper. Peel and core the apple, cut into ½-inch dice and toss with the cinnamon. Grind ⅓ cup of the almonds (reserving the remainder) and combine evenly with the rye flour and baking powder in a bowl. In a small saucepan gently heat the butter with the corn syrup and muscovado sugar until smooth and the sugar is dissolved – don't let it simmer. Remove from the heat and beat in the milk and then the eggs, stir all this into the almond–rye flour mixture and fold in the cinnamon-coated apple pieces.

Scrape the mixture into the pan, bang the pan a few times to dislodge any air bubbles, then sprinkle the top with the remaining sliced almonds and a light dusting of Demerara or brown sugar. Heat the oven to 350°F and bake for 40 to 50 minutes or until a skewer comes out with just a few tiny moist crumbs stuck to it. Cut when perfectly cold.

Saffron peach cake

During a gray British winter, nuts, spices and canned fruit are useful standbys to inject some color into baking. But peaches from a can have little flavor so combining them with saffron and almonds is utterly acceptable in my house, and rather good when brought together in this cake.

butter for the pan
a good pinch of saffron
¼ cup boiling water
10 tablespoons unsalted butter, softened
⅔ cup super-fine sugar
2 eggs
1¾ cups ground almonds

a few drops almond extract
1⅓ cups all-purpose flour
1 teaspoon baking powder
a 14-ounce can peach halves, well drained
handful of sliced almonds
confectioners' sugar

Butter the inside of an 8-inch square baking pan and line the bottom with parchment paper. Soak the saffron in the boiling water for 15 minutes to draw out the color. Beat the butter and sugar until light, then add the eggs and beat again for a couple of minutes until light and evenly mixed through. Add the ground almonds and almond extract, stir well, then sift in the flour and baking powder a little at a time, folding this through alternately with the saffron infusion. Give it one good quick beat at the end to make sure it's smooth. Spread the mixture over the bottom of the pan, then cut each peach half into quarter segments and press these into the mixture randomly. Sprinkle the sliced almonds over the top and bake at 350°F for 35 to 40 minutes. Leave to cool, then dust with confectioners' sugar and cut into fingers to serve.

Sticky lemon and poppy seed cake

This is one of those cakes you dream you'll find in a corner sandwich bar but never (okay, rarely) do. The lemon zest goes into the cake mixture, and a syrup of juice and sugar soaks the cake afterward. Finely ground oatmeal makes each mouthful chewier, and the oil keeps it softer than simply using all butter.

FOR THE CAKE
1 cup super-fine sugar
9 tablespoons unsalted butter, softened
½ cup sunflower oil
finely grated zest of 3 lemons
4 eggs
¼ cup hot water
2 cups all-purpose flour
2 teaspoons baking powder
1 cup fine oatmeal, or rolled oats finely ground
¼ cup poppy seeds

FOR THE SYRUP
⅔ cup super-fine sugar
½ cup lemon juice

super-fine sugar to finish

To make the cake, line a deep 8-inch square cake pan with parchment paper. Beat the sugar with the butter, oil and lemon zest until pale and fluffy, then add the eggs, one at a time, and beat well. Whisk the hot water into the mixture till smooth. Sift the flour and baking powder two or three times, then toss the oatmeal and poppy seeds in with the flour and beat this through the cake mixture. Pour the batter into the pan and bake at 350°F for 40 to 50 minutes or until a skewer inserted comes out with just a few tiny moist crumbs stuck to it.

To make the lemon syrup, heat the sugar with the lemon juice in a saucepan until dissolved.

Poke a skewer deep into the cake dozens of times, then spoon all of the syrup over it. Allow to cool, then dredge it with super-fine sugar before serving.

Brown sugar chocolate cake

Stirring crumbled chunks of good dark chocolate into boiling water avoids having to melt it in a bowl over a simmering pan, while the dash of baking soda with the chocolate turns the crumb a rather beautiful reddish brown in this fluffy moist chocolate cake. Serve on its own, or with thick chocolate icing spread over the top, such as the Molasses Chocolate Fudge Frosting (page 332).

¼ cup cold water
¼ cup cocoa powder
⅜ cup boiling water
2 ounces dark chocolate, chopped into little pieces
½ teaspoon baking soda
½ cup (1 stick) unsalted butter, softened

¾ cup muscovado sugar
½ cup condensed milk
2 eggs
2 teaspoons vegetable glycerine
1½ cups all-purpose flour
2 teaspoons baking powder

Line the bottom and sides of a 7½-inch long loaf pan or similar with parchment paper. Stir the cold water with the cocoa to make a smooth paste then whisk in the boiling water. Immediately stir in the chocolate and baking soda and leave it to melt. In another bowl beat the butter, sugar and condensed milk with an electric mixer until very smooth, then beat in the eggs and glycerine. Stir together the flour and baking powder. Beat half of it thoroughly into the egg mixture, followed by the chocolate mixture, then beat in the remaining flour until smooth, again using an electric mixer.

Scrape the mixture evenly into the pan and bake at 350°F for 40 to 50 minutes or until a skewer comes out with only a few crumbs sticking to it. Remove from the oven, leave to cool in the pan and peel off the parchment paper when cold.

THAT SINKING FEELING

Cakes with a high proportion of fat and sugar to flour are susceptible to collapse using all-purpose flour. If you have problems with cakes collapsing in the middle, the two remedies you can try, separately or in tandem, are: (i) add an extra 2 tablespoons of flour (this will thicken the consistency of the batter and it should sit higher) and (ii) add an extra tablespoon of egg white (this will help the sugar and fat stay bound in the flour mixture).

Chocolate and almond fudge cake

This is a chocolate cake with a darker, less sweet flavor and a heavier, moister crumb than most chocolate cakes. I've used a cooked mixture of fine oatmeal and milk, which allows the sugar to be reduced without losing the "fudge" texture that usually occurs because of . . . you guessed it, the sugar. It puffs then sinks back down, as flourless cakes usually do, and sets firm when chilled.

¾ cup milk
⅔ cup fine oatmeal, or ⅓ cup
  gluten-free cake flour
2 tablespoons cocoa powder
2½ tablespoons corn syrup
8 ounces dark chocolate, chopped
10 tablespoons unsalted butter,
  chopped

3 eggs, separated
1 cup ground almonds
½ cup super-fine sugar, plus
  extra to finish
whipped cream, Pedro Ximénez
  sherry and grated chocolate
  to serve

Line the bottom and sides of a 7-inch round cake pan with parchment paper. In a saucepan whisk the milk, oatmeal, cocoa and corn syrup together and heat to the first "plop" of a boil, stirring all the time. Remove from the heat, stand the pot somewhere warm and beat in the chocolate and butter with a wooden spoon. It will separate a little but don't worry.

Beat in the egg yolks, one at a time, until well mixed through, then stir in the almonds with about half the sugar until combined. In a clean bowl, beat the egg whites using an electric whisk, gradually adding the remaining sugar to form a soft meringue. Beat a third of the meringue through the chocolate mixture in the saucepan, then pour this back in with the remaining meringue and gently fold the two evenly together as lightly and quickly as you can. Bake at 350°F for 40 minutes, then cool and chill before serving with lightly whipped cream flavored with a little sherry and some grated chocolate.

Oats are gluten-free, but can acquire traces of it during the harvesting and milling process, so if you're making this cake for someone sensitive to gluten, do check the packaging for the manufacturer's assurance that it's definitely GF. However, some people are also sensitive to avenin, a protein found in oats, so do check with the person you're baking for, or use gluten-free flour.

Chocolate passion cake

I was asked for a soft and fluffy vegan-friendly cake that didn't crumble when cut, which can happen when eggs are left out. In this recipe, a purée of dates emulsifies with the oil the same way yolks do, and the combination of grated carrot and bread flour replaces the egg white that holds the rich crumb together. Baking the mixture in layers also means there isn't as much "structure" to be held together, so the crumb can be a bit more delicate.

FOR THE CAKE
¾ cup boiling water
⅔ cup chopped dates
⅔ cup sunflower oil
1 tablespoon cider vinegar
⅔ cup chopped pecans
1⅓ cups grated carrot
⅔ cup super-fine sugar
1⅓ cups bread flour
3 tablespoons cocoa powder
1 teaspoon ground mixed spice
    (cinnamon, nutmeg,
    ginger and cloves)
1 teaspoon ground ginger
1 tablespoon baking powder

FOR THE ICING
½ cup confectioners' sugar
2 tablespoons cocoa powder
2 tablespoons boiling water

To make the cake, line the bottoms of two 7-inch round pans with parchment paper. Pour the boiling water on the dates, leave for 10 minutes to soften, then put the dates and water into the blender with the oil and vinegar. Purée until it is utterly smooth, tip the mixture into a large bowl and stir in the pecans, grated carrot and sugar until evenly combined. Sift together the flour, cocoa, spices and baking powder and beat this into the mixture. Divide the mixture between the pans, smooth the tops and bake at 350°F for about 25 minutes, or until a skewer inserted into the center of the cake comes out with only a few crumbs sticking to it. Allow to cool in the pans, then remove and peel away the parchment paper.

To make the icing, beat the confectioners' sugar and cocoa with the boiling water, adding the water gradually.

Use half of the icing to sandwich the layers together and the rest to spread over the top.

Hazelnut wafer cake

My mother made this recipe for my tenth birthday, and for a few more after that. I can still remember the chewy layers that tasted like Topic bars; it was the first cake I ever dreamed about.

FOR THE WAFERS
4 tablespoons unsalted butter, melted, plus extra for the baking sheets
⅓ cup all-purpose flour, plus extra for the baking sheets
4 egg whites
⅔ cup super-fine sugar
1¼ cups toasted and ground hazelnuts

FOR THE CHOCOLATE CREAM
⅓ cup super-fine sugar, plus 2 tablespoons
⅓ cup milk
3 tablespoons cocoa powder
4 egg yolks
2 ounces dark chocolate, chopped
2½ cups heavy cream
1 teaspoon vanilla extract

confectioners' sugar to serve

To make the wafers, heat the oven to 350°F. Butter and flour two large baking sheets, then mark two 7-inch circles on each, to guide you. Whisk the egg whites with the sugar till thick and meringue-like. Fold the hazelnuts, flour and butter through until combined, then spoon and spread the mixture to cover each of the four circles. Bake for 25 minutes until the wafers are golden. Remove from the oven and loosen from the bottoms of the baking sheets with a knife when cool.

For the chocolate cream, whisk the ⅓ cup sugar with the milk and cocoa in a pan and bring to a boil. Cool for 2 minutes, then beat in the egg yolks and stir in the chocolate. Leave until cooled and thickened, then whip three-quarters of the cream until thick and fold this in. Chill the mixture, then spread it evenly over three of the wafers. Whisk the remaining cream with the vanilla extract and the remaining 2 tablespoons sugar. Divide this evenly over the chocolate-covered wafers, then carefully stack one on top of another, finishing with the uncovered wafer on top.

Dredge with confectioners' sugar to serve.

Marbled chocolate crumble cake

Blobs of vanilla and double chocolate-chip pound cake mix are swirled together and covered under a mountain of chocolate–brown sugar crumble. Very, very good warmed slightly and served with thick hot custard or cold cream.

FOR THE CRUMBLE
TOPPING
1 cup all-purpose flour
2 tablespoons cocoa powder
⅓ cup light brown sugar
5 tablespoons unsalted butter

FOR THE CAKE
¾ cup super-fine sugar
¾ cup (1½ sticks) unsalted butter, softened
3 eggs
2 teaspoons vanilla extract
1⅓ cups all-purpose flour
2 teaspoons baking powder
2 tablespoons cocoa powder
4 ounces dark chocolate, roughly chopped

To make the crumble topping, rub the flour, cocoa, brown sugar and butter together with your fingers until combined, adding a few drops of cold water at the end to make it crumbly rather than dusty, then set this aside while you make the cake.

To make the cake, first line a deep square 8-inch cake pan with parchment paper. Beat the super-fine sugar and butter until light and fluffy, then beat in the eggs, one at a time, until combined, then add the vanilla. Sift the flour and baking powder together and beat this through the butter mixture, then spoon three-quarters of it in blobs into the pan, leaving gaps here and there. Beat the remaining mixture with the cocoa until smooth, then stir in the chocolate. Spoon this into the gaps in the pan, then swirl the mixtures together with the spoon handle. Bake at 350°F for 25 minutes, then sprinkle the topping over, bake for another 10 minutes, check whether it's cooked with a skewer, then remove from the oven and leave to cool in the pan.

The alchemist's chocolate cake

This chocolate cake has a delicate moist texture and flavor, but very little fat or refined sugar, and it's quick to make. If you cut it into ten slices, you will have about 220 calories a piece, with only half the fat and a quarter of the carbs of a typical un-iced caked. You might up the calories a little by serving it with a spoonful of low-fat crème fraîche or a drizzle of melted chocolate.

14½-ounce can pear halves in juice	¼ cup walnut oil
⅔ cup cocoa powder	3 eggs
⅔ cup super-fine sugar	1¾ cups all-purpose flour
1 tablespoon vanilla extract	2½ teaspoons baking powder

Drain the pears well, reserving ½ cup of the juice. Measure the cocoa, sugar and pear juice into a saucepan, madly whisk it all together and bring to the first "plop" of a boil. Then spoon it with the pears into a mixing bowl and leave for 15 minutes. Meanwhile, line the bottom and sides of an 8-inch round cake pan with parchment paper and heat the oven to 325°F. Spoon the pears and cocoa mixture with the vanilla and oil into a blender and purée until smooth. Pour this back into the bowl, then beat in the eggs. Stir the flour and baking powder together, sift this into the bowl and beat well until smooth. Scrape the mixture into the cake pan and bake for 40 minutes or until a skewer comes out with only a few crumbs sticking to it.

Vienna chocolate cake

A simplified Sacher torte rich and moist with chocolate, almonds and apricot jam.

FOR THE CHOCOLATE
GLAZE
½ cup water
⅔ cup super-fine sugar
1 tablespoon cocoa powder
½ teaspoon lemon juice
4 ounces dark chocolate, chopped into pieces

FOR THE CAKE
5 tablespoons unsalted butter, softened
⅓ cup super-fine sugar
2 eggs
1¼ cups ground almonds
⅓ cup all-purpose flour
¾ teaspoon baking powder

½ cup good apricot jam, thinned with a little water or brandy and warmed

To make the chocolate glaze, whisk the water, sugar, cocoa and lemon juice till smooth, then bring to a boil in a deep saucepan and simmer for 1 minute. Cool for 5 minutes, stir in the chocolate until melted and keep warm in a measuring cup.

To make the cake, heat the oven to 375°F. Line the bottom and sides of an 7-inch round cake pan with parchment paper. Whisk the butter, sugar and one egg for about 2 minutes until fluffy. Separate the remaining egg, saving the white in a clean bowl and beating the yolk, ground almonds and half the chocolate glaze in with the cake mixture. Using a separate bowl, beat the egg white with a clean electric whisk to form soft peaks. Sift the flour and baking powder onto the cake mixture, fold through evenly, then quickly and lightly fold in the egg white. Gently scrape this into the pan, secure a sheet of foil over the top and bake for about 35 minutes until firm and a skewer inserted comes out with just a few tiny moist crumbs stuck to it. Cool, still covered, in the pan, then slice horizontally into three or four thin layers. Spread each layer generously with jam, reassemble, then pour the remaining chocolate glaze over the top and sides.

Sour cream butter cake

What's a pantry cake? To me, it's a cake made with ingredients that keep well and that I'm likely to have in the house, rather than a lot of things that are very seasonal or involve a trip to a specialty store. This sour cream cake is very buttery and best eaten cold. The mixture is versatile, and will happily fit into an 8-inch round or 7-inch square pan or can be used for small cupcakes.

¾ cup (1½ sticks) unsalted
  butter, softened
1 cup super-fine sugar
3 eggs

1⅔ cups sour cream
2¼ cups all-purpose flour
1 tablespoon baking powder

Line the base of an 8-inch round or 7-inch square cake pan with parchment paper. Cream the butter and sugar until light and fluffy, then add the eggs, one at a time, and beat well until combined. (An electric mixer really does the best job here.) Beat in the sour cream till it vanishes into the mixture, then sift the flour and baking powder together and beat this through.

Spoon the mixture into the pan, heat the oven to 350°F and bake for 45 minutes (shallow cake) to an hour (deep loaf pan with a collar) or until a skewer inserted comes out with just a few tiny moist crumbs stuck to it.

COLLAR CHIC

I also like to bake this cake in a large loaf pan. As the quantity of batter here would normally spill over the sides, I make a foil collar, which gives the cake an extra bit of height and elegance. It's a trick that you can employ to make a deeper cake in a smaller pan, or if you think there's more batter in a recipe than will fit the pan you have. Line the pan with parchment paper, then take a sheet of aluminium foil three times the length of the pan and fold the upper and lower thirds inward. This will produce one very long narrow foil collar. Carefully bend the foil so it sits upright and tight against the insides of the pan, smooth side facing inward, and pinch the ends together to secure.

Coconut milk layer cake

This is a very seductive, fluffy and light coconut sponge, soaked with fresh lime juice and white rum before being filled with meringue buttercream icing. If you have some homemade lime curd (see page 342), you can use it in place of the meringue buttercream icing.

⅔ cup canned coconut milk
⅔ cup shredded coconut
½ vanilla pod, scraped, or
   2 teaspoons vanilla extract
¼ cup white rum,
   plus 3 tablespoons
1½ cups super-fine sugar
1 cup (2 sticks) unsalted
   butter, softened

3 eggs
2¼ cups all-purpose flour
2½ teaspoons baking powder
2 tablespoons freshly squeezed
   lime juice
Meringue Buttercream Icing
   (page 327)

Line the bottoms of three 8-inch round cake pans with disks of parchment paper. Heat the coconut milk till boiling, then remove from the heat and stir in the shredded coconut, vanilla and rum. Leave to soak for 30 minutes so the coconut softens. Place the sugar and butter in a bowl and beat until light and fluffy, then beat in the eggs, one at a time, until evenly combined. Sift the flour with the baking powder two or three times, then gradually fold this into the sugar, butter and eggs, alternating with spoonfuls of the coconut mixture (remove the vanilla pod here if you used one) until smooth. Divide between the pans and smooth the tops. Heat the oven to 350°F and bake for 30 to 35 minutes or until a toothpick inserted comes out with just a few tiny moist crumbs stuck to it.

Leave to cool in the pans, then remove carefully. Sprinkle 2 teaspoons lime juice and 1 tablespoon rum on each layer. Top each of the sponges with icing as you assemble the cake, finishing with a layer of icing over the top and sides.

Marmalade layer cake

A delicate cream sponge flavored with bitter orange marmalade and layered with vanilla cream. The only tricky bit is folding flour into the beaten eggs, but be quick and light-handed and you'll have the airiest cakes in town.

FOR THE CAKE
¾ cup bitter fine-cut
   marmalade
½ cup heavy cream
3 eggs
⅔ cup fine unrefined
   or super-fine sugar
1¼ cups all-purpose flour
1 teaspoon baking powder

FOR THE VANILLA CREAM
½ cup heavy cream
1 tablespoon milk
1 teaspoon vanilla extract
1 tablespoon fine unrefined
   or super-fine sugar

To make the cake, line the bottoms of two 8-inch round cake pans with a disk of parchment paper on the bottom of each. (Have a fine sieve for the flour and a rubber spatula for folding the ingredients together ready at hand.) Heat the oven to 350°F.

Gently warm the marmalade and cream together over low heat, then leave to cool. In a clean bowl, beat the eggs with the ⅔ cup sugar using an electric whisk until very thick and creamy. Lightly beat in the cream and marmalade, then sieve in the flour and baking powder. Fold the flour and cake batter together quickly and evenly using the spatula, so the mix does not deflate. Evenly divide it between the pans, and bake for 25 to 30 minutes or until risen and barely firm. Remove from the oven and leave to cool before removing the pans and paper bottoms.

To make the vanilla cream, whip the heavy cream, milk, vanilla and sugar together until fluffy. Spread half of the cream over the top of each cake layer. Then stack one on the other, wiggle them to get them even, and serve.

Caramel hazelnut layer cake

You can now buy cans of "caramel" made from condensed milk, very much like dulce de leche from Latin America, so no more terror in having to boil the cans at home.

FOR THE CAKE
¾ cup (1½ stick) unsalted
    butter, softened
½ cup light brown sugar
⅔ cup caramel or dulce de leche
2 eggs
4 ounces hazelnuts, toasted,
    skinned and ground
1⅓ cups all-purpose flour
1 tablespoon cocoa powder
2 teaspoons baking powder

FOR THE TOPPING
4 tablespoons unsalted
    butter, softened
½ cup caramel or dulce de leche
1½ cups confectioners' sugar, sifted
1 teaspoon vanilla extract

To make the cake, line two 7-inch round cake pans with a disk of parchment paper. Heat the oven to 350°F. Beat the butter with the brown sugar and caramel until smooth, then beat in the eggs, one at a time, until smooth once more. (Don't worry if it looks slightly curdled.) Beat in the ground hazelnuts, then sift the flour, cocoa and baking powder together and beat this through. Divide the mixture between the pans and bake for 25 to 30 minutes or until a toothpick inserted into the center comes out with only a few crumbs sticking to it. Leave to cool in the pans before lifting out and removing the paper bottoms.

To make the topping, beat the butter with the caramel until smooth, then work in the confectioners' sugar and vanilla to make a thick creamy icing.

Spread half of the icing between the cake layers and the rest on top so it cascades gently over the edge and down the sides.

I toast the hazelnuts by putting them in the oven on a baking sheet at 350°F for 15 to 20 minutes until golden. When I try toasting them in a pan, I always seem to get little burnt bits, which this method avoids.

By adding a touch of cocoa to any recipe that uses toasted nuts, you can enhance the nutty flavor considerably without making it taste overtly of chocolate.

Sherry and cherry cake

The cake is studded with little gems of dried cherry. You could, if you like, substitute the glacé ones, but halve or quarter and then wash them briefly before drying on a cloth or paper towel and then tossing in a little of the flour. Me? I save the syrupy cherries for a whisky sour.

½ cup (1 stick) unsalted
  butter, softened
⅔ cup super-fine sugar
2 eggs
4 to 5 ounces dried sour
  cherries, quartered

1¼ cups all-purpose
  flour
1½ teaspoons baking powder
2 tablespoons sweet sherry
Demerara sugar to finish

Line the bottom and sides of a 7-inch long loaf pan or similar with parchment paper. Heat the oven to 325°F. Beat together the butter, super-fine sugar and one egg with an electric mixer for 2 to 3 minutes until the sugar has almost dissolved. Add the other egg and beat well for 1 to 2 minutes. In another bowl toss the cherries, flour and baking powder together, then sift out the cherries and put them to one side. Fold a third of the flour through the butter mixture, stir in the sherry then fold in the remaining flour and beat until smooth. Spoon half the mixture into the pan and sprinkle on half the cherries, then add the remaining mixture and sprinkle the rest of the cherries over that, pushing them in slightly with a teaspoon. Scatter Demerara sugar over the

top and bake for about 40 minutes, then test with a skewer in the center. If it comes out with just a few crumbs sticking to it, bingo. When cold, take out of the pan and peel off the parchment paper.

Swedish almond cake

Though you can probably buy something like this in a box at Ikea, imagine all the travelling time you'll save by making it at home. It's a simple butter cake best served on the day it's made, as the top is crisp then and the bottom still soft and moist. Serve it barely warm with a dollop of ice cold and very softly whipped cream, or some vanilla ice cream.

FOR THE CAKE
4 tablespoons unsalted butter
2 tablespoons dry white
    breadcrumbs
2 medium eggs
½ cup super-fine sugar
1 teaspoon vanilla extract
2 tablespoons heavy cream
¾ cup all-purpose flour
¾ teaspoon baking powder

FOR THE TOPPING
2 tablespoons unsalted butter
½ cup sliced almonds
2 tablespoons super-fine sugar
1 teaspoon all-purpose flour
1 tablespoon heavy cream

To make the cake, melt the butter and use some to brush the insides of a 7-inch flan pan that you then dust generously with the breadcrumbs. Heat the oven to 350°F. Break the eggs into a large clean bowl and whisk until frothy. Slowly add the sugar and beat until thick. Thoroughly stir in the vanilla and cream, sift in the flour and baking powder and fold through, followed by the remaining melted butter. Spoon into the pan and bake for 25 minutes until the middle is barely firm.

To make the topping, melt the butter in the same saucepan you used before, then add the almonds, sugar, flour and cream and stir over the heat until bubbling.

When the cake is cooked, remove it from the oven and turn the heat up to

400°F. Spoon the almond topping over the cake, return to the oven and bake for another 5 to 7 minutes until golden. Remove from the pan while warm.

Coffee and ricotta marbled cake

I must admit to having an affection for marbled cakes, and they make a sweet addition to the tea table for very little extra effort. Drizzle this one with a simple coffee water icing (see page 335) to finish, if you want to dress it up a little.

2 tablespoons finely ground
    roasted coffee beans
2 tablespoons boiling water
9 tablespoons unsalted butter,
    softened
1 cup super-fine sugar

1½ cups all-purpose flour
5 ounces ricotta
3 eggs
2½ teaspoons baking powder
2 tablespoons Marsala or dark rum

Line the bottom and sides of a 7-inch long loaf pan or similar with parchment paper and heat the oven to 350°F. Stir the ground coffee and boiling water together in a cup and leave for 10 minutes to infuse. Beat the butter and sugar until soft and light, then add the flour, spooning about a quarter of it in with the butter mixture, and beat until smooth. Beat in the ricotta and then the eggs, one at a time. Sift the baking powder and the remaining flour into the mixture and beat lightly. Divide the mixture in half and beat the coffee mixture through one half and the Marsala through the other. Spoon the mixture in alternate blobs into the pan, tap the pan firmly on the work surface to knock out any air bubbles, swirl the batter gently with a skewer, then bake for 50 to 60 minutes.

THE FLOUR BATTER METHOD

Beating a little flour in with the butter and sugar at the start ensures that the wet ricotta and eggs form an emulsion in the cake mixture. This helps the cake bake with a finer crumb texture and stops it from sinking so easily.

SHORT & SWEET

Double espresso brazil nut cake

The sweet butteriness of the brazil nuts works so well here, and it avoids the slight bitterness you can get with some walnuts. The fleck from the ground coffee is hidden in the mixture of whole-wheat and all-purpose flour, but it adds a very rich intense coffee flavor.

½ cup milk

2 teaspoons instant coffee

1 tablespoon finely ground roasted coffee beans

¾ cup (1½ stick) unsalted butter, softened

½ cup light brown sugar

½ cup super-fine sugar

3 eggs

¾ cup all-purpose flour

1 cup spelt, rye or whole-wheat flour

2 teaspoons baking powder

½ cup brazil nuts, finely chopped

coffee water icing (see page 335)

Line two 8-inch round cake pans with disks of parchment paper. Combine the milk, instant coffee and ground coffee in a saucepan and bring to a boil, then remove from the heat and leave until warm. Beat the butter, brown sugar and super-fine sugar together until light and fluffy, then beat in the eggs, one at a time. Beat in the coffee mixture until evenly combined. Stir the two flours and baking powder together, then beat this through with the chopped brazil nuts. Divide the mixture between the pans, heat the oven to 350°F and bake for 25 to 30 minutes or until a toothpick inserted comes out with just a few tiny moist crumbs stuck to it.

Leave to cool before removing the pans and peeling off the paper. Sandwich together and drizzle with the icing.

Dark aniseed cake

This dense licorice-flavored eggless cake uses spelt flour, which helps to keep the crumb moist, as the bran it contains absorbs liquid while the cake cooks in the oven. Slather dollops of thick orange icing over the top for an enhanced "licorice allsort" (a type of candy) effect.

FOR THE CAKE
1½ cups boiling water
6 ounces pitted prunes
⅔ cup blackstrap molasses
⅓ cup dark ale
¾ cup (1½ sticks) unsalted
    butter, softened
¾ cup muscovado sugar
4½ cups spelt flour
4 teaspoons baking powder
4 teaspoons anise or
    fennel seeds

FOR THE ICING
2½ cups confectioners' sugar
finely grated zest of 1 orange,
    plus 3 tablespoons orange juice

To make the cake, line the bottom of an 8-inch square cake pan with parchment paper. Pour the boiling water over the prunes, leave to soak for 5 minutes, then purée in a blender with the molasses and ale until smooth. In a warm bowl, beat the butter and sugar until fluffy and pale, using an electric mixer and stopping from time to time to scrape down the bowl sides and break up any hefty sugar lumps. Slowly beat in the prune mixture until combined into a dark creamy liquid. Sieve the spelt flour to remove lumps but add back any bran bits that get caught in the mesh. Toss the baking powder and seeds through the flour before beating this quickly and evenly through the cake mixture. Tip the mixture into the pan and smooth the top. Heat the oven to 350°F. Bake the cake for 50 minutes or until a skewer stuck into the center comes out with just a few tiny moist crumbs stuck to it. Cool in the pan then transfer to a plate.

To make the icing, beat the confectioners' sugar, orange zest and juice together. Spread the icing over the top of the cake.

An alcohol-free version

If you'd prefer a cake made without alcohol, or worry about opening a bottle of beer for just ⅓ cup, you can substitute cold tea. Try toasting half the aniseeds, or using other seeds such as caraway, poppy or some of the larger ones, such as sunflower or even pumpkin, to vary the flavor and texture of the cake.

Rum cake

If you have a ring pan — the shape of a giant "O" with the center removed — this is the perfect cake to bake. The combination of whole-wheat bread flour (more often seen in bread making) and all the fruit and sugar would otherwise make for a dense mixture, and a conventional round pan would leave the center of the cake underbaked. But best of all, this cake has lots of flavor; keeps well in the refrigerator, too.

FOR THE CAKE
butter for the pan
2 cups whole-wheat bread flour,
   or spelt flour
2 teaspoons baking powder
1 teaspoon baking soda
5 ounces dates, chopped
4 ounces brazil nuts, chopped
8-ounce can pineapple,
   chopped and drained
½ teaspoon ground black pepper
¼ teaspoon ground cloves
½ teaspoon ground cinnamon
1¼ cups muscovado sugar
3 eggs
⅔ cup corn oil
⅓ cup dark rum

FOR THE SYRUP
½ cup super-fine sugar
¼ cup water
½ cup dark rum

To make the cake, butter a deep 8-inch ring pan and heat the oven to 350°F. Combine the flour with the baking powder and baking soda, and mix together the dates, nuts and pineapple.

In a large bowl, mix together the spices and muscovado sugar, then add the eggs and beat with an electric mixer for 3 to 4 minutes until light and fluffy. The odd small lump of sugar is no bad thing. Beat the oil and rum into the eggs and sugar, and then gradually add the flour mixture, mixing until smooth. Beat in the pineapple, dates and nuts, then spoon the mixture into the pan. Bake for 40 minutes until risen and firm to the touch.

To make the syrup, in a saucepan, boil the super-fine sugar with the water, then remove from the heat and cool before adding the rum.

Spoon half of the syrup over the cake in the pan then leave for 30 minutes. Ease the cake away from the pan with a knife, then invert onto a plate and spoon over the remaining syrup.

A lighter cake

Whole-wheat flour typically bakes to a denser finish, so if you wanted a lighter result, you could try a mix of 50/50 white and whole-wheat.

Quinoa hazelnut cake

This cake isn't actually difficult to make, though there are perhaps more steps to go through than with many other recipes in this book. Quinoa is one of those ancient grains, very high in protein compared to wheat or rice. This gives you a nutrient-packed cake that's low in fat, and if filled with fresh fruit, makes a good addition to your diet. Toasting the seeds lightly replaces the grassy flavor with something nutty, and if toasted hazelnuts are added as well, the result is excellent.

Baking powder is made up of a combination of cream of tartar and baking soda, and in most cake recipes it is sifted with the flour. But in a flourless cake recipe it is difficult to achieve the same even distribution. I solve this by beating the egg whites with the baking powder in this recipe. This allows the cream of tartar to strengthen the meringue as well as evenly distributing the baking soda without activating it.

¾ cup quinoa

¾ cup hazelnuts

1⅔ cups water

2 tablespoons unsalted butter

4 eggs, separated

1 teaspoon baking powder

¾ cup light brown sugar

1 teaspoon ground cinnamon

2 tablespoons cornstarch

⅔ cup heavy cream

1 tablespoon milk

½ cup berry jam, any sort

⅔ cup soft ripe berries

Line the bottom and sides of an 8-inch round springform cake pan with parchment paper. Tip the quinoa onto one baking sheet, the hazelnuts onto another, and place in an oven preheated to 400°F for about 20 minutes until both are golden brown.

Pour the quinoa into a saucepan with the water, bring to a boil, then stick the lid on tight and leave over a gentle heat for about 15 minutes until the water is absorbed and the grains burst and are soft. Spread on a dinner plate to cool. Grind the hazelnuts in a food processor or blender. Lower the oven to 350°F. Heat the butter in a saucepan until it just turns nut brown, then remove from the heat and leave somewhere warm.

Using an electric whisk, first beat the egg whites with the baking powder and about half the sugar until thick. Then, in a separate bowl, beat the yolks with the remaining sugar until very thick and beige-colored. Fold the quinoa, hazelnuts, cinnamon and cornstarch through the yolks, then fold in the egg whites and the melted butter. Pour the mixture into the pan and bake for 45 minutes or until the center of the cake feels firm to the touch. Remove from the oven and leave to cool. Whip the cream and the milk to soft peaks, stir in the jam until smooth, then spread this over the cake and decorate with berries.

Cinnamon honey fruitcake

Like a puppy, a fruitcake is not just for Christmas. A slice of this to nibble later in the day will help ward off that midafternoon slump and keep you perky enough to enjoy any family get-together or simply one of those evenings after work. I think that this recipe would work equally well in a larger, flatter pan, giving you fruitcake bars for a lunch-box treat.

1⅓ cups raisins
1⅓ cups dried apricots, chopped
1¼ cups dried figs or prunes, chopped
⅓ cup light brown sugar
5 tablespoons unsalted butter, softened
¼ cup honey, acacia or orange blossom is good
2½ tablespoons blackstrap molasses
2 teaspoons ground cinnamon
3 eggs
⅓ cup brandy or cold tea
1½ cups all-purpose flour
1½ teaspoons baking powder

Line the bottom and sides of an 8-inch round cake pan with parchment paper. Measure the fruit out first as it's a bit of a pain to be scrabbling around the cupboard when you've mixed everything else together. (Substitute where you need to: if you hate figs but love dates, they'll do nicely. If you like whole almonds, then pop ½ cup in with the fruit.)

Beat the sugar, butter, honey, molasses, cinnamon and one of the eggs together until creamy and smooth. Then add the other eggs one at a time with the brandy and beat well. The mixture will look dark and curdled but for this fruitcake that's quite alright. Sift the flour and baking powder together into the bowl and beat well. Finally, add the fruit and fold through until evenly combined. Spoon into the pan, smooth the top and bake at 325°F for about an hour and a half.

Black Christmas cake

No, I'm not wishing you a Black Christmas — in fact, this cake should banish any unseasonal doom and gloom.

13 ounces dried mixed fruit
5 ounces prunes, cut into quarters
1 teaspoon orange extract
¾ cup chopped crystallized ginger
2 cups stout
1 cup (2 sticks) unsalted butter
1 teaspoon ground cinnamon
1 teaspoon ground mace

1 teaspoon ground cloves
1 teaspoon ground nutmeg
1 cup muscovado sugar
½ cup blackstrap molasses
3 eggs
2½ cups spelt or whole-wheat flour
½ teaspoon baking powder

Stir the dried fruit, prunes, orange extract and crystallized ginger in a bowl. In a large saucepan, bring the stout to a boil, watching it doesn't bubble over, then simmer for 15 minutes or so, until reduced to just 6 tablespoons. Add the butter to the pan and let it melt, then remove from the heat, leave to cool and stir in the spices. Beat in the sugar and molasses, then pour all of this over the fruit in the bowl. Beat the eggs and stir them in. Sift the flour and baking powder together, adding back the bits caught in the sieve, and beat this in to the mixture with the fruit.

Line the bottom and sides of an 8-inch round cake pan with parchment paper, spoon the mixture in and bake for 2½ hours at 325°F or until a skewer inserted comes out with just the odd crumb stuck to it and the top of the cake feels firm.

LONG SLOW BAKING

This cake takes quite a long time to bake, and I find that the difference between 2 hours and 3 hours when your oven is set low isn't too great. The final moistness is rather more about the stickiness of the crumb caused by the malt (from the stout) and the molasses and sugar.

Marrakesh Express loaf cake

This spiced moist date loaf stays soft for days, and contains a high-protein flour, ground from hemp seeds once the oil has been removed. The recipe uses an easy and old-fashioned method where everything ends up in the saucepan, then gets stirred together.

1¼ cups freshly brewed black coffee	5 tablespoons unsalted butter
the crushed seeds of 6 to 8 cardamom pods	1 cup chopped dates
	2 eggs
1½ teaspoons ground cinnamon	¾ cup chopped walnuts or pecans
finely grated zest of 1 small lemon	2 tablespoons sesame seeds
2 tablespoons honey	1½ cups spelt or whole-wheat flour
2 tablespoons pomegranate syrup	¾ cup hemp flour
⅔ cup dark brown sugar	2 teaspoons baking powder

Line the bottom and sides of a 7-inch long loaf pan or similar with parchment paper. Pour the coffee into a large saucepan and add the spices, lemon zest, honey, pomegranate syrup, sugar, butter and dates. Bring to a boil, then leave until cool. Beat in the eggs, stir in the walnuts and sesame seeds. Add the spelt flour, hemp flour and baking powder straight into the saucepan, stir everything thoroughly together and spoon it into the pan. Heat the oven to 350°F and bake for about 40 minutes or until a skewer poked in comes out with just a few tiny moist crumbs stuck to it. Let it cool, remove from the pan and wrap well in waxed paper or parchment paper. It's even better the day after baking.

CLOSER TO HOME

At the heart of this recipe lies a very good date and walnut loaf, and replacing the pomegranate syrup with blackstrap molasses, and the hemp with whole-wheat flour, won't hurt it a bit.

Caramel Christmas cake

A classic burnt-sugar caramel, rich with cream, gives the edge to this extra soft fruitcake, ready to ice and decorate as you please.

1 cup super-fine sugar
¼ cup water
⅔ cup heavy cream
2½ tablespoons honey
2½ tablespoons blackstrap
   molasses
finely grated zest of 1 orange
   and 1 lemon
4 teaspoons mixed spice
   (cinnamon, nutmeg,
   ginger and cloves)

½ cup (1 stick) unsalted butter
3 eggs
2 cups bread flour
¼ teaspoon baking soda
1½ cups each currants, raisins
   and chopped prunes or figs
14 ounces natural candied cherries
1⅔ cups walnut halves

Place the sugar and water in a deep heavy saucepan and boil hard for 5 to 6 minutes until it cooks to a dark reddish caramel. Pour in the cream, being very careful to stand back in case it spits, stir, then remove from the heat and add the honey, molasses, zest and mixed spice. Stir well, then add the butter and beat that through as it melts. Pour into a mixing bowl and beat in the eggs, one at a time, then stir in the flour and baking soda until smooth, and finally stir in the fruits and nuts.

Heat the oven to 325°F and line the bottom and sides of a 7-inch round cake pan with 2 to 3 layers of parchment paper. Spoon the mixture into the pan and bake for about 2 hours or until a skewer inserted comes out with only a few crumbs sticking to it.

Small things

Small things

All the excitement around cupcakes, whoopie pies, French macarons and every individually baked thing relates to an essential truth: sometimes, we like to have our own cake rather than a piece of someone else's. Sure, there's something lovely about a large cake you can cut a slice from and share, but that's exactly the problem for the greedy monster in our heads: it isn't ours exclusively, and though refusing to share is held up as the ultimate sin, there are days when you feel less like Mother Teresa and more like Billy Bunter.

Small cakes are not all about gluttony. When you have that cupcake on a plate, all yours and beautifully decorated, maybe there's less of a temptation to eat half a dozen, in a panic or a careless moment. You know, when you let your concentration slip and find you've eaten half a 12-portion layer cake. With a small cake it's easier to enjoy it slowly in a carefully "deconstructed" manner until the last crumb is squished with the back of the fork and eaten.

They can be as rich or as simple as you like. A classic scone, light with a crisp just-baked top crust and spread with fresh and fruity jam and yellowish heavy cream, has a pared-down magnificence that to my taste is far more dramatic than a cluttered mess of piped ganache, tuiles and glazes. But when glamour is just the ticket – when only more is enough – a mini-layer cake gleaming with baubles and glitter is easier to pull off when your surface is only 3¼ inches across.

One of the liberating things about making small pretty cakes today is that, finally, it's OK to be out and proud and say, "I like cakes to look beautiful." I remember a time when "pretty" was an unfashionable concept in baking, ensuring that decorated cakes stayed out of public view from the mid-1980s until just a few years ago. At home you could dress up a cupcake like a Fabergé trinket, but out in public it took all your talent to reverse this appearance and make it look as "man" made and as crude as possible. Pastry bags were banished, palette knives looked on with suspicion, and the only acceptable tool for the young pastry cook was a spoon.

In London it was a German pastry chef, Gerhard Jenne, who began the counterattack in 1992 with Konditor & Cook, a shop that made unashamedly brightly colored and camp fondant fancies called "magic cakes," that used food coloring in the way that gastropub cooks use olive oil. A rainbow of cake cubes decorated with words, icons and hearts became the fashion crowd's wedding cake du jour, but it took a decade more for other pastry chefs to really lose their inhibitions and join the dolled-up revolution.

Even simple baking can shine with a little effort, without having to resort to colorings. A banana bran muffin can have disks of fresh banana dipped in lemon juice placed on top before baking, or be brushed with a little Jamaica rum syrup while hot. Hazelnut brownies can have skinned whole nuts scattered over the top. And unbaked scones can have their tops brushed carefully with a little beaten egg so they shine when baked. It's about sticking with it, and doing that last little bit with the same care you put in at the start.

For basic tips on making small cakes, have a look at the Cakes chapter (see page 105) and the Desserts chapter (see page 355).

Preparing the pans

When I'm baking bars, cakes or brownies, I usually put a sheet of parchment paper on the bottom and butter the sides of the pan, or press one large sheet of foil across the bottom and up the sides. For muffins and cupcakes I go for paper muffin liners, or squares of greaseproof paper (not nonstick) pressed into the pan with your fingers before filling. Greaseproof, because you actually want some of the outer layer to stick to the paper, both to make the muffin easier to hold and to reduce the amount of crust you have to eat. If you must go "bare," a liberal brushing with clarified butter works best.

Sizes and measuring the mixture

You usually want a batch of individual small cakes to all turn out the same size, and this requires a little more planning than when you bake the mixture as one large sheet or bar and cut it into portions after baking. For scone dough it's as simple as patting the dough out to a certain thickness and then using one cutter. Muffins and cupcakes are more tricky, but don't require scientific precision. Volume is the easiest way to judge it; just fill each muffin cup to the same level. The downside is that you can't be too sure with a new recipe exactly how many you'll get.

If having an exact number is absolutely crucial, and you don't mind it getting a bit tricky, use a calculator and electronic scale for precision. After mixing up the batter, place it on the scale to get the total weight. Divide that by the number of cakes you need, and that will give you the amount of each portion. Then place a dinner plate on the scale, put your baking sheet or muffin pan on that so it's lifted up above the display and spoon the mixture into the individual cups.

Baking

You can usually slightly underbake small cakes as they will continue cooking for a few minutes after they come out of the oven.

Finishing the cakes

All of the icings in the Sugar Sugar chapter (see page 291) can be used here, but you might want to halve the quantities if you only have a few cakes to ice. I've never heard anyone complain about a cupcake being too tall, so keep the consistency of the icing very thick, perhaps reducing the liquid in the recipe. If you're using a pastry bag, practice your swirls on a sheet of paper first and, for a less formal effect, have a test cake and practice on that. Plan how the elements will work together before you put them in place. If you drag the decoration around on a small cake, it can end up looking a bit messy.

Make your own vanilla extract

Do what many pastry chefs do, and stuff a clean empty bottle with old vanilla pods, then add cheap brandy to fill and 1¾ cups sugar (light brown is good) for every 4½ cups of spirit. Leave it a week or so before using, then glug away instead of using store-bought vanilla extract.

Chocolate custard muffins

Simply the best chocolate muffin you'll ever eat. A swirl of Meringue Buttercream Icing (page 327) or some leftover Molasses Chocolate Fudge Frosting (page 332), perhaps topped with a crystallized violet or rose petal, looks great on these.

MAKES 12

½ cup cornstarch
3 tablespoons cocoa powder
½ cup dark brown sugar
1 cup cold water
5 tablespoons unsalted butter, cubed
4 ounces dark chocolate, broken into small pieces

⅓ cup sunflower oil
2 teaspoons vanilla extract
2 eggs
⅔ cup super-fine sugar
1 cup all-purpose flour
2½ teaspoons baking powder

Place the cornstarch, cocoa, brown sugar and water into a saucepan and whisk together constantly over medium heat until boiling and very thick. Remove from the heat and beat in the butter and chocolate until melted and absorbed. Add the oil, vanilla and one of the eggs and beat again until combined, then add the remaining egg with the super-fine sugar and beat until smooth and thick. Measure the flour and baking powder into a small bowl, stir together, then sift this directly onto the custard and beat through until combined.

Heat the oven to 350°F. Spoon into paper muffin liners sitting in the cups of a muffin pan, and bake for 25 minutes. Leave to cool on a wire rack.

Banana bran muffins

This recipe makes lots, but also doubles as a simple moist cake so you could line a large shallow pan with parchment paper and bake, to freeze or eat straight away drizzled with a little lemon water icing (see page 335).

MAKES 18 to 20

1 cup boiling water

2⅓ cups wheat bran

3 ripe mashed bananas

1 cup muscovado or dark brown sugar

½ cup super-fine sugar

2 eggs

9 tablespoons unsalted butter, melted

¾ cup Greek yogurt

2 teaspoons vanilla extract

2½ cups all-purpose flour

1½ teaspoons ground cinnamon

1½ teaspoons baking soda

1½ teaspoons baking powder

2 cups raisins

Pour the boiling water over the bran and leave for 15 minutes to soak up the liquid. Place the bananas, muscovado and super-fine sugar and one of the eggs in a bowl and beat until smooth. Then beat in the remaining egg followed by the melted butter, yogurt and vanilla. Sift the flour, cinnamon, baking soda and baking powder together two or three times so the leavening agents and spice are evenly distributed.

Heat the oven to 400°F. Take a 12-cup muffin pan and line with paper liners.

Beat the bran through the banana mixture, then fold in the dry ingredients and the raisins. Spoon into the paper liners and bake for 25 minutes or until a toothpick comes out with just the odd crumb stuck to it, then remove from the oven and let the muffins cool on a wire rack.

Clementine and oat muffins

Clementines have a subtle flavor, so this recipe has zest and juice mixed in both the glaze and batter, to capture the delicate tang.

MAKES ABOUT 6

FOR THE MUFFINS
finely grated zest of
   3 clementines, plus ½ cup
   juice and pulp
⅔ cup super-fine sugar
⅓ cup sunflower oil
2 eggs
⅔ cup rolled oats
1½ cups all-purpose flour
2½ teaspoons baking powder

FOR THE GLAZE
finely grated zest of
   1 clementine, plus 1 to 2
   tablespoons juice
1 cup confectioners' sugar

To make the muffins, heat the oven to 350°F and place paper liners in six cups of a muffin pan.

Using an electric whisk, beat the clementine zest with the sugar, oil and eggs for 3 to 4 minutes until pale and thickish. Stir in the juice and pulp, add the oats, then sift the flour with the baking powder and fold this in until smooth but barely combined. Spoon into the paper liners, filling them four-fifths of the way up. Bake for 25 minutes or until golden in color and a toothpick inserted comes out with just the odd crumb sticking to it, then remove from the oven.

To make the glaze, stir together the clementine zest and juice with the confectioners' sugar.

Spoon a little of the glaze over each muffin while hot. Let the muffins get cold before eating.

Dark blueberry bran muffins

Good all year-round, but during one wintry season of colds and coughs, I thought a dairy-free treat might be good for all those feeling a bit blocked up. Or you can make it with cow's milk and rely on a boost from the minerals and iron in the muscovado sugar and molasses.

MAKES 12

¾ cup soy milk

1⅓ cups wheat bran

½ cup dark muscovado sugar

1 tablespoon blackstrap molasses

finely grated zest of 1 orange

⅔ cup sunflower oil

2 eggs

1½ cups all-purpose flour

1 tablespoon baking powder

⅓ cup super-fine sugar

roughly 2 cups fresh blueberries

Heat the oven to 400°F and line 12 cups of a muffin pan with paper liners. Bring the soy milk almost to a boil in a saucepan, then pour this over the bran and muscovado sugar in a mixing bowl. Beat to a smooth mush and leave for 5 minutes. Then, beat in the molasses, orange zest, oil and eggs until smooth. Sift the flour, baking powder and sugar together, then fold this through lightly. Fold in the blueberries, spoon the mixture into the paper liners and bake for about half an hour until a deep rich brown color on top and firm to the touch. Cool on a wire rack.

Weetabix muffins

Weetabix, Oatibix or a generic "whole-wheat" breakfast cereal are right for this recipe.

MAKES 9

3 biscuits Weetabix
   or similar
⅔ cup raisins
¾ cup all-purpose flour
¾ cup whole-wheat
   or rye flour
1½ teaspoons baking soda
1½ teaspoons baking
   powder

1½ teaspoons ground
   cinnamon
½ cup light brown sugar
1 egg
1¼ cups low-fat plain yogurt
⅓ cup milk
¼ cup sunflower oil
2½ tablespoons corn syrup
zest of 1 orange

Heat the oven to 400°F and drop nine paper liners into the cups of a muffin pan. Crumble the Weetabix into a bowl and add the raisins. Sift together both flours, the baking soda, baking powder, cinnamon and sugar two or three times, then add this to the Weetabix and raisins and toss together. Beat the egg, yogurt, milk, oil, syrup and orange zest together. Stir this quickly and evenly through the dry ingredients then immediately spoon into the paper liners, filling to the top. Bake in the oven for 20 to 25 minutes until well risen, and if a toothpick inserted comes out with only the odd crumb sticking to it, bingo, they're ready. Cool on a wire rack.

BREAKFAST BAKING

If you want to impress with freshly baked muffins while everyone else is still bleary-eyed in the morning, the trick is to measure the dry ingredients the night before and have the liquid part mixed in the fridge, with the paper liners ready in the muffin pan. The following morning go to the kitchen at some ungodly hour, turn on the oven, mix the batter, spoon into the liners and bake the muffins. Then put the kettle on and start your day.

Blueberry crème fraîche cupcakes

This slightly odd cake method produces a very delicate and moist crumb, and stops the blueberries from sinking to the bottom. The icing might seem a bit like overkill but hey, it's a cupcake. And in my book a cupcake demands icing.

MAKES 12

FOR THE CUPCAKES
3 egg whites
2 cups confectioners' sugar
5 tablespoons unsalted butter, softened
1¼ cups crème fraîche
1 teaspoon vanilla extract
½ teaspoon almond extract
2¼ cups all-purpose flour
2½ teaspoons baking powder
2 cups fresh blueberries

FOR THE ICING
¾ cup crème fraîche
3 cups confectioners' sugar

To make the cupcakes, in a clean bowl, whisk the egg whites with an electric beater until they begin to fluff up, then gradually add half the confectioners' sugar and beat to a soft meringue. In another larger bowl, beat the butter until fluffy then add the crème fraîche with the vanilla and almond extract, beat lightly to combine, then add the remaining confectioners' sugar with ¾ cup of the flour and beat for 1 minute until thick and smooth.

Beat about a third of the meringue through the butter mixture until smooth, then a third of the remaining flour sifted with the baking powder, and repeat until all the meringue and flour have been added. No need to be delicate here, put some elbow into it. Fold in the blueberries then line 12 cups of a muffin pan with paper liners, and spoon in the mixture. Heat the oven to 350°F and bake until risen and golden, 25 to 30 minutes. Cool on a wire rack.

To make the icing, beat the crème fraîche with the confectioners' sugar for a minute till it is light and smooth.

Swirl a blob of icing on top of each cooled cupcake.

Pumpkin ginger cupcakes

What seems like a mountain of raw grated pumpkin vanishes magically into the crumb and simply leaves a moist texture and a subtle sweet flavor.

MAKES ABOUT 12

FOR THE CUPCAKES
½ cup crystallized ginger
¾ cup muscovado or dark brown sugar
9 tablespoons unsalted butter, softened
2 eggs
3¾ cups raw grated pumpkin or butternut squash
1½ cups all-purpose flour
2 teaspoons baking powder
1½ teaspoons ground ginger
1½ teaspoons ground allspice
¼ teaspoon ground nutmeg
¼ teaspoon ground cloves
1 cup chopped pecans or walnuts

FOR THE ICING
2 cups confectioners' sugar
5 tablespoons unsalted butter, softened
4 ounces full-fat cream cheese
3 tablespoons crystallized ginger, finely chopped

shredded ginger to finish

To make the cupcakes, heat the oven to 375°F and line the cups of a muffin pan with paper liners.

Finely chop the ginger. Beat the sugar and butter until smooth, then beat in the eggs, one at a time. Stir the pumpkin and ginger through, sift the flour, baking powder and spices into the mixture, add the nuts and stir again until smooth. Spoon the mixture into the paper liners, almost to the top, and bake for 25 minutes. Cool on a wire rack.

To make the icing, beat the confectioners' sugar, butter and cream cheese till smooth and stir in the ginger.

Swirl a dollop of icing on each cupcake and decorate with just a pinch of shredded ginger.

Vanilla cupcakes

What makes cupcakes look so appealing is their size, as they're baked in muffin liners, with a jaunty swirl of butter frosting to give them a dab of Dior glamour. But underneath beats the heart of an old-fashioned pound cake, with a touch more flour to give them a soft volcano peak.

MAKES 8

FOR THE CUPCAKES
⅔ cup super-fine sugar
9 tablespoons unsalted butter, very soft
2 eggs
2 teaspoons vanilla extract
1¼ cups all-purpose flour
1 teaspoon baking powder

FOR THE FROSTING
5 tablespoons unsalted butter, very soft
2½ cups confectioners' sugar
⅓ cup condensed milk
⅓ cup heavy cream

To make the cupcakes, in the bowl of a stand electric mixer, beat the sugar, butter, eggs and vanilla for about 3 minutes on the highest speed until light and fluffy. Sift the flour and baking powder together two or three times as this will stop "tunnels" from forming in the crumb. Add the flour to the butter mixture and beat for about 30 seconds. Spoon the batter into eight paper liners placed in the cups of a muffin pan, then leave to rest at room temperature for 30 minutes. Heat the oven to 350°F. Bake for 20 to 25 minutes until golden and firm, then cool on a wire rack.

To make the frosting, get the butter as soft as possible without melting, then place it in a bowl with the remaining ingredients. Whisk everything together with an electric beater until smooth and fluffy.

Swirl the frosting thickly over the top of each cupcake. The sugar in the frosting will make sure it keeps its shape at a cool room temperature.

MIXING BY HAND

Making cupcakes or any butter-rich cake by hand with a wooden spoon requires a slightly different — but traditional — method to get the right

result. Warm your mixing bowl with a splash of boiling water, then wipe it dry. Measure the sugar and butter into the bowl, making sure the butter is very soft. Beat them together with a spatula or wooden spoon until smooth and slightly fluffy. Beat the eggs in a separate bowl then add them, a quarter at a time, to the butter and sugar, beating well after each addition. An electric mixer can produce a great result with the butter, sugar and eggs in all at once; this more gradual method works best when working by hand. Beat the flour into the butter mixture in batches, a quarter at a time. Finish beating as soon as the mixture is smooth. And be sure to sift your dry ingredients together first, to get the lightest result. For years I never bothered, but I went back and checked some of my habits and found that yes, you do get a lighter result if you sift your dry ingredients together. Spoon into the paper liners and leave to sit for a lighter result (or bake right away if you're in a hurry, the difference is slight). When baked, the paper should be dry and free from grease, and when broken open, the texture of the cakes should be very light and fluffy.

Green fairy cakes

The green fairy here is two little spoonfuls of absinthe on each lime and almond cake, which turns these into an "adults only" treat. Perfect for those intimate moments when a little absinthe might make the heart grow fonder.

MAKES 9

¾ cup super-fine sugar

½ cup (1 stick) unsalted butter, plus extra for the pan

finely grated zest of 2 smallish limes, plus 1 tablespoon lime juice

1 egg

1¾ cups ground almonds

½ cup milk

1¼ cups all-purpose flour

1 teaspoon baking powder

⅓ cup absinthe

¾ cup confectioners' sugar

1 small piece of tarragon, shredded into spiky pieces

Heat the oven to 350°F. Cut 4-inch squares of parchment paper and press them down into the buttered cups of a deep muffin pan — the mixture will weigh the paper down and the corners should poke up like handkerchief points around the cakes. Beat the sugar, butter and lime zest until light and fluffy. Add the egg and almonds and beat until creamy. Then add the milk and beat until fluffy again — if it looks slightly curdled, everything's still OK. Sift together the flour and baking powder, then stir this into the egg mixture until smooth. Divide the mixture evenly between the cups and bake for 30 to 35 minutes until risen and golden.

Remove and leave until almost cold, then spoon 2 teaspoons of neat absinthe over each. Beat the confectioners' sugar with the lime juice and drizzle a psychedelic swirl over each cake, then decorate each one with a pinch of tarragon.

Spelt and hazelnut cupcakes

I was once sent a box of glorious spelt cupcakes (ahhh, the perks of the job), which showed that even bran-rich flour can produce a light and delicate cake. As spelt doesn't contain as much gluten as regular flour, this also helps keep the crumb tender.

MAKES 12

10 tablespoons unsalted butter, softened
⅔ cup super-fine sugar
2 eggs, separated
1½ cups spelt or whole-wheat flour
1¼ teaspoons baking powder
¼ cup sherry or milk
½ cup hazelnuts, toasted and finely chopped
lightly sweetened and whipped heavy cream
confectioners' sugar to dust

Heat the oven to 400°F and line the cups of a 12-hole muffin or cupcake pan with paper liners.

Beat the butter and sugar until light and fluffy, then add the egg yolks and beat again until combined. Sift the flour and baking powder together, tipping the bran that gets sifted out right back in again, then beat this through the butter mixture alternately with the sherry. Finally, stir in the hazelnuts, then in a clean bowl with a clean whisk, beat the egg whites to a stiff froth and fold them gently but evenly through the mixture. Spoon into the paper liners almost to the top and bake for 25 minutes, or until a toothpick inserted comes out with just the odd crumb stuck to it.

Leave until cold, then use a sharp knife to cut out the center of each cake. Spoon whipped cream in, cut the removed piece of cake in two, stick these in to make "wings" and dust with confectioners' sugar.

Madeleines de Commercy

These morsels of sponge cake perhaps sit more comfortably here than anywhere else. Henri-Paul Pellaprat was the most revered and influential professor at the elite Le Cordon Bleu cooking school in pre-WWII Paris, and this version is inspired by his 1937 book on desserts. I've added a trick of my own, spooning a little cold butter on top just before baking, as this results in that sensuous nipple rising in the center of each little cake. If you have a madeleine pan, use that instead of a muffin pan.

MAKES 12

2 eggs, at room
    temperature
⅓ cup super-fine sugar
2 teaspoons vanilla extract
5 tablespoons unsalted butter,
    plus extra for the pan and to finish

¾ cup all-purpose flour
½ teaspoon baking soda

Warm the mixing bowl, then break the eggs in with the sugar and beat with an electric whisk for 3 to 4 minutes until thick and doubled in volume. Add the vanilla and beat a moment more.

Melt the butter and set aside. Heat the oven to 425°F and butter 12 muffin pan cups. Sift the flour and baking soda together, then sift them into the egg mixture and fold through very gently, followed by the butter, until lightly and evenly combined. Spoon some of the mixture into each muffin cup, filling them about one-third full (three-quarters if you're using a madeleine pan). Put

a small flat piece of butter (about ¼ teaspoon) in the center of each madeleine, place the pan in the oven and bake for about 10 minutes until well risen and slightly scorched at the edges.

Chocolate whoopie pies

A good whoopie pie should be chewy and slightly soft, with a hint of crispness at the edges. Pipe these using a pastry bag with a wide nozzle if you want them to look perfect, but I just spoon them onto the baking sheet and don't mind the odd wobbly edge or bumpy top. You can fill them with Simple Lemon Cream Cheese Frosting (page 330), but for me, it ain't a whoopie without marshmallow cream and the recipe I use here is quick and easy, and soft to eat. I've deliberately made my pies small, as I find a giant whoopie just a bit too much of a mouthful.

MAKES ABOUT 5

FOR THE "CAKES"	FOR THE MARSHMALLOW CREAM AND ICING
5 tablespoons unsalted butter	4 ounces white marshmallows
3 ounces dark chocolate	2 tablespoons milk
1 egg	9 tablespoons unsalted butter, very soft
¾ cup dark brown sugar	2 cups confectioners' sugar
1 cup sour cream	½ cup cocoa powder
2 tablespoons cold milk	about 3 tablespoons water
1 teaspoon vanilla extract	
2 cups all-purpose flour	
¼ cup cocoa powder	
¾ teaspoon baking soda	

To make the cakes, line a baking sheet with parchment paper and heat the oven to 350°F. Melt the butter in a saucepan, then break the chocolate into it and heat gently until that is also melted, then leave to one side. In a mixing bowl, beat the egg until light and fluffy using an electric mixer, then gradually beat in the brown sugar, a third at a time, until thick and glossy. Beat in the melted butter and chocolate, sour cream, milk and vanilla. Sift the flour, cocoa and baking soda into the mixture and beat through until smooth.

Pipe or spoon ten balls of the mixture, the size of a small unshelled walnut, onto the baking sheet, spaced 1½ inches apart, flatten them slightly with wet fingers and bake for 13 to 14 minutes until cooked. If the cakes are underbaked, they tend to shrink as they cool. Allow to cool slightly, then transfer to a wire cooling rack and bake the remaining mixture.

To make the cream and icing, heat the marshmallows and milk in a saucepan over low heat. When melted, take off the heat, beat with a hand whisk until smooth, then leave until almost set. Beat the butter until creamy, then gradually beat this into the marshmallow mixture until whipped and smooth. Sift the confectioners' sugar and cocoa into a small bowl and gradually add the water until you get the right consistency for the icing.

Sandwich two cakes together with the marshmallow cream, and decorate the top with a little of the cocoa icing.

Vanilla whoopie pies

FOR THE "CAKES"
½ cup (1 stick) unsalted butter
1 egg
¾ cup super-fine sugar
1 cup sour cream
2 tablespoons cold milk
1 teaspoon vanilla extract
2¼ cup all-purpose flour
¾ teaspoon baking soda

FOR THE MARSHMALLOW
  CREAM AND ICING
4 ounces white marshmallows
2 tablespoons milk
9 tablespoons unsalted butter,
  very soft
2 cups confectioners' sugar
2 to 3 tablespoons water

To make the cakes, line a baking sheet with parchment paper and heat the oven to 350°F. Melt the butter in a saucepan, then leave to one side. In a mixing bowl, beat the egg until light and fluffy using an electric mixer, then gradually beat in the sugar, a third at a time, until thick and glossy. Beat in the melted butter, sour cream, milk and vanilla. Sift the flour and baking soda into the mixture and beat through until smooth.

Pipe or spoon ten balls of the mixture, the size of a small unshelled walnut, onto the baking sheet, spaced 1½ inches apart, and bake for 13 to 14 minutes until almost evenly golden on top. If the cakes are underbaked, they tend to shrink as they cool. Allow to cool slightly, then transfer to a wire cooling rack and bake the remaining mixture.

To make the cream and icing, heat the marshmallows and milk in a saucepan over low heat. When half melted, take off the heat, beat with a hand whisk until smooth, then leave to cool. Beat the butter until creamy, then gradually beat this into the marshmallow mixture until whipped and smooth. Sift the confectioners' sugar into a small bowl and gradually add the water until you get the right consistency for the icing.

Sandwich two cakes together with the marshmallow cream, and decorate the top with a little of the icing.

OTHER FLAVORS

These all use the basic ingredients and method of the vanilla whoopie pies, marshmallow cream and icing, with additions to achieve a variety of flavors. In each case, by using only half the vanilla batter, one basic recipe enables you to try two other flavors.

Hazelnut and black cherry whoopie pies

Take half the vanilla batter and stir in 1 to 1½ tablespoons black cherry preserves, 3 ounces chopped dried sour cherries and ⅓ cup chopped toasted hazelnuts. Sprinkle extra chopped nuts over before baking. To finish, take half the marshmallow cream and beat in 1 tablespoon black cherry preserves. Leave the tops plain, no icing.

Apricot and almond whoopie pies

Take half the vanilla batter and stir in ¾ cup finely chopped soft dried apricots. To finish, take half the marshmallow cream and beat in the seeds of a vanilla pod (or 1 teaspoon vanilla extract) and 1 tablespoon sour cream. For the icing, sift 1 cup confectioners' sugar into a small bowl, add the seeds of half a vanilla pod (or ½ teaspoon vanilla extract) and gradually add 1 to 2 tablespoons water until you get the right consistency, and top each pie with toasted sliced almonds over the icing.

Passion fruit whoopie pies

Take half the vanilla batter and use as is. To finish, take half the marshmallow cream and beat in the pulp from two passion fruit. For the icing, sift 1 cup confectioners' sugar into a small bowl, stir in the pulp from one passion fruit and just enough water to get the right consistency.

Raspberry ruffle whoopie pies

Take half the vanilla cake batter and stir in ½ cup shredded coconut and an additional 1 tablespoon milk, and sprinkle extra coconut over before baking. To finish, take half the marshmallow cream and beat in 1 tablespoon raspberry preserves. Dust with confectioners' sugar, instead of icing.

Lemon or orange whoopie pies

Take half the vanilla cake batter and stir in the finely grated zest of one large unwaxed lemon or orange. To finish, take half the marshmallow cream and stir in the finely grated zest of half a lemon or orange. For the icing, sift 1 cup confectioners' sugar into a small bowl with the finely grated zest of half a lemon or orange, and just enough of the juice to get the right consistency.

PLAN AHEAD

The cake halves can be baked and frozen, unfilled; assemble at the last minute, as they are best freshly filled and iced. Decorate the tops with chocolate or colored sprinkles, tiny candies or citrus zest over the icing, or simply dust with confectioners' sugar.

Banana blondie

If Carmen Miranda ever wondered what to do when her bananas ripened, she should have gotten some of her personal stash of baking powder out (I hear she'd hide it in the heel of her shoe) and made these.

1½ cups super-fine sugar
2 tablespoons cold water
½ cup brazil nuts, roughly chopped
oil for the baking sheet
½ cup (1 stick) unsalted butter

8 ounces white chocolate
1 egg
2 bananas, peeled and chopped
2 teaspoons vanilla extract
1¾ cups all-purpose flour
¼ teaspoon baking powder

Put ⅓ cup of the super-fine sugar in a pan with the cold water, bring to a boil and let it bubble away till the sugar turns to a reddish-golden caramel and a drop poured from a teaspoon into a glass of cold water sets to a hard ball. Stir in the chopped nuts, spread onto an oiled baking sheet and let it get cold. Chop the toffee up finely.

Line the bottom and sides of an 8-inch square pan with foil and heat the oven to 375°F. Heat the butter with the white chocolate in a pan over a low heat until melted, then scrape into a bowl, add the remaining sugar and beat with the egg, bananas and vanilla until smooth. Sift the flour and baking powder together and fold through the butter mixture with the chopped toffee. Spoon into the pan and bake for 35 minutes until "wobbly" set and golden on top. Leave till stone cold before slicing.

More flavors

If brazil nuts really aren't your thing, try substituting 4 ounces dark chocolate chips for the toffee, and scattering some slivered almonds over the top before it goes in the oven. Or caramelize the bananas (see the Butterscotch Banana Cake, page 126) by making a second caramel with ⅓ cup of the sugar, then fold this through after you've beaten in the sugar, egg and vanilla.

Bourbon pecan brownies

If you need to make this alcohol-free, replace the bourbon with milk, or just leave the liquid out altogether. The cocoa makes it extra chocolaty, but if you want the flavor less pronounced, you can leave that out as well. Or have a salad instead, and stop tormenting yourself.

MAKES ABOUT 16

8 ounces dark chocolate

9 tablespoons butter

2 eggs

⅔ cup light brown sugar

½ cup super-fine sugar

⅓ cup bourbon

2 teaspoons vanilla extract

1⅓ cups all-purpose flour

1 tablespoon cocoa powder

1¼ cups pecans, roughly chopped

Heat the oven to 375°F and line an 8-inch square cake pan with foil. Melt the chocolate with the butter in a saucepan and leave somewhere warm on the work surface. Beat the eggs with both the sugars until the sugars have almost dissolved and the mixture turns creamy and a light beige color. Next, beat the chocolate and butter with the eggs and sugar till evenly combined, then add the bourbon and vanilla. Sift the flour and cocoa twice, then beat this into the chocolate mixture. Finally, beat in the chopped pecans. Scrape this into the pan and bake for 25 minutes or until a poke with a toothpick through the sugary crust comes out barely clean, as the hot chocolate will cook on for at least 5 minutes after you've taken it out of the oven.

Rye hazelnut brownies

You could change the method and get a more delicate result by beating the softened butter with the oil and sugar, then the eggs, then the chocolate, coffee, flour and nuts. More work, more bowls to wash, when surely the only essentials are a magnificent flavor and a sticky moist texture. Rye flour gives them a lovely taste but use all-purpose flour if that's all you have.

9 tablespoons unsalted butter
⅓ cup hazelnut oil
1⅓ cups dark chocolate, chopped
1⅓ cups light brown sugar

3 eggs
⅓ cup strong black coffee
2½ cups rye flour
¾ teaspoon baking powder
¾ cup toasted hazelnuts, skinned

Heat the oven to 350°F and line a deep 8- to 10-inch square cake pan with foil.

Melt the butter in a large saucepan, then add the oil and chocolate and stir over a low heat until melted. Beat in the sugar and eggs, then the black coffee. Beat in the rye flour and baking power until smooth, then stir in the hazelnuts. Spoon into the lined cake pan and bake for about 40 minutes, but check it 5 minutes before the end just in case your oven runs hot and cooks it too quickly. Always better to slightly underbake brownies. Just stick a toothpick in the center and if it comes out with barely a cooked and sticky crumb stuck to it, then it's done. Leave until completely cold before cutting.

USING DIFFERENT FLAVORS

Any rye flour will contribute the lovely flavor you're after here, and a dark rye flour will also give you little pale flecks through the crumb. If you want to experiment with a gluten-free variation, try using two parts buckwheat flour to one part potato flour.

Black millionaire's shortbread

Lyle's Golden Syrup was first made with imported sugarcane at Abram Lyle's Plaistow refinery in east London in 1883. Simmered with blackstrap molasses, muscovado sugar, allspice, vanilla and butter, it makes a dark rich hit of sugar to serve with coffee.

FOR THE BASE
1 cup all-purpose flour
2 tablespoons cocoa powder
¼ teaspoon baking powder
⅓ cup muscovado sugar
½ cup (1 stick) unsalted butter, softened

FOR THE TOPPING
¾ cup muscovado sugar
2 tablespoons cornstarch
1 teaspoon ground allspice
¼ cup blackstrap molasses
¼ cup golden syrup
   or corn syrup
¾ cup (1½ sticks) unsalted butter, softened
2 teaspoons vanilla extract
8 ounces dark chocolate
2 tablespoons sunflower oil

To make the base, heat the oven to 325°F and line an 8-inch square pan with foil.

Sift the flour, cocoa and baking powder into a bowl. Add the sugar and butter, and rub together until the mixture turns to a buttery dough. Press it evenly into the bottom of the pan and bake for 30 minutes.

To make the topping, stir the sugar, cornstarch, allspice, blackstrap molasses and golden syrup together in a deep saucepan over low heat until smooth and dissolved. Add the butter and vanilla, bring to a boil and simmer for 3 to 4 minutes until a drizzle dropped into cold water can be squeezed into a soft ball between your fingers. Remove from the heat, let the bubbles subside, then pour this over the base. Leave 3 to 4 hours to cool, then carefully melt the chocolate with the sunflower oil, mix to combine and spread this over the top. Leave to set before cutting into slices or squares.

Blueberry almond bar

Lightly cooking dark fruit like blueberries, blackberries or cherries with a little starch creates a thick compote that can be folded through a rich cake batter. This means that a small quantity of fruit can be stretched to flavor an afternoon cake like this. The base should be neither as dense as a cookie nor as soft as a cake.

½ cup water
1¼ cups fresh blueberries,
   blackberries or cherries
2 teaspoons cornstarch
¾ cup super-fine sugar
1¼ cups all-purpose flour
½ teaspoon baking powder
½ cup ground almonds

½ cup (1 stick) unsalted butter,
   plus extra for the pan
1 egg
¼ cup milk
2 teaspoons honey
½ cup light brown sugar
1 cup sliced almonds

Heat the oven to 350°F and butter an 8-inch square pan. Heat the water in a pan with the blueberries, cornstarch and ¼ cup of the super-fine sugar and cook, stirring gently, until the blueberries bleed and the mixture thickens.

Measure the flour, baking powder, ground almonds and remaining ½ cup super-fine sugar into a bowl, rub in the butter, then beat the egg and work this into the mixture. Pat this into the bottom of the pan. Next, simmer the milk, honey, brown sugar and almonds in a small saucepan till slightly thickened. Spread the blueberry compote over the base in the pan, followed by the almond mixture, then bake for about 35 minutes. Leave until cool before cutting into slices.

Jammy Lamingtons

Much like Girl Scout Cookie season, every year during the infamous "Lamington Drives," Australian parents are bullied by their crazed children into buying dozens of factory-made cakes, in a fundraising frenzy. But if homemade and filled with good jam, Lamingtons are a joy, oozing redness with every bite.

MAKES 6 to 8

FOR THE CAKE

2 eggs, separated
¾ cup super-fine sugar
5 tablespoons unsalted butter, softened
1 teaspoon vanilla extract
1½ cups all-purpose flour
2½ tablespoons arrowroot or cornstarch
2 teaspoons baking powder
⅔ cup milk

FOR THE COATING

¼ cup cocoa powder
1¼ cups confectioners' sugar
½ cup boiling water
1 ounce dark chocolate, chopped
⅓ cup good quality red jam
1 cup shredded coconut

To make the cake, heat the oven to 350°F and line a deep 7-inch square pan with parchment paper.

In a very clean bowl, beat the egg whites with ¼ cup of the super-fine sugar to a soft meringue, using an electric mixer. Then in another bowl, again with the mixer, beat the remaining sugar with the butter, vanilla and egg yolks for 3 minutes until fluffy. Sift the flour, arrowroot and baking powder together and gradually beat this into the sugar, butter and egg yolks, alternating with the milk, beating until smooth; then beat in the meringue and scrape into the prepared pan. Bake for 35 minutes or until a toothpick inserted comes out with just a few tiny moist crumbs stuck to it.

To make the coating, whisk the cocoa and confectioners' sugar with the boiling water, then stir in the chocolate and leave till cold.

Trim the cake into six to eight rectangles, slice these in half lengthwise and fill with a few teaspoons of jam. Reassemble and carefully dip each one into the coating and then roll in the coconut to finish.

Marmalade oat bars

Brown sugar, orange zest and blackstrap molasses give these bars the flavor of a dark Oxford-cut marmalade. The texture is lighter and softer than the usual cookie bar, and not quite as rich.

1⅓ cups raisins	¾ cup orange marmalade
boiling water	finely grated zest of 2 oranges
1 cup (2 sticks) unsalted butter	2 tablespoons blackstrap molasses
⅔ cup dark brown sugar	5 cups rolled oats

Heat the oven to 350°F and line a 10-inch square pan or similar with foil.

In a bowl, cover the raisins with boiling water, leave for 10 minutes to soften and swell, then drain. Melt the butter in a large saucepan, add the brown sugar, marmalade, orange zest and molasses and bring just to a boil. Remove from the heat and stir in the oats and drained raisins. Spoon the mixture into the pan and pack it down evenly, right into the corners. Bake for about 25 minutes until lightly colored at the edges. Slightly tricky to get right; if you bake it too long the bars turn rock hard when they're cold, too little and they crumble, but 25 minutes should do it. Remove from the oven and leave until warm before cutting into squares.

USING OTHER FRUITS

You can use lemon or lime marmalade and zest from the matching fruit, in place of orange marmalade and zest, or use chopped apricots or cranberries instead of the raisins, to vary the flavor.

Everyday scones

Baking in a deep, clean roasting pan makes for a softer scone, as less moisture is lost during baking. You may not get a perfect shape, but the softness and flavor more than make up for that. A little cream in the dough also helps to give a richer, more tender result.

MAKES 6 to 8

1 cup low-fat plain yogurt

2 tablespoons heavy cream

2 tablespoons super-fine sugar

3 cups all-purpose flour, plus extra for dusting

½ teaspoon fine salt

2 teaspoons cream of tartar

1 teaspoon baking soda

4 tablespoons unsalted butter, softened

beaten egg to finish

Stir the yogurt, cream and sugar together and leave for a few minutes so that the sugar dissolves. Sift the flour, salt, cream of tartar and baking soda into a large mixing bowl and rub the butter through lightly. Mix the yogurt mixture into the flour, then quickly and gently work everything to a soft sticky dough. Some cooks use a knife to stir the dough, to avoid being heavy-handed.

Scoop the dough onto a well-floured work surface, and lightly dust the top with flour. Pat it out until 1½ inches high, then push a 2½-inch biscuit cutter firmly through the dough without twisting. Place on the bottom of a roasting pan or very large deep cake pan lined with parchment paper, spaced ¾ inch apart.

Heat the oven to 425°F, brush the tops lightly with beaten egg and bake for 12 to 14 minutes until just colored on top. Cool on a wire rack, covered with a tea towel to keep them moist.

FOR PERFECT SCONES

The baking soda can produce little brown speckles on the crust of a pale scone. To avoid this, dissolve the baking soda in a little water and add it to the yogurt.

You can replace the all-purpose flour, baking soda and cream of tartar with self-rising flour. Still makes a good scone but they don't rise quite as well and are a little heavier.

Sifting makes the dough a little lighter, but you still get OK scones without sifting. If you add some beaten egg to the mixture in place of the cream, it makes the crust softer, but turns the crumb darker.

Once the scones are cut and in the pan, leave them for about 15 minutes before baking if you can as this will help them rise more evenly.

Sweet buttermilk scones

Before you even ask — yes, you can use yogurt instead. These sweet buttery fruited scones are best served warm, with more butter and a dollop of good berry jam.

2 cups all-purpose flour, plus
  extra for dusting
2½ teaspoons baking powder
3 tablespoons super-fine sugar,
  plus more for the tops
3 tablespoons butter, softened

⅔ cup raisins
1 egg
⅓ cup buttermilk or low-fat plain
  yogurt, possibly a spoonful
  more, plus more for the tops

Heat the oven to 425°F. Measure the flour, baking powder, sugar and butter together into a bowl, and rub it all together with your fingertips so it turns cream-colored and slightly crumbly. The odd fleck of butter is no bad thing. Add the raisins. In a small pitcher, beat the egg with the buttermilk, then stir this into the flour. Combine to a firm ball of dough, adding a little more buttermilk if the dough seems dry, and knead lightly for 10 seconds, no more. Flour the work surface and the top of the dough and roll or press out until 1½ inches thick. Either cut with a knife into 4-inch squares, or use a round biscuit cutter the same diameter. Place on a baking sheet or deep pan lined with parchment paper, about 1¼ inches apart, brush the tops with extra buttermilk and dredge with extra sugar if you like.

Bake for 15 to 20 minutes until risen and lightly colored. Cool on a wire rack, covered with a tea towel to keep them moist.

Dalwhinnie fruit scones

As Scotch whiskies go, Dalwhinnie isn't cheap. But it has a sweet smoky honey flavor that works very well in baking.

4 ounces mixed dried fruit (raisins, currants and mixed citrus peel in equal measure are my preference)
boiling water
⅓ cup Dalwhinnie 15-year-old single malt Scotch whisky
⅓ cup dark brown sugar
⅔ cup whole-wheat or spelt flour

1¾ cups all-purpose flour, plus a little more for dusting
1 tablespoon baking powder
4 tablespoons unsalted butter, softened
1 egg
a little milk, if needed
1 beaten egg for the tops

At least a day before you want to bake, take the mixed dried fruit, place in a bowl and pour boiling water over them. Leave for 5 minutes then drain thoroughly before covering the fruit with the whisky and dark brown sugar. Stir, to mix evenly, then cover the bowl and leave overnight.

The next day, sift both flours and the baking powder into a bowl, then rub in the butter until it disappears. Beat the egg, and add with the fruit and its liquid, then work this through the dry ingredients to form a soft dough, adding a little milk if necessary. Roll on a well-floured surface until 1½ inches thick. Cut out rounds using a sharp biscuit cutter and place on a lightly floured baking sheet or deep pan lined with parchment paper, spaced no more than 1 inch apart so they stay moist.

Heat the oven to 425°F, brush the tops with beaten egg, and bake for 18 to 20 minutes until a rich golden brown. Leave to cool on a wire rack, covered with a tea towel.

Rocky road rock cakes

The bottom half is an easy chocolate cake, loaded with nuts and chocolate chunks, while the top half is all soft chocolate and marshmallows. Totally Willy Wonka insane.

FOR THE CAKES
1¾ cups all-purpose flour
1 teaspoon baking powder
1 teaspoon ground cinnamon
½ cup cocoa powder
5 tablespoons unsalted butter
1 cup salted peanuts, or
    walnut pieces
4 ounces dark chocolate, roughly
    chopped
1 cup condensed milk

FOR THE TOPPING
8 ounces dark chocolate
5 tablespoons butter
⅓ cup condensed milk
¼ cup boiling water
4 ounces mini or chopped
    marshmallows

To make the cakes, sift all the dry ingredients into a mixing bowl and rub in the butter. Add the nuts and the chocolate, then stir in the 1 cup of condensed milk to make a firm but sticky dough. Heat the oven to 400°F. Line a baking sheet with parchment paper, spoon on golf ball–sized dollops of the batter, then slightly flatten the top of each one with the back of the spoon. Bake for just 15 minutes until lightly colored then leave until cold.

To make the topping, melt the chocolate with the butter, add the ⅓ cup condensed milk with the boiling water and beat well until smooth and creamy. Leave until just warm, then stir in the marshmallows and spoon some topping over each of the cakes so they look like mini volcanoes. Chill to set the chocolate, then return to room temperature to serve.

If your chocolate-butter-condensed milk topping mixture curdles when you pour boiling water onto it, don't worry. Odd as it may sound, the solution is to beat it more and add more boiling water as you do so, a scant 1 tablespoon at a time. It curdles because the fat content is too high — chocolate and butter both vary in fat content, but there will be a point where cautiously adding more water brings it back together and you can continue with the recipe.

The instruction to "add a little more boiling water" will seem contrary to what you expect — you want it to emulsify. But by adding a tablespoon of boiling water, beating well, then checking it again, you'll see that you get to a point where it turns to a creamy chocolate mixture rather than a dark oily-looking one.

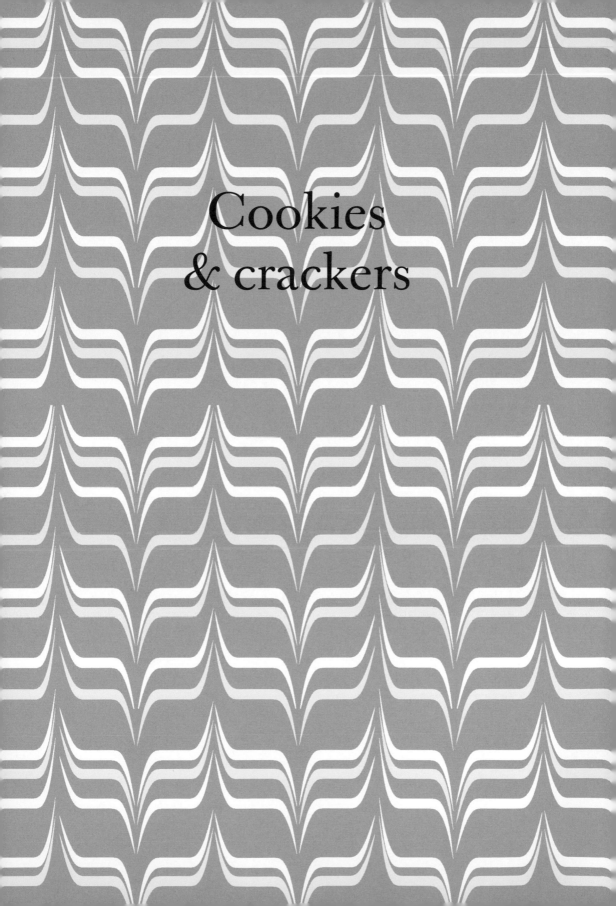

Cookies
& crackers

Cookies & crackers

A stack of homemade cookies just warm from the oven is something I find irresistible. I can't get past them without trying another. Where a slice of cake might seem like an indulgence, cookies almost count as diet food. One more cookie isn't going to break the fat bank. And as I've made them, I know exactly what's in them.

When I was just leaving childhood, about twelve and home alone after school, I learned to make a batch of oatmeal cookies quickly and eat all of them; committing the crime then eating the evidence. From my love of cookies grew a fascination with short and sweet baking, because the perfect cookie has a crispness at the edges when freshly baked, a moist and slightly chewy heart and, most important, a rich buttery flavor.

To make a cookie with vegetable shortening is a crime. A little lard or oil can add more crispness or chewiness, but at a cookie's heart there must be at least a little butter. If that makes it unhealthful, then I'm happy to alert every guest to the perilous danger that oatmeal cookies pose but meanwhile I'll devour my poison with hot coffee and a good book.

Cookies or crackers are the ultimate in foolproof baking. There's so little to go wrong. You can usually mix everything together at once or at least very quickly; they bake immediately and only for minutes, and the dough can even be stored in the fridge or freezer for raiding late at night for some nocturnal comfort baking.

If you have an allergy or dislike, then the recipe ingredients can usually be exchanged for something else, and that's a rare event with baking recipes. Making it gluten-free is simply a matter of swapping the wheat flour for a gluten-free flour mix, and you should still get a lovely result. Chunks of moist dried fruit can replace, or be replaced by, pieces of chopped nut. Replacing a spoonful of the flour with cocoa is a quick way to turn a plain cookie into a chocolate fix. There is a paradise of tweaks and simple changes that can be made to most recipes, enough to keep an inventive cook busy for a decade.

As gifts, wrapped in cellophane with a jaunty bow holding them tightly inside, cookies are without equal. Small enough to say thank-you without looking too grand, yet still containing enough effort and imagination to be a pleasure to receive. I look for handsome jars in the shops a few months before Christmas and keep them for later filling with sugary cookies as gifts. Or sometimes just for us to enjoy at home during the holidays.

Flour

For most cookies the sort of flour you use doesn't matter too much. I like using bread flour for chewy chocolate chip cookies, and all-purpose flour for shortbread, but these are preferences of mine rather than strict rules. Gluten-free flour works well in most cookie recipes in place of wheat flour. Semolina and finely ground rice add a gritty crunch to cookies and are particularly good in simple all-butter cookies as they help to soak up excess moisture from the butter, and produce an even crisper texture after baking. American chef Shirley O. Corriher told me that if you activate the gluten in white wheat flour by rubbing a few tablespoons of water through it first, then leave it for 10 minutes before beating it with the other ingredients, the resulting cookies are much chewier.

Sugar

Granulated sugar and super-fine sugar have different roles in cookie making. The coarser texture of granulated gives cookies more of a crunchy texture when first mixed and then quickly baked, compared to super-fine sugar. If the dough is left in the refrigerator overnight, this difference vanishes and they'll both produce a softer chewier texture in a lightly baked dough. Brown sugar can make cookies slightly softer but can be interchanged easily with white sugar. Syrups, like honey, corn syrup or molasses, can be added in place of some of the sugar. But these syrups make the texture much softer, so use them sparingly.

Butter

Most of the time I prefer all butter in cookies as it gently softens the flavors of other ingredients like dark brown sugar, chocolate and spices. The idea of pork lard in a cookie may even sound mildly alarming, no matter how fashionable it has become in many top restaurants for adding a particular crispness to cookies and pastries that can't be matched with butter alone. If the idea appeals to you, experiment with lard in place of no more than one quarter of the butter, in recipes where crispness rather than chewiness is the goal.

Eggs

You could halve the egg in most cookie recipes that include it and hardly notice, so if you have some beaten egg left over in the refrigerator from another recipe, use it in place of one whole egg when making cookies. The reason less egg still works is that most cookies rely on the trio of fat, sugar and flour for their luxurious texture and the egg only needs to hold the cookie crumb gently intact, not bind it into a rubbery disk. Your cookie will bake slightly crisper but that's no bad thing. If you want to leave the egg out entirely, you should be fine if you like your cookies very crumbly, but for more chewiness think about adding a tablespoon of puréed date or raisins to the dough instead.

Chocolate and vanilla

One simple rule: choose the chocolate you and your family like to eat, and use that. There's no point buying a dark single-estate Peruvian if you're happier with milk chocolate, though typically the more expensive varieties will give you a more intense chocolate "hit." However, once mixed with lots of other ingredients, the finer points are likely to be completely lost, so buy thoughtfully but don't go overboard. And you'll have a lot more choice if you buy it as a bar, rather than as chocolate chips.

When it comes to vanilla, buy extract not flavoring, and good plump vanilla bean pods are always welcome. Just like chocolate, the nuances of the finest vanilla types can disappear in a complex mixture, but cheap vanilla extract seems so heavily diluted nowadays that it isn't worth using.

Baking . . .

A good, solid flat metal baking sheet that fits in the oven, with enough space between the edges and the oven walls for hot air to circulate, is essential for baking cookies effortlessly. Cover the bottom of this tray with parchment paper, to make removing the baked cookies very simple. The paper can be reused four or five times so you'll get your pennies back.

Typically, cookies are baked at around 350°F for about 15 minutes for a chewy texture or much longer at a lower temperature for a very crisp crunch. For example, I bake ¾-inch-thick fingers of shortbread at 325°F for about 40 minutes to get them crisp. So play with raising or lowering the temperature to get the texture you prefer. Cookies baked at a low temperature for a long time have a much more dense snap to them.

After baking, carefully move the cookies onto a wire rack if you want them to cool quickly, or leave on the baking sheet if you're not in a hurry. Fragile soft chewy cookies are best left for at least 5 minutes on the baking sheet, to set.

. . . or not baking

Most cookie dough can be kept in a covered container for a week in the fridge, or be frozen for months, and still produce an excellent, smoother-textured cookie. The smoother texture occurs because the sugar dissolves slightly into the moisture in the dough when it's stored in the fridge or freezer. So soft-baked cookies become even chewier and more mellow if baked the following day or even later.

The easiest way to store the dough is one that relates to the size you want the cookie to be. I like to roll the dough into a log, the diameter of the piece I'll eventually want on the baking sheet, then I wrap this in plastic wrap or parchment paper with the ends twisted tightly like a candy, then it's stored in the fridge or freezer. To use, slice off disks of dough, space them out on the baking sheet and bake: either when slightly defrosted (if frozen) or straight from the fridge.

For more complicated shapes, or balls of dough, it's useful to freeze them. Make the shapes you want and sit them quite close together on a baking sheet, lined with parchment paper, that will fit inside your freezer. Place the shaped cookies in the freezer and when frozen move them into a container where they can be stored, with nonstick paper between each layer. To use, simply take out as many as you need, leave for 15 minutes to defrost, then bake as suggested in the recipe.

And will they keep?

I've always had a sixth sense regarding cookies that have been in the cupboard a bit too long, even in an airtight container. They just don't do it for me. Keeping the unbaked dough in the freezer is convenient and baking another baking sheet of cookies just takes minutes, so try not to bake more than you'll use in a week.

Cookie or biscuit?

To Americans, *cookie* refers to any number of hand-held, flour-based sweet cakes, while a *biscuit* is a small quick bread. Across the pond in Britain, the terms *cookie* and *biscuit* are practically interchangeable today. The *Oxford English Dictionary* has a reference from about 1730, but the British population appeared to stop using the word *cookie* in the early 1900s. It then reentered their vocabulary through American baking, attached to recipes with a previously unheard-of richness and delicacy. Dutch settlers took the word "koekje" across to America, but back it came redefined with a generous and indulgent meaning. I love what I call biscuits but, sometimes, I just hanker for the exuberance of a cookie.

Chestnut chocolate cream cookies

Rich double-decker cookies sandwiched with a dark chocolate cream. You really need to use a food processor for this recipe. Then you won't need to sieve the mixture to avoid any knobbly bits of chestnut left behind, turning curiously tough during baking.

5 ounces cooked peeled chestnuts
(I use the canned ones)
¾ cup dark brown sugar
1 cup (2 sticks) unsalted
butter, softened
1¾ cups all-purpose flour

¼ teaspoon baking powder
cocoa powder for dusting
4 ounces dark chocolate
2 tablespoons heavy cream
2 tablespoons brandy
1¼ cups confectioners' sugar

Whiz the chestnuts and brown sugar to a smooth paste in a food processor, then add ¾ cup of the butter and purée again. Spoon this into a bowl, work in the flour and baking powder evenly, then scrape onto a sheet of parchment paper on a baking sheet and chill for 30 minutes.

Heat the oven to 300°F and line a baking sheet with parchment paper. Roll the dough until about ¼ inch thick and cut out small round cookies about 2 inches across. Lay these on the baking sheet and dust with cocoa. Bake for 35 minutes, then leave to cool on a wire rack.

Melt the chocolate, then leave until barely warm but still soft. Beat the remaining 4 tablespoons butter, the cream and brandy with the chocolate until smooth, then add the confectioners' sugar and beat again. Spread a good dollop on half of the cookies, then sandwich another on top of each.

USING CHESTNUTS

Ideally, you want "dry" canned chestnuts for this recipe, moist but no more than that. If yours come in liquid, drain them and leave them overnight on a few layers of paper towel to dry out. If you want to cook fresh chestnuts, make sure to get them extra dry before using.

Dark chocolate chunk cookies

Cookies need bits in them: crystallized ginger, rolled oats or granola, dried fruit like raisins or apricots, seeds and nuts, or, in this case, a generous quantity of dark chocolate chips. You can make the mixture ahead and keep it in the freezer, in 2-inch-diameter logs rolled in parchment paper. Then just defrost it a little and slice off disks of dough as you need them.

MAKES LOADS

9 tablespoons unsalted butter, softened

¾ cup dark brown sugar

2 tablespoons super-fine sugar

2 teaspoons vanilla extract

1 egg

1⅓ cup all-purpose flour

¼ cup cocoa powder

1 teaspoon baking soda

11 ounces dark chocolate, chopped roughly into chips

Heat the oven to 350°F and line a baking sheet with parchment paper.

Beat the butter, both sugars and vanilla until light and fluffy. Beat in the egg, then sift the flour, cocoa and baking soda together and stir that through, then finally stir in the chocolate chips. Roll tablespoon-sized scoops into balls with your hands, place on the baking sheet spaced 1½ to 2 inches apart and bake for 12 to 14 minutes until barely puffed and just starting to color at the edges. Leave to cool on the baking sheet for a few moments to firm slightly, then move with a spatula to a wire rack to cool.

A COOL IDEA

I like to make my own ice-cream sandwiches with these, sticking a scoop of homemade chocolate or vanilla ice cream (see page 350) between two large cookies.

Mint cream chocolate cookies

In the 1880s, Mitcham, still then a village in Surrey, was renowned for the mint and lavender grown and distilled into oils by Joe Jakson & Co., prized around the world. One journal at the time described it as having the "purist [sic] white color, with a tremendous strength and delightful aroma." Now all that remains of Jakson's farm is a pub named after him. Summerdown, an herb farm in Hampshire, distills peppermint grown from the same variety, called Black Mitcham, into an oil that's perfect for these cookies. Sandwiched together with creamy peppermint icing, these bittersweet chocolate cookies make the most of this special oil.

MAKES 12

5 tablespoons unsalted butter, softened

⅓ cup super-fine sugar

3 ounces good dark chocolate

1 cup all-purpose flour

1 tablespoon cocoa powder

¼ teaspoon baking powder

2 cups confectioners' sugar

⅓ cup heavy cream

8 to 10 drops peppermint oil

Beat the butter and the super-fine sugar until fluffy, then melt the chocolate and beat this through. Sift the flour, cocoa and baking powder together and beat this in. While the mixture is still fresh and relatively soft, make 24 balls (about ½ ounce each) and carefully press them onto a baking sheet lined with parchment paper. They should sit about ¼ inch high, and though the dough will crack around the edges as you press, it bakes firmly.

Heat the oven to 350°F, bake for 25 minutes, then remove and leave to cool on the baking sheet. Beat the confectioners' sugar with the cream and peppermint oil until firm and sandwich the cookies together with the icing.

Toll House yo-yos

If ever you're stuck for a way to add fiber and increase the food value of a cake or cookie, look to the humble blender. Bran, as well as various cereals such as oats and millet — the rolled or flaked sort rather than whole grains — can be pulsed to a powder in seconds, and makes a healthful addition to many a baking mix. And the blender will do a far better job than the food processor.

MAKES ABOUT 14 to 16

FOR THE COOKIES
1 cup good quality rolled oats
10 tablespoons unsalted butter
1¾ cups confectioners' sugar
1⅓ cups all-purpose flour
½ cup cornstarch
2 teaspoons vanilla extract
2 tablespoons milk
5 ounces good dark chocolate,
    chopped into ¼-inch chips

FOR THE ICING
3 cups confectioners' sugar
1 tablespoon vanilla extract
a little cold milk

To make the cookies, grind the oats to a powder in the blender. In a mixing bowl, beat the butter and confectioners' sugar until light and creamy. Add the powdered oats, flour, cornstarch, vanilla, milk and chocolate and mix to a soft dough, then roll into a log about 16 inches long and 2 inches in diameter, wrap in parchment paper and chill for 30 minutes.

Heat the oven to 350°F. Line a baking sheet with parchment paper, unwrap the dough and slice into disks ½ to ¾ inch thick. If the dough crumbles a little just press it back into shape. Place the disks on the baking sheet spaced 1 inch apart and bake for 25 to 30 minutes until risen and golden but still a little soft. Remove and leave to cool.

To make the icing, beat the confectioners' sugar with the vanilla and just enough milk to give you a smooth consistency.

Sandwich the cookies together with the icing to serve.

Walnut chocolate cookies

An easy gluten-free cookie recipe that can be dolled up with chocolate chips, dried sour cherries, raisins or slivers of toasted almond.

⅔ cup finely chopped dates

¼ cup boiling water

½ cup (1 stick) unsalted
butter, softened

⅔ cup brown sugar

⅔ cup super-fine sugar

¼ cup cocoa powder

2 teaspoons vanilla extract

2 cups cornstarch

½ teaspoon baking powder

½ teaspoon baking soda

1 cup walnuts, roughly chopped

Place the dates in a mixing bowl, cover with the boiling water and leave for 5 to 10 minutes. Then add the butter and sugars and beat till smooth and light so the dates start to mash down into the mixture. Add the cocoa and vanilla and beat again till smooth. Add the cornstarch, baking powder and baking soda and beat well, then mix in the walnuts.

Heat the oven to 350°F. Line a baking sheet with parchment paper, roll walnut-sized nuggets of dough into balls with your hands, then press them lightly onto the baking sheet, spaced 2 inches apart, and bake for about 15 minutes. Leave to cool on the baking sheet for 5 minutes so that they firm, then carefully move onto a wire rack with a spatula, to cool. Then bake any remaining dough, or you can store it in a tub in the fridge for a few weeks, or roll it into a log, wrap in parchment paper and freeze.

Passion fruit melting moments

Think of these as custard creams from Down Under. This is one of my mum's recipes and, having eaten my way through a truckload as a child, it's still one of my favorite cookies. My mum's trick is to use custard powder in place of cornstarch if she runs out of vanilla extract.

2 large passion fruit
1 cup (2 sticks) unsalted butter, softened
1 cup confectioners' sugar
1 teaspoon vanilla extract
2 cups flour, plus extra for dusting
⅔ cup cornstarch

FOR THE ICING
1½ cups confectioners' sugar
¼ cup heavy cream
1 large passion fruit

Cut the passion fruit in half and scrape all the pulp out. You can either use the pulp, seeds and all, or press it through a sieve with the back of a spoon, extract the juice (about ¼ cup) and discard the seeds. They bake to a nice crunch but if you don't fancy it leave them out. Then beat the passion fruit pulp, butter, confectioners' sugar and vanilla until light and fluffy, add the flour and cornstarch and work everything to a soft smooth dough. Line a baking sheet with parchment paper, take spoonfuls of the dough rounded into balls the size of a quail's egg, place on the baking sheet spaced 1 inch apart and lightly flour the tops. Press the balls down gently with the back of a fork. Bake at a very low heat, 300°F, for 30 to 40 minutes until crisp and lightly colored.

To make the icing, beat the sugar with the cream and the pulp of the passion fruit.

Sandwich the cookies together with the icing when cold.

Peanut butter cookies

These are very good on their own, but they also make a great sundae broken into rough chunks and layered with vanilla ice cream and a drizzle of dulce de leche.

MAKES ABOUT 30

¾ cup crunchy peanut butter

9 tablespoons unsalted butter, softened

¾ cup super-fine sugar

¾ cup brown sugar

2 teaspoons vanilla extract

1 egg

¾ cup to 1 cup whole-wheat or spelt flour

1 teaspoon baking soda

1¼ to 1½ cups rolled oats

Line a baking sheet with parchment paper. Beat the peanut butter, butter, both sugars, vanilla and egg until creamy and evenly mixed. Beat in the flour and baking soda until smooth, then beat in the oats until evenly combined. Spoon pieces the size of an unshelled walnut (about 1 ounce each) onto the baking sheet, spaced about 1½ inches apart as they will spread in the oven. Heat the oven to 350°F and bake for about 20 minutes until lightly colored on the top but still moist underneath. Remove from the oven, then leave to cool on the baking sheet for 5 minutes before carefully transferring with a spatula to a wire rack to cool completely. Store in an airtight jar.

SMART COOKIES

If you keep the flour and oats down to ¾ cup and 1¼ cups, respectively, you'll end up with a thinner, chewier cookie, albeit one that will need more resting time after baking (about 10 minutes) and be more fragile. You could jazz up the cookies by adding ¾ cup chopped roasted peanuts (rinse most of the salt off first) to the batter or the same amount of dark or milk chocolate, cut into pea-sized chunks.

Orange almond butter cookies

These white sugar–coated cookies look smart stacked in a large canning jar in layers, and this way the jars make good gifts too. In Greece they have similar cookies known as kourambiedes, made without the orange. Other nuts, like pecans or hazelnuts, give a slightly different but equally good flavor.

MAKES ABOUT 40

1 cup (2 sticks) unsalted butter, softened

finely grated zest of 2 oranges

1 cup confectioners' sugar

1 egg yolk

1 tablespoon vanilla extract

2 tablespoons Cointreau or brandy

1¾ cups finely chopped blanched almonds

2¼ cups all-purpose flour

½ teaspoon baking powder

lots of extra confectioners' sugar to finish

Beat the butter, zest and confectioners' sugar until smooth and light, then beat in the egg yolk, vanilla and Cointreau. Stir in the almonds, then add the flour and baking powder and work to a smooth dough. Pinch nuggets of dough from the bowl, about the size of small unshelled walnut (¾ ounce if you want to do it the way I did), and roll these between your hands to make smooth balls. (They freeze well at this point.)

Line a couple of baking sheets with parchment paper or foil, then space the balls about 1 inch apart (and if baking from frozen leave 30 minutes to soften). Heat the oven to 325°F and bake for 30 minutes. Sift more confectioners' sugar into a bowl, toss in the hot cookies three or four at a time so they get thickly coated in sugar, then cool on a paper-lined baking sheet with a little more confectioners' sugar sieved over the top.

Butter shortbread

Really simple to make and bake, but it absolutely benefits from being left overnight in the refrigerator before baking. While it sits, the semolina will absorb some of the liquid from the butter, resulting in a slightly crisper shortbread. The luxurious amount of butter in the recipe means that it does spread slightly during baking, so I find it's best suited to thick chunky fingers rather than rolled into delicate shapes.

2½ cups all-purpose flour, plus extra for rolling	¾ cup super-fine sugar
1 tablespoon semolina or rice ground in a spice grinder	½ teaspoon fine salt
	1 cup (2 sticks) unsalted butter

Spoon the flour, semolina, sugar and salt into a mixing bowl. Cut the butter into pieces and rub this through the flour until it starts to look crumbly, then continue to work it quickly with your hands until it becomes a smooth dough. If the mixture starts to soften too much and feel oily before it's evenly combined, just chill it in the fridge for 15 minutes before continuing. Once the mixture is evenly mixed, wrap it well and chill overnight.

Line a baking sheet with parchment paper and heat the oven to 325°F. Remove the dough from the fridge and let it soften until workable first, then roll it till about ¾ inch thick using extra flour to stop it from sticking. Cut the dough into thick fingers, then sit them almost touching on the tray. Bake for about 40 minutes until golden, or less if the dough is rolled thinner. Large pieces of shortbread can be scored again with a knife the moment they come out of the oven to make them easier to break into pieces when cold.

Gingerbread cookies

Intensely spiced ginger cookies like these can be baked, then decorated with a simple lemon water icing (see page 335) and used as Christmas tree decorations, or cut out into gingerbread pigs for bonfire night as they used to do in Yorkshire.

2 cups all-purpose flour,
  plus extra for rolling
2 tablespoons cocoa powder
¾ teaspoon baking powder
a pinch of salt
10 tablespoons unsalted butter
1 tablespoon each ground ginger
  and cinnamon

½ teaspoon each ground cloves
  and nutmeg
½ cup muscovado sugar
1 tablespoon runny honey
1 egg
small candies or the sugar
  decorations of your choice

Sift the flour, cocoa, baking powder and salt into a bowl. In a saucepan melt the butter with the spices, then add the sugar and honey. Any lumps of sugar should break up in the warmth when squashed with a spoon. Remove from the heat, leave to cool for 2 to 3 minutes, then beat in the egg. Stir this in with the flour and mix everything to a soft smooth dough. Wrap the dough in wax paper or plastic wrap and chill or freeze until required.

To bake, let the dough soften at room temperature, then roll on a floured surface and cut into shapes, with a hole for a ribbon if you need one. Heat the oven to 350°F and line a baking sheet with parchment paper. Lift the shapes carefully with a spatula, place on the baking sheet and bake for 15 minutes. Leave to cool on the baking sheet, then decorate as desired.

Short and spicy

Vary this recipe according to your taste; add cardamom, black pepper, anise or slivers of crystallized ginger. The dough is a bit delicate because

of all the butter, so go for simple shapes and lots of care when you move them to the baking sheet. They bake rather crisp and short so they should survive a week or so in a cookie tin or dangling on the tree.

Spelt and ginger cookies

While spelt flour can be awkward to work into a light aerated loaf of bread, in this cookie dough the heaviness is rather good, as it adds to the chewiness of the texture, and it also adds a nutty complexity to the flavor.

MAKES ABOUT 35

4 tablespoons unsalted butter

2½ tablespoons corn syrup

2 ounces crystallized ginger, chopped into pea-sized chunks

¼ cup super-fine sugar

¼ cup light brown sugar

1 egg yolk

1½ cups spelt flour

1 teaspoon ground ginger

½ teaspoon baking soda

Warm the butter, corn syrup and crystallized ginger in a saucepan until the butter has melted. Then remove the saucepan from the heat, beat in the two sugars and the egg yolk, followed by the flour, ground ginger and baking soda. Stir to a smooth soft dough.

Heat the oven to 400°F. Line a baking sheet with parchment paper, then place teaspoon-sized balls (½ ounce or so) on it, spaced 2½ to 3 inches apart, as they spread as they bake. Bake in batches in the oven for 7 to 8 minutes until they puff up like macaroons with a golden tinge at the edges. Remove from the oven and let them sink back down, and cool off enough to lift off the baking sheet with a spatula without breaking. Leave to cool on a rack while you bake the remaining dough.

Macarons

These are so easy to make. The pasteurized egg white powder isn't strictly necessary, but it will give your macarons an extra "lift" when you bake them. Make sure that your fresh egg white has not so much as a speck of yolk in it.

MAKES ABOUT 10 to 12

½ cup ground almonds
½ cup confectioners' sugar
1 egg white
½ teaspoon egg white powder
¼ cup super-fine sugar

Easy Lemon Curd (page 342) or Meringue Butter-Cream Icing (page 327)

Take a sheet of parchment paper and, using a soft pencil, heavily mark it with 20 to 24 circles, 1¼ inches in diameter, spaced 1 inch apart.

Mix the almonds with the confectioners' sugar in a bowl. Separately, and using an electric whisk, beat the fresh and powdered egg white until stiff, then gradually add the super-fine sugar, beating for 1 to 2 minutes after each spoonful, until thick and glossy. Use a little of this meringue mix to fix the parchment paper drawn-side down on a baking sheet.

Fold the almond mixture into the meringue, and spoon or pipe onto the baking sheet, to evenly cover the circles. Tap the baking sheet on the work surface to pop any air bubbles, and leave uncovered for 30 to 60 minutes, so they dry out slightly. Bake at 325°F for 10 to 12 minutes, until puffed at the base and crisp on top. Leave to cool, then gently indent the bottom of each disk with a knife, and sandwich them together with a little lemon curd or icing.

If you want vividly colored macarons, use the more intense "paste" coloring available from cake decorating shops. For a more pastel shade, a few drops of liquid food coloring will be fine. I like to give my macarons a Scottish twist by sandwiching them together with a little thickly whipped heavy cream and some good Dundee marmalade. Best to avoid too many chunky bits of peel though.

Rye and raisin cookies

As the steel-gray color of the flour can be a little off-putting to a rye novice, the dark cocoa makes it a compelling cookie. If you really don't have a sweet tooth, reduce the sugar by ¼ cup.

MAKES 15 to 18

9 tablespoons unsalted butter, softened, plus extra for the baking sheet
⅔ cup brown sugar
⅔ cup super-fine sugar
2 tablespoons cocoa powder

1 egg white
1 teaspoon vanilla extract
1½ cups rye flour
½ teaspoon baking soda
1½ cups raisins

Heat the oven to 350°F and lightly butter a rimmed baking sheet (or line it with parchment paper). Using an electric mixer, whisk the butter, sugars and cocoa until smooth and light, then beat in the egg white, followed by the vanilla. Add the flour and baking soda and, with a wooden spoon, beat everything together until smooth. Stir in the raisins, then roll the mixture into lumps slightly smaller than a golf ball — about 2 ounces each. Sit these 3 to 4 inches apart on the baking sheet, and bake for 12 to 15 minutes until the raisins puff and pop through the sugary crust of each cookie. Leave to cool on the baking sheet for 5 minutes, then gently twist each off and place on a cooling rack while you roll and bake any remaining dough.

Oat and sour cherry cookies

So many new things have appeared in our supermarkets over the last decade that sometimes I'm torn between the joy of the new and encouraging you to bake with a more traditional ingredient. So this recipe manages to face both ways, combining the chewiness of oats with the slight sourness of dried cherries.

MAKES ABOUT 50 COOKIES

1 cup (2 sticks) unsalted butter, softened
1¾ cups light brown sugar
¼ cup super-fine sugar
1 tablespoon vanilla extract
2 eggs

2¼ cups all-purpose flour
1 teaspoon ground cinnamon
2 teaspoons baking soda
2⅓ cups rolled oats
8 ounces dried sour cherries

Beat the butter, sugars and vanilla until light and fluffy. Beat in the eggs, one at a time, then sift the flour, cinnamon and baking soda together and stir that through, followed by the rolled oats and dried cherries, until you have a consistent mixture.

Heat the oven to 350°F and line a baking sheet with parchment paper. Spoon tablespoon-sized dollops of the dough onto the baking sheet spaced 1½ to 2 inches apart, and bake for 12 to 14 minutes until barely puffed and just starting to color at the edges. Leave to cool for a few minutes, then transfer to a wire rack to finish cooling, while you continue to bake or freeze half to use later.

Coffee cardamom cookies

My friend Martin Prior, who ran a bakery in Malaysia for many years, achieved an amazing flavor by omitting the cinnamon, and using the seeds of four green cardamom pods, ground with 1 tablespoon roasted coffee beans instead.

Banana fudge cookies

A heavy dusting with confectioners' sugar before baking, so thick that you can't see the dough, gives these soft cookies a sugary crisp and cracked crust. If you only like crunchy cookies, then these aren't for you, but if you like a tender cookie and spy a couple of mushy soft bananas in the fruit bowl, they'll do nicely.

MAKES ABOUT 25

⅔ cup super-fine sugar

⅔ cup light brown sugar

2 very ripe bananas, peeled and mashed

1 cup (2 sticks) unsalted butter, softened

2 teaspoons vanilla extract

1½ cups all-purpose flour

½ cup cocoa powder

2 teaspoons baking soda

2¼ cups rolled oats

lots of confectioners' sugar

Beat the sugars, bananas, butter and vanilla until fluffy. Sift the flour, cocoa and baking soda together, and beat this in followed by the oats. Cover and chill the mixture for 30 minutes.

Line a baking sheet with parchment paper, and heat the oven to 350°F. Spoon nuggets of dough the size of unshelled walnuts out of the bowl, roughly shape into balls then press these onto the baking sheet spaced 1½ inches apart. When the baking sheet is full, return the bowl to the fridge, then get cracking with the dusting. Using a tea-strainer, heavily sift a load of confectioners' sugar over each unbaked blob so it disappears under the whiteness.

Bake for 15 to 20 minutes until the cookies are richly colored and beginning to firm, then remove from the oven and leave for a moment before easing them off the baking sheet with a spatula, onto a wire rack. Repeat with the remaining dough.

Lemon curd cookies

These lemon shortbread rounds are spread with a mixture of cream, oats and lemon curd that bakes to a bumpy chewy topping.

MAKES ABOUT 10

⅔ cup rolled oats
¼ cup heavy cream
½ cup Easy Lemon Curd
   (page 342)
½ cup (1 stick) unsalted
   butter, softened

½ cup super-fine sugar
finely grated zest of 1 lemon
1¼ cups all-purpose flour
2 tablespoons rice ground
   in a spice grinder

In a small bowl combine the oats, cream and lemon curd and stir until evenly combined. Cover and leave while you prepare the other ingredients. Cream the butter and sugar with the zest until fluffy, then add the flour and ground rice and work into a soft dough. Roll the dough into a cylinder about 2 inches in diameter and 10 inches long, wrap in parchment paper and chill for an hour until firm.

Heat the oven to 350°F. Line a large baking sheet with parchment paper, then unwrap the dough and slice into ¾-inch disks. They'll crumble as you cut them but just press the dough back together. Space them 1½ to 2 inches apart on the baking sheet. Spoon a teaspoon of the oat-curd topping onto each disk of dough and spread it to cover. Bake for 25 to 30 minutes until the cookies have risen and the tops have gently browned. Cool for a few moments before removing from the baking sheet and placing on a wire rack to get cold.

SHORT & SWEET

Ginger macadamia cookies

You can use unsalted macadamia nuts but I like a slight salty tang set against the buttery sweetness of the cookie.

MAKES ABOUT 35

9 tablespoons unsalted butter, softened	1½ cups all-purpose flour
1 cup light brown sugar	2 teaspoons ground ginger
1 egg	½ teaspoon ground allspice
3 nuggets of crystallized ginger	1 teaspoon baking soda
⅔ cup shredded coconut	1 cup salted macadamia nuts, chopped into flakes

Line two baking sheets with parchment paper and heat the oven to 350°F. Beat the butter and brown sugar until smooth and light, then beat in the egg until evenly mixed through. Chop the crystallized ginger into slivers and stir this in to the butter mixture along with the coconut. Sift the flour, ground ginger, allspice and baking soda together and stir this through, then mix in the chopped macadamia nuts. Divide the dough into balls about the size of a walnut, press onto the baking sheets 2 inches apart and bake for about 15 minutes. Leave on the baking sheets for a few minutes, then lift off with a spatula onto a wire rack to cool. Repeat with the remaining dough.

One-a-day cookies

An all-time favorite in our house. When you bake sweet things, if you can mix a little whole-wheat flour into the recipe, or tender grains or toasted seeds, you bring mineral and fiber goodness to offset the sugar negative. One of these cookies a day is a healthful start. You could replace the super-fine sugar with grated apple, but the finish will be less crisp. The thinner the baking sheets, the more the cookies will spread in the oven.

MAKES 12 to 14

9 tablespoons unsalted butter, softened
½ cup super-fine sugar
½ cup muscovado sugar
1 egg
1 teaspoon vanilla extract

¾ cup whole-wheat flour
1 cup lightly toasted seeds
   (try a mixture of pumpkin
   and sunflower)
1¼ cups good quality rolled oats

Heat the oven to 350°F and line two baking sheets with parchment paper (or bake in two batches). Beat the butter and both sugars until smooth, then add the egg and beat again until thoroughly combined. Stir in the vanilla, then lightly beat in the remaining ingredients. Divide the mixture into 12 to 14 spoonfuls (each about the size of an overly large unshelled walnut) on the baking sheets and flatten them gently. (I find I can only get about six on each baking sheet as they spread to twice the diameter as they bake.)

Bake for 10 to 12 minutes, or until the cookies are lightly brown on the edges. Remove from the oven, leave to cool for a minute, then with a spatula transfer to a wire cooling rack. When cold, store in a paper bag or an airtight container.

Sesame, date and ginger cookies

These are great little cookies to serve with an espresso midmorning, or post-dinner with a shot of grappa or arak. The unbaked dough keeps well for a week or so covered in the fridge, ready to be baked when it suits.

MAKES 15 to 18

¼ cup dark brown sugar

2½ cups blackstrap molasses

9 tablespoons unsalted butter, softened

1 egg yolk

1⅓ cups all-purpose flour

½ teaspoon baking soda

¾ teaspoon baking powder

2 teaspoons ground ginger

2 teaspoons mixed spice

1¼ cups chopped dates

about ⅔ cup sesame seeds

Place the brown sugar, molasses and butter in a bowl and beat until creamy. Add the egg yolk and beat until fluffy, then spoon in the flour, baking soda, baking powder and spices and stir everything until smooth. Add the dates, beat the mixture until combined, then cover the bowl and stick in the fridge for 30 minutes to firm.

Heat the oven to 350°F and line a baking sheet with parchment paper. Divide the dough into walnut-sized balls, sprinkle the sesame seeds onto a dinner plate, then flatten the dough balls into them. They should end up less than ½ inch thick, about 1½ to 2 inches wide, and coated evenly in seeds. Lay them on the baking sheet and bake for 15 to 20 minutes until a rich even golden brown and firm at the edges. Remove from the oven, leave to cool on the baking sheet and store in an airtight container when cold.

FAVORITE FLAVORS

You can exchange most of the ingredients for ones you love more, figs or cranberries for the dates, poppy seeds or oats for the sesame seeds, or cinnamon with a hint of cardamom for the ginger.

Blue cheese and oatmeal crackers

Store-bought cheesy crackers often taste nasty because, at some point, the good cheese and decent butter get ditched for cheap or artificial substitutes to bring the cost down. Make them at home and you can be as lavish as you want. Substitute another cheese for the blue if it's not your thing. They're good served with cold dry sherry. This dough is best prepared and either chilled for 4 hours, left overnight in the fridge or stored frozen before baking.

MAKES ABOUT 60

1 cup rolled oats

7 ounces blue cheese, like Shropshire Blue or Stilton

½ cup (1 stick) unsalted butter, softened

2 teaspoons powdered mustard

2 egg yolks

1 tablespoon cold water

¾ cup all-purpose flour

½ cup spelt, whole-wheat or rye flour

½ teaspoon fine salt

Toast the oats on a baking sheet in a 350°F oven for about 10 minutes until just golden brown, then leave until cold. Mash the cheese, butter, powdered mustard, yolks and water together until smooth, using a food processor, mixer or wooden spoon. Add the toasted oats, both flours and salt and work to a smooth dough. Line a loaf pan, 7½ inches long or similar, with plastic wrap or parchment paper, press the dough down flat into it with another sheet of plastic or paper, and chill or freeze.

Heat the oven to 350°F and line two baking sheets with parchment paper. Use the dough straight from the fridge, or leave to soften out of the freezer. Trim the block and cut into wafers about ⅛ inch thick then, if you like, cut these in half again to make fingers. These crackers don't spread while baking, so make sure the shape is what you'll finally want it to be! Bake for about 15 minutes until crisp and golden.

Cheese and black pepper buttons

Odd bits of cheese, even the ones that have gone a bit dry and crusty at the end, can be used to make these. Look on the Parmesan and other cheeses given below as mere suggestions, and check the deli counter at the supermarket for those odd leftover pieces they sell cheaply.

MAKES 25 to 30

5 tablespoons unsalted butter, softened

½ teaspoon coarsely ground black pepper

1 small garlic clove, grated to a paste

¼ teaspoon fine salt

⅓ cup finely grated Parmesan

⅓ cup grated hard cheese, like Cheddar or Double Gloucester

¾ cup all-purpose flour

Beat the butter, pepper, garlic and salt till smooth. Stir in the cheeses and the flour, and work into a soft evenly mixed dough, adding a scant 1 teaspoon or so of water if it seems dry. Chill the mixture for about 30 minutes in the bowl, covered if you need to leave it longer.

Heat the oven to 325°F. Line a baking sheet with parchment paper, take teaspoonfuls (about ⅓ ounce) of the mixture between your hands, shape them into very smooth balls and press them onto the tray so they flatten slightly. Or press them with the end of a spatula if you want them extra smooth on top. With the end of a toothpick, poke four evenly spaced holes in the middle of each one, just like a button. Bake for 25 to 30 minutes until crisp and golden.

Buttermilk oatcakes

These delicate rounds taste a little like oatmeal crackers, but have a much wilder and more ragged look compared to what you buy in the stores. I've used rolled oats pulverized in the blender, but if you can get fine oatmeal use that.

2⅓ cups rolled oats, ground
  to a powder in a blender,
  plus extra to finish
½ teaspoon baking soda

2 to 3 tablespoons sugar
½ teaspoon fine salt
4 tablespoons unsalted butter
¾ cup buttermilk or
  low-fat natural yogurt

Place the ground oats, baking soda, sugar and salt in a mixing bowl. Chop the butter into small pieces, then rub this through the oats until the lumps vanish and the mixture looks like a fine oatmeal crumble. Stir in the buttermilk to form a soft paste.

Line a baking sheet with parchment paper and heat the oven to 350°F. Place heaped teaspoonfuls of the dough on the baking sheet, sprinkle them thickly with ground oats to finish, then press them out thinly with your fingers into rounds about ¼ inch thick. You don't need to leave a space between the oatcakes as they hold their shape and won't spread. Bake for 25 to 30 minutes until firm in the middle and just beginning to color at the edges. Leave to cool on a wire rack while you bake the remainder of the dough.

Chili almond rounds

Make the dough in advance and keep a batch in the freezer. That way, you've got something you can serve at 30 minutes' notice with a drink before dinner, or you can doll them up in cellophane and ribbon for a last-minute gift. They're only mildly hot, and a pleasure to nibble.

MAKES ABOUT 40 to 50

¾ (1½ sticks) unsalted butter, softened

1½ cups grated strong Cheddar

1 teaspoon red chili flakes

¾ teaspoon fine salt

2 teaspoons paprika, sweet smoked is perfect

1 small garlic clove, crushed to a paste

1⅓ cups all-purpose flour

2 tablespoons ice-cold water or milk

1 cup whole blanched almonds, Spanish Marconas are good

Chop the butter roughly and beat it with the Cheddar, chili flakes, salt, paprika and garlic until smooth. If you're mixing by hand it's easiest to beat the ingredients in one by one, or if you're using a food processor, just let it whiz away for a minute. Add the flour and water, work everything together to a smooth soft dough, then stir in the almonds — by hand, so the food processor doesn't shred them!

Spoon half the mixture onto a sheet of parchment paper and roll it up into a cylinder about 1½ inches in diameter and 8 to 10 inches long; repeat with the remaining dough on a second sheet. Chill or freeze until firm. To bake, cut 1-inch-thick slices and place them about 1 inch apart on a parchment paper–lined baking sheet. Heat the oven to 350°F and bake for 20 to 25 minutes until golden.

Extra thin rye crispbreads

There's something reassuring about the ease with which simple crackers like this can be made. If I get a move on, I can have the first batch out of the oven within 20 minutes of taking the bag of flour out of the cupboard. I sometimes flavor these by brushing the tops with water, and either sprinkling with sesame or anise seeds or giving a dusting of coarsely ground black pepper just before baking. Serve them with herring stirred with a little sour cream and fresh dill, or slices of beet and spoonfuls of thick strained yogurt, given some bite with a dusting of chili powder and a few flakes of coarse sea salt.

MAKES 16 to 18

2½ cups rye flour, plus extra
   for flouring and rolling
1 teaspoon sugar
½ teaspoon baking powder

1 teaspoon fine salt
2 tablespoons unsalted butter,
   cut into small cubes
⅔ cup cold milk

Spoon the rye flour into a large mixing bowl with the sugar, baking powder and salt. Rub in the butter until it vanishes, then stir in the milk and mix to a soft sticky dough. At first the dough will seem impossibly sticky but that's one of the odd characteristics of rye flour. Don't be tempted to add more flour, as it will firm up over the next few minutes and become easier to work with.

Heat the oven to 400°F and flour a baking sheet. You next need to roll the dough incredibly thinly, about the thickness of a thin sheet of cardboard if that makes sense. The way I do it is by pinching off pieces of dough about 1 ounce each, flouring both them and a patch of countertop, then, with a rolling pin, working the dough as thin as I can while checking every so often that it's not sticking. It's easier than it sounds, as dough made with rye flour doesn't spring back annoyingly like dough made with wheat flour does. Place about three pieces on the floured baking sheet, leaving the edges ragged, though you could trim them neatly if you like. Bake for 8 to 10 minutes until they just begin to color. Remove to a cooling rack, then bake the rest.

Doughnuts, batters
& babas

Doughnuts, batters
& babas

This chapter is all about those simple flour mixtures that get eaten the moment they're golden and set after cooking, even while they're still sizzling and steaming from the pan. Cakes and bread have that annoying waiting time, until you can cut a slice and judge whether the effort was worth it. Whereas these gems are best enjoyed in the kitchen and close to the action.

Cooking on a hot, flat surface or in a pot of boiling fat are both very old methods that turn simple raw grains and flour into good food, and arguably in their simplicity they predate the use of an oven. If you build a fire, it's possible to cook raw dough on the hot stones tucked in close to the heat, and a dish collecting fat, as it drips from a beast roasted whole on a spit, might be hot enough to cook dough in and give it a crispness and darker color as the flames lick around it. A pan of oil or a heavy frying pan, or a griddle or metal bakestone are simply the convenient domestic successors to these methods.

Sometimes when I'm standing by the stove, lowering doughnuts into oil or ladling pancake batter into the frying pan, I think about the history of it all. And for a moment, when I'm not cursing the pan for being too hot or too cold, or unevenly heated, what I'm doing feels more like an ancient craft than a repetitive bore. Halfway through, I may think, "How much mixture is left?" and wonder when it will end. But then I feel upbeat again as I cook the last few, and glowing with pride by the final one.

With softer batter mixtures, there is the possibility of tweaking or getting creative after the first spoonful is cooked. I usually taste the first one, to check that it's sweet or salty enough, and to see if the flavor is bold or delicate in a way that suits how I'm serving it or what's going with it. It's also the time to check that the pan is the right temperature. If I burn the first one, or flip it when it's flabby rather than golden, then so be it. No regret or guilt for the first few; they're testers and absolutely expected.

As you're so exposed to the heat of the pan, even more so when it's filled with hot fat, I do see it as something to do when you're sober, calm and well organized, and of an age where you can take responsibility in the kitchen. A chef somewhere talked about how he loved to fry doughnuts with his children; he may also have taken them for a jog along the highway, or left them to polish his gun collection. Deep-fat frying and children aren't a good mix, even if doughnuts and little ones seem perfectly suited. Understand the difference between frying and consumption, and all will be happy and safe.

Take your time and be prepared

Being prepared takes all of the stress away from pancake or doughnut making. Before starting the mixing, I make sure that my heavy-bottomed frying pan is ready to go, or if I'm frying, I make sure I have enough fresh clean oil in the cupboard. A metal pan lined with absorbent paper towel is useful to spoon the cooked pancakes or doughnuts onto, and clear the space around the stove and have some light on the area where you're working.

Nearly all flour-based mixtures (except cakes) turn out better if left for some time before cooking or baking; as little as 30 minutes but much longer if possible, as tenderness is usually the goal. This applies equally to yeasted doughs and pancake batters. With yeasted dough, this rest is usually explained by the need to "let the dough aerate," but the complete reason is more complex. Flour mixtures will produce a more tender crumb the longer they are left, and some ingredients help this to happen. Naturally occurring enzymes in the flour, activated when water is added, start the process but other ingredients like milk, yogurt and butter have their own natural chemistry that helps this change. So when old cookbooks insisted that pancake mixtures or Yorkshire pudding batter should be made hours before they were required, they were right and not simply wasting your time.

This rule applies much less to gluten-free flours and to batters expected to stay ultracrisp. In something like a tempura batter, usually made by mixing wheat flour with potato or rice starch, the minimal mixing, cold ingredients and speed of use all act to prevent a chewy character forming before it is fried. If you want an extra crisp yeasted beer batter, it's best to mix in a little cornstarch or potato flour with the all-purpose flour, because this lowers the proportion of potentially "chewy" gluten in your dry ingredients.

Frying in oil

I need to tell you a depressing truth: frying in hard fats, the fats that are the worst for your arteries and general health, produces the best-textured, crispest, lightest doughnuts and fritters. Even pancakes are better when fried in butter or hard fat. And frying in beef fat — known as dripping, suet or tallow — produces the crispest texture and richest flavor of all. Though dripping is often described as the least healthful of fats, the truth is much more complex. Beef dripping is high in saturated fats, but a small amount might in fact be beneficial. And though it's sometimes implied that vegetable oils, by contrast, are a healthful alternative, it appears that they have far more impact on the liver.

So the best advice I can give you is to keep fried food as an occasional, rather than an everyday, part of the diet. If you like food fried in beef fat then don't get piggy about it. The classic advice: eat in moderation, and have a widely varied diet, still seems to me to be the best.

Grapeseed and canola oils are best suited to very high-temperature frying but can be a little characterless. They can be reused a few times, if filtered to remove fine particles of batter when cooled. But if you've fried fish in your oil, that's it; from that point on it can only be used for fish and even then just a few times before it should be discarded. It's a myth that frying in olive oil is bad for you or the oil. Though it does have a low smoking point (the temperature the oil breaks down at) of around 410°F, that's well above the optimum temperature you should be frying at. It does have a pronounced flavor, and that may put you off, but sometimes I like the rich peppery-fruit flavor it gives the batter. For me, eating sliced apples dipped in batter, fried in olive oil and dusted with coarse sugar is one of the greatest, simplest desserts I know of.

Getting the perfect color

Having a deep-fry thermometer that clips on to the side of the pan has meant that, for me, burnt or soggy fried mixtures are a thing of the past. They cost relatively little and mean that you always know the exact temperature of the oil. Aim for a temperature of around 375°F, though if it moves slightly above or below it will be OK. The moment you put the mixture into the oil, the heat will drop slightly and will take a minute to get back to temperature. Don't overload the pan as this will cause the heat to drop too much; things will stick to each other and be difficult to flip easily.

If you want to avoid the dough absorbing too much oil, you can lift things out when moderately colored, drain them and finish cooking them in the oven on a baking sheet lined with absorbent paper towels at about 350°F for 10 to 15 minutes. This will enable the dough to cook through properly.

With members of the pancake family, get the pan evenly hot, add a little butter or oil, then, as it melts, rub it over the surface of the pan with a crumpled-up clump of paper towels before spooning the mixture in. The first one sometimes sticks, so if this happens, console yourself with the knowledge that it's doing the same for most cooks around the world. Before flipping the pancake over, you want to see bubbles forming in the surface, which should still be moist in the center, with just the outer fifth around the edge of the mixture almost set. On the first one, check the color when you flip it over, and if it's too dark or light adjust the heat underneath.

Adding extra sweetness and flavors

When a mixture is cooked directly touching the heat source, or in hot fat, it colors very quickly. So avoid adding too much sugar or fat to the mixture if it needs a longer cooking time for the heat to get right through to the center, as with a doughnut for example. It's often better to use flavorings, like vanilla or lemon, that have a sweet association and then serve them with something sweet like an icing, preserve, sauce or compote.

Pieces of fruit, like chopped apple or tiny cubes of dried apricot, can be stirred into the batter at the last minute to add sweetness before frying. If the dough is firm, like some doughnut batters, it's sometimes easier to pat it out on a floured countertop, sprinkle the apple or whatever over it, then roll the dough up tightly to capture the ingredient inside. Leave the dough to rest for 5 minutes, then it can be divided and reshaped more easily.

Batters are usually fairly robust. You can stir in a handful of herbs, spices or pepper without worrying too much. Be careful about overly wet, dry, sweet or oily ingredients as these can affect the way the mixture cooks. Small amounts of big flavor ingredients are the best way to go.

The right tools

A deep-fry or candy thermometer that clips on to the inside of the saucepan makes judging the temperature much easier. But do make sure you use a candy thermometer, which can read temperatures up to at least 390°F – don't go putting the one out of your medicine cabinet into hot oil as it'll go bang.

Raised Doughnuts

Homemade jam and hot sugared doughnuts are an outstanding pairing, the bright acidity of the newly made jam tempering the rich oily crust.

MAKES 6

½ cup warm milk

1 teaspoon instant yeast

2 cups bread flour

1 egg

2 tablepoons super-fine sugar

2 tablespoons unsalted butter, melted

1 tablespoon vanilla extract

2 teaspoons vegetable glycerin, (optional but helps to keep them soft)

½ teaspoon fine salt

sunflower oil for kneading and frying

warm jam for filling

confectioners' sugar and ground cinnamon for dusting

Mix the milk, yeast and ¾ cup of the flour and leave, covered, for 2 hours. Whisk the egg and sugar until thick and pale with an electric mixer then beat with the yeast mixture, melted butter, vanilla and glycerin until smooth. Add the remaining flour and the salt and squish it into a sticky dough. Give the dough a short knead (see pages 13 to 14) on a lightly oiled work surface, then return it to the bowl and leave for 1½ hours, briefly kneading the dough two or three times more during that time.

Divide the dough into six pieces, shape into balls, place on an oiled plate and cover with a tea towel for 1 hour. Quarter-fill a deep-sided saucepan, 7 inches in diameter (or similar) with sunflower oil, and heat until a cube of bread dropped into the oil turns golden brown in about a minute, 350 to 375°F. Fry two or three doughnuts at a time, for 1 to 1½ minutes on each side. Drain on paper towels. Spoon the warm jam into a small pastry bag fitted with a long nozzle, poke a hole into each doughnut and squeeze in the filling. Dust the doughnuts with confectioners' sugar, maybe sifted with a little cinnamon. If you leave them unsugared, they can be reheated later in a hot oven and will taste as if they're fresh from the oil.

Oliebollen

A traditional New Year's Eve fruity doughnut from Amsterdam.

MAKES ENOUGH FOR 3 to 4 BRITS
   OR 1 NETHERLANDER

½ cup warm water

½ cup dark ale, at room
   temperature

2 teaspoons instant yeast

1 egg

zest and juice of ½ lemon

1 small apple, peeled and finely
   diced

⅓ cup raisins

⅓ cup currants

⅓ cup candied citrus peel

2 cups bread flour

½ teaspoon fine salt

1 tablespoon super-fine sugar

1 teaspoon ground cinnamon

lard or oil for deep frying

confectioners' sugar for dusting

Scald a mixing bowl with boiling water, tip this out, then add the warm water, ale and yeast. Stir well then beat in the egg, lemon juice and zest. Tip the apple, dried fruit and candied peel into the bowl, add the flour, salt, sugar and cinnamon and beat well with a wooden spoon to a smooth batter. Leave in a warm part of the kitchen for 1 hour, beat again to knock the gas out of it, then leave for another hour.

   In a deep-sided saucepan, 7 inches in diameter (or similar), heat 2 to 3 inches of lard or oil to 350°F. Drop a small spoonful of the batter into the fat: it should puff and turn golden brown after about a minute, not much sooner. Dip two spoons into the hot oil then scoop up a tablespoon of the batter without knocking the gas out of it and slide it from the oily spoons into the oil. Fry three or four at a time, turning them in the fat so they cook evenly. Drain on paper towels, fry the rest of the batter and serve with a hefty dredge of confectioners' sugar.

Chestnut blinis

This make-and-chill batter can sit on standby in the fridge all day, or even overnight, ready for guests as and when they call. Serve a trio of these as a snack with mulled wine or champagne or as a starter, topped with smoked eel, mackerel or salmon with sprigs of fresh dill or chive, and a dollop of sour cream mixed with horseradish or mustard.

2 eggs, separated
8 ounces whole cooked
   chestnuts
¼ cup heavy cream
⅔ cup cold milk

⅓ cup all-purpose flour
½ teaspoon each of fine salt
   and pepper
oil or melted butter for frying

Place the egg yolks in the food processor with the chestnuts, cream and milk. Process to a smooth purée, then add the flour, salt and pepper and beat till combined. Scrape into a container, cover and chill till you're ready to cook them. Just before you put the pan on, whisk the egg whites to soft peaks in a clean bowl and fold the chestnut batter through evenly. Heat a smidgeon of oil in the pan and spoon in the batter in blobs about 2 inches in diameter. I won't hide the fact that they burn very easily and flip in a slightly disconcerting wobbly way, so do watch the heat under the pan and flip quickly and with care. The second side only takes a moment to set, then lift each blini out and keep them on a warm dinner plate while you make the others. They do keep but are really best eaten within 10 to 15 minutes of cooking, so round up other bods to dress and serve them.

Betsy's Scotch pancakes

Betsy Morrison is a renowned home baker who lives on the Black Isle in Scotland, and I watched her effortlessly whisk up a batch of these pancakes in front of a crowd of people one summer at a food festival in Cromarty (a historic royal burg, complete with 18th-century merchants' houses, fishermen's cottages, a skull and crossbones graveyard and an alarming number of ghosts). Her way has become my way, and hopefully yours too.

2⅔ cups all-purpose flour
¾ teaspoon baking soda
1½ teaspoons cream of tartar
⅓ cup super-fine sugar

3 eggs, beaten
about 1 cup cold milk
butter
jam for serving

Have a smooth and heavy-bottomed frying pan or griddle ready, and a little butter and a few sheets of paper towel at hand. Sift the flour, baking soda, cream of tartar and sugar together into a bowl: "a very important step if you want them to be light," says Betsy. Add the eggs and nearly all the milk, then beat to a thick batter, but "only add the last of the milk if need be," she says. Heat the pan with a smidgeon of butter until it sizzles, then wipe the butter over the hot pan with a few folds of paper towel. Drop about 2 tablespoons' worth of batter onto the surface for each pancake, frying two or three at a time. When the air bubbles pop on top, flip them over so they are cooked on both sides. "Not back and forth, mind," she says, "that only makes them tough." Lay a clean tea towel over a wire cooling rack, place the cooked pancakes on it and fold the cloth lightly over to keep them covered so they stay soft, while you cook the rest of the batter.

Eat while very fresh, with a little butter, or butter and jam. The best butter and jam, mind.

Crêpes Suzette Tour d'Argent

In the 1950s, American writer Elsie Lee interviewed Henri Charpentier, the likely inventor of the Crêpes Suzette, for one of Cyril Ray's beautiful and intelligent "Compleat Imbiber" books. He explained that his version began as the dish of pancakes with fruit sauce his foster mother made for him as a child on very special occasions, and the addition of liqueurs was something chefs in Paris did. As a child it was one of the first desserts I tasted where alcohol was part of the flavor (sherry trifle was the other), and I've no doubt that it inspired, at least in part, my curiosity toward food.

MAKES 8

10 tablespoons unsalted butter, plus a little extra for frying
¼ cup each Cointreau, Grand Marnier and champagne or white wine
zest and juice of 1 or 2 oranges
¼ cup super-fine sugar, plus extra for the sauce

1½ cups milk, plus a little extra
1 vanilla pod, split
4 eggs
1 cup all-purpose flour
confectioners' sugar and brandy to finish

Melt the butter in a saucepan, then remove from the heat. Beat in the Cointreau, Grand Marnier, champagne, orange zest and juice, plus sugar to taste and set aside till the last minute. In another pan, bring the milk to a boil with the vanilla pod, then leave until cold. Beat the eggs and ¼ cup sugar together until combined, beat in the milk (remove the vanilla pod first), then beat in the flour gradually until smooth. Leave this batter in the fridge for a few hours to thicken.

Lightly butter a hot frying pan, dilute the batter to the consistency of thin cream with a little extra milk, cook the thinnest crêpes you can, then remove to a warm plate. Dust with confectioners' sugar and keep warm while you cook the remaining batter. Warm the sauce, fold the crêpes and pour the sauce liberally over them. Sprinkle with confectioners' sugar, flame with brandy and serve.

Walnut and berry blintzes

Ground walnuts, toasted in butter and mixed into the batter, give you pink-tinted, walnut-flavored crêpes, to fill with a sweet, orange-flavored cheese curd and fresh or frozen berries.

MAKES 6 to 8

FOR THE FILLING
1½ cups cottage cheese
⅔ cup cream cheese
1 egg yolk
¾ cup confectioners' sugar
finely grated zest of 2 oranges

FOR THE BLINTZES
⅔ cup walnuts, finely ground
4 tablespoons unsalted butter,
    plus extra for frying
¾ cup milk, plus a little extra
3 eggs
1 tablespoon super-fine sugar
¾ cup all-purpose flour

fresh or frozen berries
confectioners' sugar to serve

To make the filling, break up and gently mix the two cheeses together, then place in a sieve and leave to drain for 2 to 3 hours. Then beat the cheeses, egg yolk, confectioners' sugar and orange zest together in a food processor until smooth.

To make the blintzes, cook the nuts with the butter in a pan to a golden brown. Remove from the heat, add the milk, then beat in the eggs, super-fine sugar and flour. Chill this batter for 2 to 3 hours. Heat a clean, smooth nonstick frying pan and melt a little butter in it to stop the blintzes from sticking. Add extra milk to the batter if needed so it's the consistency of light cream. Ladle a few spoonfuls into the hot pan whilst twirling it so the batter is spread evenly and thinly across the base. Return to the heat and flip when the edges of the crêpe turn brown. Remove the crêpe to a warm plate and repeat with the remaining batter.

Place some berries and a large spoonful of the filling in each crêpe, then roll each one into a neat, tucked-up parcel — tricky as the filling is runny. Fry the filled crêpes in a little butter, and serve with a dusting of confectioners' sugar.

Parsley crumpet fry-up

There was a time when it wasn't potatoes with everything, when the great British breakfast was simply one modest helping of protein, hot tea, whole-wheat bread or griddle cakes, and a brisk walk to work. Today's greasy fry-up owes zilch to the Edwardians, and that plate of piled-up, overprocessed rubbish is just a consequence of a postrationing feeding frenzy. You still can be lean while eating a traditional British menu. Serve these with crisp bacon and tomatoes.

⅔ cup rolled oats
2 cups boiling water
½ teaspoon instant yeast
1½ cups bread flour
½ small onion, finely chopped
1 egg
just under 1 teaspoon fine salt

½ teaspoon baking powder
a good handful of parsley,
    roughly chopped
some good bacon
some ripe tomatoes

The night before, place the oats in a large mixing bowl, pour the boiling water over them and leave until warm. Then beat in the yeast, 1¼ cups of the flour and the onion. Cover the bowl and leave overnight at room temperature. In the morning beat in the egg, the remaining flour, salt, baking powder and parsley. Leave this for 30 minutes while you get set up. Start by frying the bacon and grilling the tomatoes, then keep these warm on a plate. Return the unwashed frying pan to the stove top. When the pan is hot, ladle in the batter to make small pancakes, and flip them when the top is barely set. Keep warm while you cook the rest, and serve with the bacon and tomatoes.

TENDER IS THE NIGHT

The yeasted oat mixture sits overnight to produce a more tender crumpet, with the morning addition of baking powder giving an extra hint of lightness. But if you're out of yeast, just soak the oats and onion in water overnight, then in the morning add all the flour and maybe increase the amount of baking powder to 1 teaspoon.

Beer batter for fish

One summer, we went looking for the best fish and chips in Britain, with The Galleon, Rhos-on-Sea, North Wales, near the top with ever-so-crunchy batter, and chips on the soft side of crisp. Couldn't find any chippies (chip shops) using beer batter, but a shameful few were using frozen fish prebattered in something yellow. Copy this recipe and hand it to any offending chippy.

SERVES 3 to 4

2 cups light ale

2 teaspoons instant yeast

2⅔ cups all-purpose flour, plus
   a plate of all-purpose flour,
   seasoned with salt and pepper,
   for dipping

⅔ cup cornstarch, potato flour
   or extra all-purpose flour

1½ teaspoons fine salt

a little cold water

lard, peanut or sunflower
   oil for frying

fresh fish (white-fleshed
   fillets about 1 inch thick)

Lightly stir the ale, yeast, flours and salt together, cover the bowl, let it sit for 2 to 3 hours, then add just enough cold water to reach the consistency of pouring cream.

Choose your frying medium: lard will produce a very crisp and rich-tasting batter and chips, peanut or sunflower oil the cleanest flavor. Barely half fill the pot with oil, heat to 355°F using a suitable thermometer and, if you have many fillets to fry, heat the oven to 375°F. Dip the fish lightly into the seasoned flour, double-dip it into the batter and then straight into the oil, using tongs, one or two fillets at a time. Fry the fish until a deep golden color, then pop the battered fillets in a warm oven and cook the rest.

Onion rings

If there's only one or two of you and you think you'll have batter left over, make your own onion rings (the frozen ones on sale at the supermarket are just so dismal). Slice a large white onion and separate the layers into rings. Dip these into the batter and fry in small batches until lightly golden.

Leave to cool on a baking sheet lined with parchment paper, and freeze until required in a ziplock bag, then simply bake in a hot oven until crisp.

Basic Babas

These are so easy to make, and so good to eat, that I don't know why we're not all making them every week. They should strictly be made with both currants and sultanas – but better without as they then cut into clean, beautiful halves. You want them to really soak in the syrup while they are still warm from the oven.

MAKES 5 OR 6
½ cup warm milk
1½ teaspoons instant yeast
1¼ cups bread flour
1 egg, plus 1 yolk
1½ teaspoons super-fine sugar
¾ teaspoon fine salt
4 tablespoons unsalted butter,
    softened, plus more for
    the molds

FOR THE SYRUP
3 cups super-fine sugar
2 cups water
a strip of lemon zest
1 vanilla pod, split lengthwise

dark rum and whipped cream
    to serve

Rinse the bowl of a stand mixer with boiling water to warm it, wipe it dry, then add the milk, yeast and ⅓ cup of the flour. Stir well and leave for 15 minutes until it turns foamy. Then add the remaining flour, egg and yolk, sugar and salt and beat for 2 minutes. Finally, add the butter and beat for another 2 minutes. Cover and leave in a warm place for 45 minutes until doubled in height.

Butter the insides of five or six stainless-steel 4-ounce baba molds, or the pockets of a deep muffin pan, and barely half-fill them with the batter.

To make the syrup, heat the sugar, water, lemon zest and split vanilla pod, and simmer for 5 minutes.

Heat the oven to 400°F. When the batter reaches the top of the molds, bake for 25 minutes. Take them out, remove from the cups, place in a deep bowl and pour the hot syrup over them. Sit a plate over the top to keep them dunked, and serve when barely cold, split lengthwise, with a splash of rum and some soft unsweetened whipped cream.

WHY SO MUCH YEAST?

Think of this mixture as a batter rather than a dough in order to get it light and airy. The recipe uses a heck of a lot of yeast for a small amount of flour but there is a reason behind it. First, it keeps the recipe quick, but more important, it helps produce this crisp, dry and very light result. We're not looking for a moist crumb but one that will be open and tender yet sturdy enough to hold its shape in the syrup. Usually we cut back on yeast to help keep the crumb moist, but here we want an almost abnormally dry finish so it can soak up the syrup without falling apart.

Sugar sugar

Sugar sugar

Confessing that you love sugar is like saying you love gin. First choose who you're going to tell, and decide whether they'll deal with it in an adult way or look down on you as a deranged sugar junkie. A secret handshake would help, something Masonic and subtle that involves the pinkie finger tickling the other's palm, signaling the caramel-eaters among your friends.

While the gift of a loaf of homemade bread suggests you possess a quiet earthy calmness, giving someone caramels wrapped in wax paper hints at something much racier and more subversive. Toffees, especially if poured into a sheet that has to be smashed into shards with a hammer, have the same combination of tradition and rebellion as firecrackers. Fudge, the soft grainy sweet related to the much older tablet, has something fun about it. And icing? Well, that's the start of a party.

There's a basic pantry quality to sugar confectionery, needing little more than a bag of sugar to get started. Barely dissolved, boiled fiercely until a drop sets hard in a glass of water, then poured onto an oiled baking sheet, you have the simplest of golden clear toffees. But add other ingredients, alter the way you cook it, and a door is opened into a sweetshop of ideas.

The combination of different sugars and syrups cooked with varying degrees of heat means that you can fine-tune the result to suit your creativity. If your caramel is too pale, or your marmalade too yellow, a little brown sugar can be added late in the cooking to turn the color deeper. Or say you have a delicately fragrant orange juice that you must avoid heating, as it will lose its freshness: confectioners' sugar stirred in will turn this into a glaze or syrup that can be spooned over a cake to capture all of its natural vibrancy.

Cream and butter soften the set, and will start to turn a brittle toffee recipe into something tender and chewable. Crème fraîche, clotted cream, butter and oils all give the sugar a different character when boiled and cooled. Chocolate and cocoa add a dark bitterness that tempers the sweet flavor, as do spices and the zest from citrus fruits.

When mixed into an icing, sugar transforms every cake into an event. The bare-faced rich fruitcake can just about claim the title of "health food," especially if you're planning to stride up a mountain with a slice in your pocket. But cover it with almond paste and icing and you have a serious wedding cake, at once about celebration and bliss. All because of icing. Cupcakes need sugar-rich frosting. Chocolate fudge cakes are just plain wrong without icing on top. So here's where you'll find some ideas for icing and filling your cakes and desserts.

I've also included a few very simple sauce recipes, because more often than you may realize, a simple dessert can be elevated by the addition of a sauce that's only taken you minutes to make. But let them be your starting point, rather than where you end up, an encouragement to use your imagination and go further. And finally, I've included here a few more things I do at home, from recipes for an easy lemon curd and "instant" mincemeat to the almond paste I use each Christmas, some easy ice cream and a cake syrup that I can assure you has saved many a professional pastry chef from a dry cake disaster.

So this chapter is devoted to sugar, hoping that we start to see it as potent and remarkable rather than dull and everyday. Use it less frequently, but with more gusto, and you'll rediscover just how special an ingredient it is.

Candy and icing making is time-sensitive, so have everything ready before you start: all ingredients measured and utensils set out.

For sugar cooking I have a candy thermometer ready if the recipe needs one, and a deep glass filled with room-temperature water. It's really important to use a thermometer specially designed to withstand the high temperatures needed for cooking, and not the one from the medicine cabinet. My friend Sarah at baking911.com recommends testing a candy thermometer every so often by checking the temperature of a pan of boiling water. At regular altitudes (that is, not up the side of a mountain) the thermometer should read about 212°F. So if your thermometer reads higher or lower than that, remember to make an allowance when you use it next time. And ask friends for a new one at Christmas.

Get a heavy-duty saucepan, and allow for the sugar mixture to boil much higher than its level when cold: up to six times the height. I use a hard, anodized 3-quart saucepan most of the time, but just make sure your pot is heavy. Try to avoid stainless steel as the sugar burns easily on the bottom and can be very difficult to clean.

White sugar

White sugar is all the same, no matter what brand: refined and chemically pure. Super-fine sugar dissolves very quickly but, given enough heat, granulated sugar will do the same. I prefer granulated sugar for coating the outside of fruit jellies.

Using confectioners' sugar

If you have the time, it's a good idea to sift confectioners' sugar first, as it will then mix smoothly without too many lumps. When you're adding liquids to confectioners' sugar, remember that the sugar particles are very small and dissolve easily so it will turn runny quickly if too much liquid is added. I tend to add half the liquid any recipe suggests, then cautiously add more just until the consistency looks right.

Confectioners' sugar is very good for last-minute sweetening of custards and sauces as it dissolves instantly and this means you won't have to reheat the mixture.

Using sugar substitutes

Whether you're making a cooked or uncooked sugar recipe, in some way the method will rely on the chemical composition of sugar to work well. So if you exchange the sugar for an ingredient that has a different chemical structure, then, very simply, the recipe won't work in the same way. When sugar is a small proportion of the recipe you can often get away with it: say in a fruitcake or a pudding. But in dishes where sugar is the main ingredient, it's not possible to get the same effect with a sugar substitute.

Where the physical properties of the sweetener are very similar to the one used in the recipe then, yes, you can usually exchange them, though the flavor and appearance will be different. Honey or agave nectar can replace molasses or corn syrup, for example.

Classic Caramel

A regular feature of cooking classes during my school days in suburban Melbourne were "Russian caramels," a sort of soft toffee, made with condensed milk, brown sugar and butter. And I guess I've been sold on caramel ever since. When I started working as a chef, caramel on restaurant menus was, from what I remember, a simple, dark and bittersweet affair. It might have been caramel ice cream, perhaps using a Frédy Girardet recipe; the crunch of spun sugar over a peach Melba à la Marco Pierre White; the brutish syrup bathing scorched apples in a classic tarte Tatin at Chez Panisse or Alastair Little, or perhaps the brown underbelly of a crème caramel or the delicate upper crust on a brûlée. Beyond that, caramel was viewed by many chefs as just sweetshop stuff, lacking the hormones needed for the testosterone-fueled kitchens of "fine dining." Well, that's all in the past. Caramel is now the coolest of cool.

It's still one of the cheapest treats you can brew up in your kitchen, yet one of the most sophisticated luxuries, at the same time slightly threatening with its saucepan of molten sugar, yet utterly calming in the measured steps that making it demands. Take a little time to master the basic art, and you'll find it's neither difficult nor time-consuming.

Start with the right kit

Treat yourself to a candy thermometer. Yes, there are recipes, even in this chapter, where I try to work with whatever reluctance you might have in that direction, by dripping the sugar solution into a glass of cold water to test the consistency of the "set." But for safer, reliable results, you really need a candy thermometer. I've checked, and the cost is about the same as a couple of heat-resistant glass bowls. But make sure it's heat-proof, and that the numbers won't boil off. Go for something metal and glass and decidedly old-fashioned.

Also, make sure you have a saucepan with a heavy, thick base. Try to get a pan that conducts heat evenly: hard anodized aluminium works better than stainless steel. Apart from those two items, there's nothing special you'll need: the scales, wooden spoons and pans you use in your baking will be more than good enough.

Be careful and organized, and stay relaxed

David's mother was a hard-core marmalade maker well into her eighties, and her frail manoeuvring of a pan of boiling sugar syrup always worried me. But her calm confidence, and the pleasure she derived, outweighed any fear in her mind. Caramel involves a much smaller pan of sugar and much less danger than marmalade making, but danger is relative and there are steps you should take to stay safe. Be free from any distractions, and I'd include small children and pets in that. Don't dip your fingers in to taste the mixture, even if it looks inviting. When adding new ingredients, remove the pan from the heat and expect it to bubble and spit furiously at each addition, so stand back until it subsides. And should a small drop of boiling sugar hit your skin, hold the area immediately under cold running water for a few minutes. But stay calm, and don't let the fear put you off. Have the ingredients measured out before you start, and your equipment easily at hand. If your caramel is going to end up in a pan or baking sheet, get that set up with a damp cloth underneath, so it doesn't slide about when you pour.

Start with white sugar

White sugar gives caramel a pure sweet taste, and will make gauging the color of the caramel much easier. But with practice you should be able to try unrefined ("golden") sugar, which has a "bigger" and more complex flavor, and after that, move on to using muscovado in place of some of the white sugar for an even more powerful flavor. For a tarte Tatin or crème caramel, you may be happier always using white sugar; but if you're making soft caramels or sauces, try replacing some of the white sugar in the recipe with brown sugar (any sort), but only caramelize the white sugar. Then add the brown sugar with the butter and cream.

Burnt is closer to what you want

Talking to the experts, the consensus seems to be that the darker the caramel, the better. From the moment the sugar hits the pan, it goes through visibly different stages. First a white syrup, then a clear syrup that occasionally has a frost-white crust on the top. It then begins to turn a golden caramel at the edges, and swirling the pan as it cooks further will take it to a uniform golden caramel. From this point on it will turn a rich golden caramel, a dark reddish caramel, a darker brown caramel with wisps of smoke, and finally it's burnt black. Each point along the scale has its own flavor, but for now, aim for that rich golden to dark reddish color. As your confidence grows, you may want to experiment with a darker brown, but master the techniques first.

The cooking temperature is . . .

Well, that depends. More fat (cream, butter or oil) may keep the caramel from turning too hard, but then it needs to cook to a higher temperature to achieve a firmer set. Less fat may mean cooking it to a lower temperature, to avoid it becoming brittle and hard. As a general guide, for a soft eating caramel, take the temperature to somewhere between 253 and 257°F, and to 266°F for a hard set, depending on your recipe.

Practice, practice, practice: caramel apples

Don't feel trapped by a recipe book. You can practice with simple ingredients and still make something lovely. I had a few dessert apples in the fruit bowl that had to be used up. So I peeled, cored and quartered them, then simply put ⅓ cup sugar in a frying pan with a dash of water and heated that continuously till it turned a golden caramel. Then I added 2 tablespoons butter and the apples, and cooked them gently with about ¼ cup water until they were almost tender, adding a dribble more water every so often so they stayed moist. At first, hard bits of toffee formed, but they soon dissolved in the juices from the apples. I had a little brandy in the cupboard so I added a dash, say 2 tablespoons, and let it simmer for a minute more. This gave a beautiful, simple caramel butter sauce around tender pieces of apple, and the result looked rich and luxurious even with scoops of a basic vanilla ice cream and a few sliced almonds scattered over the top. You want cheap chic? Caramel apples are it, in my book.

CARAMEL ICE CREAM

After making caramel, you'll never get it all out of the pan at the end, so don't bother. Leave a bit more in there perhaps, and add a little cream and milk to dissolve the caramel, and use this mixture as the start of some homemade ice cream. All the hard bits stuck on the pan will slowly melt into the cream and flavor it, and you can then simply continue with your normal ice cream recipe.

Basic butter caramels

These are so straightforward to make at home, and the changes you can make with different sugars, syrups and enriching ingredients make it easy to steer one basic recipe toward the type that best suits you at that moment. Make it dark and ballsy with molasses and muscovado sugar. Or delicate with cream and honey. Whatever you want, you can make it. The key is to make a note of the ingredients and measures you choose so that you can repeat it next time if it's brilliant or subtly change it to make it better.

5 tablespoons unsalted butter (or ¼ cup oil) plus more for lining the pan
1½ cups super-fine sugar
2 tablespoons water

⅓ cup corn syrup (or blackstrap molasses, honey, malt extract, or maple syrup)
¾ cup light cream (or heavy cream, or crème fraîche)
¼ teaspoon fine salt (optional)

Unless you are making this as a sauce, take a square-cornered metal loaf pan, dab a little butter on the insides, then line the pan securely with parchment paper. Make sure all the ingredients are measured and within reach.

Heat ¾ cup of the sugar with the water in a deep, heavy saucepan until it turns a rich reddish brown. Then remove the pan from the heat and add the butter or oil. Add the remaining sugar, the syrup, cream and salt, stirring after each addition; return to the heat and bring to a boil, watching that it doesn't boil over. Then reduce the heat slightly and simmer for 3 or 4 minutes. This is where you need your candy thermometer.

For an all-purpose caramel sauce, you want it to reach 235°F, at which point, let it cool slightly and it is then ready to serve. Thin with a little boiling water if necessary.

For a chewy caramel, continue to 257°F, and to 266°F for a brittle set. Then remove the pan from the heat and leave it for a minute to let the bubbles subside. Tap the pan gently on the work surface to remove any remaining bubbles, then while still hot, pour into the loaf pan, gently scraping as much as you can out of the saucepan with a spoon, and leave until cold. Lift the set caramel out of the loaf pan by the paper lining, place on a chopping board and, with a sharp, heavy knife, cut into squares or fingers. Store in an airtight container, ideally wrapped in individual scraps of parchment paper, as the caramels will start to soften almost immediately.

The following sets of ingredients, used as previously explained will, I hope, also encourage you to experiment and try ingredient and flavor combinations of your own.

Crème fraîche molasses caramels

5 tablespoons unsalted butter, plus more for lining the pan
¾ super-fine sugar
2 tablespoons water
¾ cup muscovado or molasses sugar

⅓ cup blackstrap molasses
¾ cup crème fraîche
¼ teaspoon fine salt (optional)

Dark notes from the unrefined sugar plus a gentle acidity from the crème fraîche. Make as a sauce to serve almost cold over ginger ice cream, or as a firm-set caramel to cut up and hand round after dinner.

Toasted brazil nut and orange caramels

5 tablespoons unsalted
   butter, plus more for
   lining the pan
1½ cups super-fine sugar
2 tablespoons water
⅓ cup honey

¾ cup heavy cream
¼ teaspoon fine salt (optional)
finely grated zest of 2 oranges
⅔ cup brazil nuts, coarsely
   chopped and toasted in
   the oven

A rich butter flavor accentuated by the brazil nuts and lightened by the orange to stop the sweetness from overpowering it. A magical sauce when poured hot over ripe bananas, served with ice-cold and thickly whipped cream. Good as firm-set caramels for an afternoon spent watching a film with your love. Stir the orange zest and nuts in gently at the end of the cooking time.

Olive oil and black pepper caramels

butter for lining the pan
¾ cup super-fine sugar
2 tablespoons water,
   plus ½ cup
¼ cup extra virgin olive oil
¾ cup dark brown sugar

⅓ cup malt extract
1 tablespoon cocoa powder
¼ teaspoon fine salt (optional)
2 teaspoons coarsely ground
   black pepper

Malt and chocolate provide background flavors as the olive oil and black pepper dominate. Lovely as a sauce on poached pears, chocolate or black cherry ice cream, where the chocolate becomes more apparent. As a firm caramel, perfect with a shot of espresso. Stir the cocoa, salt and half the pepper in with the ½ cup water, scattering the remaining pepper over the top as it sets.

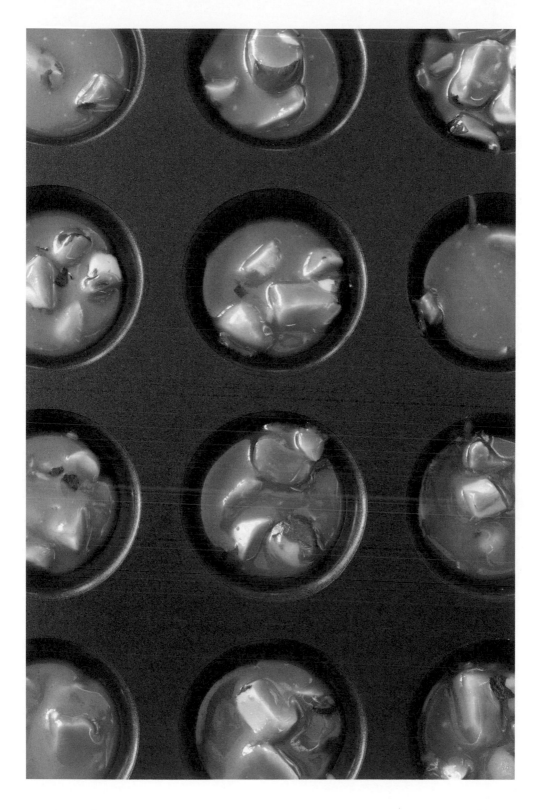

SHORT & SWEET

Firm set salted macadamia caramels

5 tablespoons unsalted
    butter, plus more
    for lining the pan
1½ cups super-fine sugar
2 tablespoons water
⅓ cup corn syrup

¾ cup heavy cream
¼ teaspoon fine salt
    (optional)
½ cup coarsely chopped
    salted macadamia nuts

Cook the sugar and water to a slightly darker caramel. After adding the other ingredients, make sure the caramel cooks for about 4 minutes till it reaches 266°F. Just before it gets to temperature, gently stir in the macadamias. Wrap the chopped-up squares individually in parchment paper, stuff them into your pocket and enjoy a trip to your local art gallery. You're never alone with a pocket full of caramels.

SWEET GIFTS

Going to a dinner party? Don't take wine, take caramels – cut into squares, wrapped first in parchment paper and then a double thickness of brown paper, and simply tied with some kitchen twine.

Black Russian caramels

These dark, chewy caramels have a slight bitterness from the principal flavors of brown sugar, coffee and cocoa, which means that they veer away from cloyingly sweet and are parked somewhere between dark and complex. If you close your eyes you can just about distinguish the three flavors, but without extra thought, they combine into something akin to a soft molasses toffee.

5 tablespoons unsalted butter, plus more for the pan
1⅓ cups sweetened condensed milk
1 cup dark brown sugar
2 teaspoons instant coffee granules
4 ounces dark chocolate

Butter the inside of a loaf pan, 7 inches long or similar, really well. Stir all the ingredients together in a deep heavy-bottomed saucepan and bring to a boil, stirring all the time. Then from the moment it starts boiling, cook for 10 to 12 minutes, stirring constantly around the bottom and edges of the pan with a wooden spoon, as it can stick and burn if you're not careful. (I can still hear my schoolteacher warn me about this.)

You'll be getting close when the caramel is very thick and starts to come away from the sides of the pan when stirred. Cook the caramel to 248 to 257°F, then remove from the heat, give it a quick stir with the wooden spoon to get it smooth and scrape it into the loaf pan. Leave to cool before removing from the pan and cutting into squares on a chopping board with a heavy, sharp knife. Wrap each caramel in waxed paper or cellophane and store in a jar.

Caramel cashew popcorn boulders

Time to be upfront: this little batch of beauties contains a lot of refined sugar. But what a way to go . . .

2 tablespoons unsalted butter, plus more for the pan
4½ quarts popped corn
1⅓ cups unsalted roasted cashews, chopped
1¼ cups super-fine sugar

2 tablespoons muscovado sugar
2½ tablespoons corn syrup
2½ tablespoons condensed milk
cold water

Butter the cups of a muffin pan and chill until needed. Mix the popped corn with the chopped cashews.

Place the remaining ingredients in a saucepan and boil until the bubbling slows and the mixture looks thick. Spoon a little of this caramel into a glass of cold water and if it firms rapidly, it's ready – if not, boil a little longer. Carefully pour the caramel over the mixed popped corn and cashews – watch, so you don't get any on your skin, as it will cause a nasty burn. Using two spoons, stir the caramel, nuts and popcorn together. You have about a minute before the caramel cools and hardens too much to stir. Then, with the spoons, pile the hot mixture into the muffin cups, pressing it into eight or nine "boulders" if you want them extra large, or 12 to 14 smaller "rocks" that can be added to a selection of other candies. Leave to cool.

Cardamom peanut brittle

Though you can leave the cardamom out and make the brittle perfectly plain, I like the way the spice stops it from tasting overly sweet. Do get a candy thermometer; it makes it so easy and you'll be hooked on toffee making.

2 tablespoons unsalted butter, plus more for the baking sheet	⅓ cup water
	1⅓ cups salted peanuts
	the seeds from 8 to 10 cardamom pods
1½ cups granulated sugar	
⅓ cup honey	½ teaspoon baking soda

Have a buttered rimmed baking sheet ready and all of the ingredients measured and at hand before you start. Place the sugar, honey and water in a pan, bring it slowly to a boil and heat to about 266°F. Add the peanuts then return to the heat and boil until it gets to about 295 to 310°F.

Remove from the heat and stir in the butter and cardamom seeds until mixed through, then beat in the baking soda. As the mixture foams slightly, pour it onto the baking sheet, then, with two forks, smash through the foam and stretch the mixture out. Leave to cool, then carefully lever it off the baking sheet with a blunt knife and break into pieces.

It does stick to the baking sheet sometimes, so if this happens, I briefly place the baking sheet over the flame on the stove to heat it from below. Just a little, as you only want to warm it, rather than get the caramel hot.

TOFFEE PULLING

One tip that some toffee makers swear by is to stretch and pull the mixture as it cools. The way to do this is to leave the toffee for a few minutes once poured onto the baking sheet, then, with a fork in one hand and a cloth to steady the baking sheet in the other, pull the toffee outward, fold it back upon itself, then finally prod and pull the toffee back out to form a thin sheet again.

Soft vanilla fudge

One of the best things about homemade fudge is how lavish you can make it: you have a fair idea of who will eat it and what they'd like best. With store-bought, there's always the sense that someone is watching the pennies, and cheapening it very slightly. Here, the seeds from a vanilla pod beaten in as the mixture cools add those speckles to the appearance and a rich true vanilla flavor. Evaporated milk makes the texture very creamy, rich and soft, thanks to the high levels of milk protein that change the way the crystals form, and gives the fudge an intense milky flavor. If you use it, leave out the glucose as this has a similar effect and the fudge will become too soft.

2 cups granulated or super-fine sugar	good pinch of salt
⅔ cup heavy cream or evaporated milk	2 teaspoons corn syrup, (optional but will reduce the graininess)
½ cup whole or 2% milk	the seeds from ½ vanilla bean pod
5 tablespoons unsalted butter	

You need a proper candy thermometer to be really sure of getting the temperature right, so have this ready as well as a loaf pan, 7½ inches long or similar, lined with parchment paper or well buttered inside. Place the sugar, cream, milk, butter, salt and corn syrup in a heavy-bottomed saucepan that holds about 3 quarts, as the mixture boils up quite high and a large pan will ensure it stays inside and doesn't boil over. Using a wooden spoon, stir the mixture over low heat until the sugar has dissolved, then bring to a boil, stirring constantly.

Reduce the heat to just under a boil and cook for 8 to 10 minutes, stirring constantly to make sure the fudge doesn't stick, until the temperature reaches 240°F. Then remove the pan from the heat and leave until the temperature drops to 230°F. Add the vanilla and beat with a wooden spoon for 8 to 10 minutes until the mixture is very thick, creamy and slightly grainy. Spoon into the pan and leave until cold before cutting into cubes with a clean sharp knife.

Rum and raisin fudge

Adding chocolate and rum as the fudge cools will stop it from turning too dry and sugary, giving a creamy soft finish without you having to play scientist.

2½ cups super-fine sugar
½ cup milk
½ cup heavy cream
1 tablespoon cocoa powder

4 ounces dark chocolate,
   broken into little pieces
⅔ cup raisins
2 to 4 tablespoons dark rum

Line the bottom and sides of a 7-inch square pan with parchment paper. Fill a glass with cold water and keep it handy, near the stove top.

In a large, deep, heavy-bottomed saucepan, stir the sugar, milk, cream and cocoa together over low heat until smooth — it's important to use a large pan as the mixture will bubble up. Heat until boiling, stirring all the time with a wooden spoon. Then watch it carefully for the next 5 minutes, stirring often, until it forms what candy makers call the "soft ball" stage (241°F). (Remember this is boiling sugar, which can burn your skin in a split-second, so be careful.) Let a few drops fall from the spoon into the glass of water: they should sink to the bottom. Dip your fingers into the glass and check that the drops squish together into a soft but definite ball of toffee. If they do, then you're ready. Remove the pan from the heat, and leave to cool for a minute until the bubbles subside. Stir in the chocolate and raisins and finally the rum. Beat the mixture well until it gets very thick but is still pourable, then tip it into the pan and leave to set. Cut into small cubes to serve.

HOT STUFF

The first time you make fudge, boil the mixture to a slightly higher temperature — say 245°F — as this way it will set very firmly but with a grainy sugar crystal texture. A lower temperature (241°F) will give you a softer set with a creamier texture but you need to be sure that your thermometer's accurate and that you're confident with the steps.

Sesame ginger halvah

This makes a type of sweet halvah similar to the sort you see in Middle Eastern stores, wrapped in foil and sometimes studded with pistachios, or a combination of chocolate and vanilla halvah swirled together, and is technically a kind of fudge. Perfect cut into little pieces to have with thick black coffee and a shot of arak after dinner.

butter for the foil
1 cup tahini (sesame seed
    paste), warmed slightly
3 ounces crystallized ginger

1 cup super-fine sugar
¼ cup water
1 tablespoon honey

Line the bottom and sides of a large loaf pan with a buttered sheet of foil. Spoon the tahini into a bowl and stir until smooth. Chop the ginger into ¼-inch bits. Place the sugar, water and honey in a saucepan and, if testing with a candy thermometer, boil until it reaches 248°F. Or bring to a boil and simmer for 5 to 10 minutes, until a drop of the caramel hardens when dropped into a glass of cold water and can be squeezed with the fingers into a hard ball. Next, add the chopped crystallized ginger and the tahini. Beat until the mixture turns grainy, then spoon it into the foil-lined pan and press down well. Cover and leave until cold before slicing.

HALVAH RESCUE

If your mixture gets too hot and you get a blobby "bread crumby" appearance when you beat the tahini in, you can either beat in a little extra water to restore the consistency, or simply pack it firmly into the pan while hot and leave it a day or two, to get the stickier, finer texture you usually see in the store-bought variety.

Victoria plum jellies

It's best to use fruit slightly on the firm side, not too ripe. The ingredient quantities sound massive but only make about 2 cups of jellies. And of course, you can use other stone fruit equally well.

1 pound plums, with the skin but without the pits
1 cup water
2 tablespoons lemon juice

2½ cups granulated sugar, plus extra for rolling
¼ cup liquid pectin

Line the bottom and sides of a square 7-inch cake pan with parchment paper. Chop the fruit and purée in a blender with the water and lemon juice until very smooth but with tiny flecks of the peel still visible.

Tip this into a saucepan with the sugar and bring to a boil. Skim off the pale scum that comes to the top, then boil for 20 to 30 minutes, stirring occasionally with a wooden spoon, as it does catch slightly on the pan, until the temperature reaches 223°F. Stir in the pectin, boil for a minute longer, then pour the mixture into the pan and leave for 3 to 4 hours to cool.

You need to dry the jellies out to stop them from "bleeding" syrup later, so heat the oven to 150°F (or leave the oven door ajar if it doesn't have a setting that low). Cut the jelly into cubes and roll them in sugar, then leave them on a baking sheet in the oven for about 2 hours. Roll once more in sugar and leave until cold.

Soft raspberry coconut ice

This has a softer texture and more complex flavor than the "old school" kind, but is easy to make. If you let it dry even more once it's cut into pieces, it gets a slight sugary crust that will protect the moist inner texture.

FOR THE WHITE MIXTURE
2½ cups confectioners' sugar
½ cup mascarpone
2 cups shredded coconut

FOR THE RASPBERRY MIXTURE
⅓ cup fresh raspberries
¼ cup mascarpone
2½ cups confectioners' sugar
⅔ cups shredded coconut

Line a 7-inch square pan with parchment paper.

To make the white mixture, beat half the sugar with the mascarpone until you have a smooth runny paste. Stir in the coconut and remaining sugar, mix well then press into the bottom of the pan. Pack the mixture in well and smooth the top.

To make the raspberry mixture, squish the raspberries with the mascarpone and half the sugar until smooth. (You can sieve the seeds out if you like but I leave them in.) Then stir in the coconut followed by the last of the sugar. Spread this carefully over the white mixture until you have it even, then press it down firmly with a spatula and your fingers.

Loosely cover the pan, with the top exposed to the air slightly, and leave overnight somewhere cool to firm. The following day, lift out of the pan by the lining paper and cut into pieces.

THE RIGHT CONSISTENCY

Coconut ice is really just icing with coconut stirred through it, and when left to sit, the dry coconut absorbs moisture from the icing and this makes it firmer. When each mixture is made it should be a very thick paste, and coconut can hold more or less moisture according to how it was processed and stored. So if it's a little too soft when mixing, try adding a little more sugar and coconut to firm it.

Chocolate truffle cubes

If the chocolate is just left to set after mixing, the texture is a little uneven and slightly coarse, as if the truffles have been dug out from the earth on a chocolate mountain. Whereas if the mixture is beaten as it cools, the texture becomes extremely smooth and elegant. Your call. The truffles will be slightly soft at room temperature so keep them refrigerated.

¼ cup confectioners' sugar
¼ cup mascarpone
1 tablespoon honey
8 ounces dark chocolate, or
    4 ounces each dark and
    milk chocolate

5 tablespoons unsalted butter
2 tablespoons brandy
cocoa powder for dusting

Stir the confectioners' sugar, mascarpone and honey in a bowl. Next heat the chocolate and butter until just melted, then stir this into the sugar mixture, and when that's mixed through, beat in the brandy. Leave the chocolate mixture to cool slightly, then beat it gently with a whisk until it starts to look very glossy and smooth. Spoon this into a loaf pan, 7 inches long or similar, lined with plastic wrap and chill or freeze until firm.

Next cut the chocolate into small cubes and toss carefully in sifted cocoa with a couple of forks. Place each cube when coated on a baking sheet covered with a sheet of parchment paper and chill until firm. Then carefully pack into a box in layers, separated with sheets of nonstick paper, and keep refrigerated.

STORING

The best way to keep the truffles at room temperature is to cut them into cubes, freeze them, then dip them into melted dark chocolate and roll in cocoa. This will create a hard shell that will protect the mixture inside.

SHORT & SWEET

Everything you wanted to know about icing but were afraid to ask

Icing can add magic to a cake, and whether it's afternoon tea or a grand birthday party, few things will cause as much excitement as a layer cake, tall and proud and covered in buttercream. So here are my top tips for getting it right.

Making sure you have enough icing

Some people like thick icing, some thin, some soft like honey, some firm and rich, so I can't say with absolute authority how much icing you need for a cake. What I do suggest, say for a cupcake, is to weigh one before and after it's been iced then compare the amount of icing used with the total amount made. That way, you can tweak the amount of icing on each cupcake to match what's available.

For a layer cake with all-over frosting, I use very little for the "crumb coat" and in-between layer, let that chill, then divide the remaining frosting evenly over the cake.

Whisks, spoons, spatulas and pastry bags

Having really comfortable and suitable utensils to work with makes any effort involved in icing a cake seem so much less. Often I'll just use a butter knife or two teaspoons, spooning a dollop onto the cake and giving it a nifty single swirl. But sometimes you think, wouldn't it be good if the icing was really evenly smooth and crisp? And without getting too "pro" about it, you can easily do this.

The good old wooden spoon is still handy for beating, as is a whisk for getting the mixture light and smooth. Get a rubber or silicon spatula, the sort with the flexible wide head and firm handle, for folding the icing and scraping around the bowl. Also, get a long stainless-steel palette knife for smoothing the icing flat. If you want a pastry bag, be bold and get two: small and very large, and a simple selection of plain, circular and star-shaped metal nozzles.

A very long serrated knife is useful if you need to split the cake into layers. Score a line around the cake where you want your layer to be, then use a sawing action to cut through the cake.

The perfect frosted layer cake in five steps

Though covering a cake with a thin layer of water icing (see page 335) has its own tricks for getting the best result, here I'm concerned with the thicker mixtures known as "frosting," and in particular the butter-rich ones. If you read through this once, you should quickly get an idea of the steps needed when you come to assemble your cake.

1. Prepare your cake. Wait until the cake or sponge layers are completely cold before starting to ice them, then trim any slightly overcooked or rough edges off with a very sharp knife. The icing will cover most little imperfections, and you don't want to spoil the taste with any burnt crumbs. If you have time, wrap the cake well and freeze it for a few hours, then ice it fresh from the freezer. This helps to give a moister cake as it will absorb moisture from the icing as it thaws. But if you're worried that the cake might be dry, it can be rescued by brushing the layers with a little Fresh Cake Syrup (page 339) before icing.

2. Put the cake on the serving plate or board where you'll want it, then cut lengths of parchment paper and slip them under and around the bottom of the cake, just under the edges. This way any icing that drips down won't spoil the presentation, and you won't have to try moving a fully iced cake. It's a bit like wearing an apron in the kitchen: it seems fussy at first, but is the best way to keep clean.

3. Spread a layer of icing or other filling over the bottom layer of the cake. Don't try to be overly generous, and do let it splurge out at the sides slightly when the next layer of the cake is added. It isn't important to smooth it perfectly, just fairly evenly. If you have more layers, add them in the same way, and continue stacking the cake.

4. Apply the "crumb coat" — a thin layer of icing to hold all the crumbs flat — first covering the top of the cake smoothly. Then load the palette knife with more icing and spread this evenly and firmly around the sides. Then with the palette knife at a 45-degree angle, trim any lumps or bumps from the top edge of the cake, dragging them smoothly in toward the center. Return any excess icing to the bowl but beware of crumbs, then chill the cake for at least 30 minutes to firm it.

5. Give the cake another coat of icing in the same way, making it as smooth as you possibly can.

Meringue buttercream icing

This is a fluffy creamy icing that spreads and swirls beautifully, with a little more elegance than Simple Lemon Cream Cheese Frosting (page 330), and it is not difficult to make with an electric hand mixer. But if you're limited to a hand whisk I might give it a miss, though my great-grandmother would have had to make it that way. It keeps well in the refrigerator, so can be made in advance, and should be whisked again just before using. Handy, too, for using up leftover egg whites.

4 egg whites	1½ cups (3 sticks) unsalted
1 cup super-fine sugar	butter, slightly softened
	2 teaspoons vanilla extract

Place the egg whites and sugar in a saucepan and stir over medium heat until the mixture is hot and the sugar dissolved. The sugar and heat kill off any bacteria and effectively sterilize the mixture. Then scrape it into a mixing bowl and blend for about 5 minutes until very thick, holding its shape and cooled.

Beat the butter into the meringue, about 4 tablespoons at a time. Stop whisking as soon as all of the butter is evenly mixed through. If it starts to look coarse and rough, then warm it very slightly in the microwave and beat again until creamy. Finally, beat in the vanilla.

SHORT & SWEET

Buttercream variations

You can make so many different versions of the basic recipe by introducing other flavors. Just to get you started, here are a few I use at home.

Cream cheese meringue buttercream icing

Replace 10 tablespoons of the butter with full-fat cream cheese, adding it at the end after the butter has been mixed through.

Lime, lemon or orange meringue buttercream icing

Simply add 2 to 3 tablespoons of grated zest from the unwaxed citrus fruit of your choice with the butter, and use lemon, orange or lime extract in place of the vanilla.

Cinnamon meringue buttercream icing

Beat 2 or 3 teaspoons of ground cinnamon, or half cinnamon and half mixed spice (cinnamon, nutmeg, ginger and cloves), in with the butter.

Chocolate meringue buttercream icing

Replace half the butter with 5 ounces melted and slightly cooled chocolate and beat this in first before the butter.

Simple lemon cream cheese frosting

This is dead simple to make and quick as well, and can be used for example on carrot and banana cakes. But do spend 5 minutes reading the tips given below, as they will steer you to the best possible result.

14 ounces full-fat cream cheese
1 cup (2 sticks) unsalted butter,
    softened
finely grated zest of 1 lemon,
    plus 2 to 3 teaspoons lemon juice

2 cups confectioners'
    sugar

Beat half the cream cheese with the butter, lemon zest, lemon juice and confectioners' sugar together until very smooth. Add the remaining cream cheese and whisk until light and fluffy.

IT AIN'T WHAT YOU DO, BUT THE WAY THAT YOU DO IT

I've found that if you beat the butter with the sugar and some cream cheese first it helps to stabilize the mixture. Then when you whisk the remaining cream cheese through, it strengthens the emulsion and keeps the frosting light and smooth. Butter in its natural state is a rough mixture of whey and butterfat. So as the sugar binds with the cream cheese and butter, it forms an emulsion, which allows the remaining cream cheese to be held in suspension as you whisk it.

Six tips for perfect cream cheese frosting

1. Go for a butter that has less water in it. Not all unsalted butters are the same, and most pastry chefs get very particular about their choice of butter for this reason. The water content in butter varies according to the price of the milk, and some brands are always softer than others. I use Lurpak unsalted or Président unsalted as they are very firm butters that produce great easy-to-roll pastries and excellent buttercream icings.

2. Go for a good firm full-fat cream cheese, and if there is any liquid in the package, drain it away. Low-fat cream cheese can cause the frosting to fail, as they use gels and gums to give the illusion of thick creaminess, and it doesn't appear to cope with being rebeaten without thinning.

3. Don't cut the mixture with sour cream, mascarpone or thick yogurt as their water content causes the icing to thin or separate.

4. Don't overbeat. I use an electric hand mixer, and after the mixture is roughly combined just beat it a little at a time until it is barely smooth.

5. Keep all the ingredients on the cool side, not too warm because it will become thin and might split, and not too cold because it will go lumpy.

6. Once the cake is iced, chill it for about an hour. This sets the icing and helps keep it firm when you serve it.

Molasses chocolate fudge frosting

This is one of those swirly, creamy icings that tastes like soft chocolate fudge. The combination of milk and dark chocolate pushes the flavor toward something meltingly childish rather than depressingly gourmet, while the combination of the starch in the cocoa and cornstarch helps to trap the natural oils and keep it creamy.

2 tablespoons blackstrap molasses
¾ cup light brown sugar
¼ cup cocoa powder
¼ cup cornstarch
1¼ cups milk

8 ounces dark chocolate (or half milk and dark), finely chopped
2 teaspoons vanilla extract
4 tablespoons unsalted butter, softened

In a saucepan, beat together the molasses, sugar, cocoa, cornstarch and milk until smooth. Bring to a boil, whisking often so it doesn't scald on the bottom, then remove from the heat and beat in the chopped chocolate until the consistency is smooth and creamy. When barely warm, beat in the vanilla and the softened butter, a chunk or two at a time. Use while warm as it will be easier to spread.

To halve or quarter the recipe, get as close as you can with the measurements; you don't have to be exactly spot on. If you want the frosting even firmer, then beat melted chocolate through it to thicken, or heavy cream to lighten it.

334

Water icing

This is the simplest icing to make, but confectioners' sugar can quickly turn from a thick paste to a watery mess when you add liquid, so don't chuck it in all at once. Try adding it gradually, and stopping as soon as it forms a very thick paste when beaten, then add more liquid almost drop by drop, to get to the consistency you need it to be.

2¼ cups confectioners' sugar

2 tablespoons cold water, plus more if needed

1½ tablespoons corn syrup, (optional but helps it set and stay glossy)

Spoon the confectioners' sugar into a bowl, add the water and corn syrup (if using) a little at a time and stir together. If more water is needed to get to the right consistency, add it cautiously and gradually.

Lemon, mandarin or orange water icing

Replace the water with the same amount of juice plus 1 to 2 teaspoons finely grated zest. Thin with a little extra juice if needed.

Coffee water icing

Dissolve 1 tablespoon instant coffee granules in the water before mixing with the sugar and corn syrup. Add ½ teaspoon grated lemon zest for a cleaner flavor.

Ginger water icing

Mix the confectioners' sugar and water. Add 3 ounces of thinly sliced crystallized ginger.

Chocolate water icing

Add ¼ cup cocoa powder to the confectioners' sugar and stir together before adding the water and corn syrup.

Cointreau sugar glaze

A deliberately very watery icing, poured over a cake while it is still hot, which covers the cake in a pale matte finish like a glaze of ice.

2 cups confectioners' sugar
4 teaspoons Cointreau
2 teaspoons orange zest,
   finely chopped

6 tablespoons orange juice

Beat all of the ingredients together, adding the fruit juice gradually, to make a thin water icing, then spoon over the cake while it is still warm.

ADULTS ONLY

There are lots of fruit-flavored liqueurs on the market now, which you could use in place of Cointreau: make a Limoncello glaze, for example, by using Limoncello instead of Cointreau and lemon juice and zest in place of orange. Or experiment with more exotic combinations, such as sour apple liqueur and clear apple juice, even Framboise liqueur with a little raspberry juice drink.

Or go for the clean-living option, and make an alcohol-free version by simply leaving out the Cointreau, and increasing the orange juice to about ½ cup.

Extra thick vanilla cream custard

This is a gloriously thick dairy cream custard that can be piped or spooned into everything from a simple éclair to elaborate layers of puff pastry. The secret to achieving that perfect extra thick pastry cream is to make a heavily thickened, sweet boiled cornstarch custard, let it cool, then beat in cold heavy cream to achieve a luxurious finish. Don't try the recipe without the muscle power of an electric mixer as hand mixing would take an immense effort.

⅓ cup super-fine sugar
½ cup cornstarch
2 teaspoons vanilla
  extract
1 cup milk

2 egg yolks
4 tablespoons unsalted butter,
  cut into pieces
⅔ cup heavy cream

In a heavy-bottomed saucepan whisk the sugar, cornstarch and vanilla with the milk until smooth, then add the egg yolks and whisk again. Over medium heat, add the butter and bring to a boil, stirring all the time, beating it furiously as it thickens to keep it smooth. Remove from the heat, tip into a bowl, cover and leave to cool, then chill until cold.

Using an electric mixer, gradually beat the custard with the heavy cream until very smooth, shiny and thick. If you want the custard to hold its shape for piping, chill it again for an hour before use.

Chocolate cream custard

Increase the sugar to ½ cup, replace ¼ cup cornstarch with cocoa powder and add 2 ounces dark chocolate with the butter to the custard.

Coffee cream custard

Replace half the milk with espresso-strength coffee.

338

Simple sweet shortcrust pastry shells can be filled with custard and slices of apples cooked in a little caramel, and the Chocolate Napoleon (page 407) absolutely needs a mixture this thick and rich.

Fresh cake syrup

Brushing a warm pound cake or layer cake with a little sugar syrup seems to enhance its soft moist texture. If you give the syrup a similar or contrasting flavor, it's a great way to boost a simple original taste into something much more intense. Gluten-free cakes in particular work well with a little syrup spooned on after baking. What I find works best is to make the syrup quite thick, and then thin it down with a little water or other liquid before use, and use just a little at first to avoid getting a wet cake. For an example of how this syrup can be used, look at the Rum Cake recipe on page 163.

½ cup super-fine sugar   flavoring (see below)
⅓ cup cold water

Bring the sugar and water to a boil, simmer for a minute or so to reduce slightly, then remove from the heat, stir in the flavoring and leave to cool.

To use, prick the top of the cake lightly with a fork, then spoon a little of the syrup over. Use 6 to 8 teaspoons of syrup for a 7- to 8-inch cake, or more if you prefer a heavier syrupy texture to the crumb.

FLAVORINGS

Try flavorings such as vanilla extract or vanilla bean, other essences and extracts from your pantry, spirits like rum or brandy, freshly grated citrus zest, spices like cardamom or anise, chopped toasted almonds or hazelnuts (left to infuse, then sieved out before using).

Homemade marzipan (almond paste)

The texture of homemade almond paste has an appealing roughness, giving you the realization that it was made with nuts, rather than some weirdly smooth artificial concoction. Still, to imitate the smooth rolling consistency and softness of store-bought, we have to add a few other ingredients. Egg yolks and glycerin help to keep the paste malleable and smooth with a delicate yellow color, while the corn syrup helps to keep it soft and stop it from hardening too much.

2⅓ cups ground almonds
1 cup confectioners' sugar
⅔ cup super-fine sugar
3 egg yolks
1 tablespoon plus
   2 teaspoons corn syrup

1 teaspoon vegetable glycerin
½ to 1 teaspoon almond extract
   (optional)

Mix the ground almonds and confectioners' sugar in a bowl. In a saucepan over a low heat, whisk the super-fine sugar and egg yolks until light and pale, then add the corn syrup and glycerin and whisk constantly until scalding hot but not simmering: this will cook and sterilize the yolks.

Add the almond extract, if desired. Pour this mixture in with the ground almonds and sugar, and stir or knead to a thick paste. Store in a sealed container and leave for 2 to 3 hours to set or, even better, until the following day before using. Knead again before use.

Easy lemon curd

Very simple to make, but keep it in the fridge.

1 egg plus 5 egg yolks
finely grated zest of
   3 unwaxed lemons,
   plus ½ cup lemon juice

¾ cup super-fine sugar
1 cup (2 sticks) unsalted butter,
   cut into small cubes

Have ready a large sieve placed over a clean mixing bowl. In a saucepan whisk the whole egg, yolks, lemon zest and juice with the sugar until evenly combined, then add the cubes of butter. Bring to the first "plop" of a boil, stirring all the time across the bottom of the pan with a wooden spoon to check it isn't sticking. Quickly spoon the mixture into the sieve and press through with the wooden spoon to remove the zest, then cover and leave until cold before using.

Orange or lime curd

Use the zest and juice from unwaxed oranges or limes in place of the lemon to give it a different fruit flavor.

PERFECT PARTNERS

The recipe for Lemon Meringue Sundae (page 452) not only goes perfectly with this homemade lemon curd; it also uses up the 5 egg whites you'll be left with.

Tripe and suet mincemeat

You know how everyone says, "It used to be made with meat"? Well, this one still is. The thought of tripe or tongue sounds odd in a sweet mincemeat, but it does taste good. This recipe is adapted from one I found in a dusty manuscript from the early 1700s in the Cheshire records office. If you must omit the meat, add the same quantity of roasted and chopped hazelnuts to give it a rich, smoky flavor, and use vegetarian suet. Make at least 4 weeks ahead of the time you plan to use it.

6 ounces fresh beef suet, minced
3 ounces honeycomb tripe
   or calf's tongue, cooked
   and finely chopped
12 ounces apples (Granny Smith,
   Bramley or Blenheim Orange),
   peeled, cored and chopped
1 cup raisins
⅔ cup sultanas
1 cup currants

1¼ cups mixed candied citrus
⅔ cup dark brown sugar
zest and juice of ½ lemon
½ teaspoon fine salt
¾ teaspoon ground cloves
½ teaspoon ground nutmeg
½ teaspoon ground mace
½ teaspoon ground cinnamon
¼ cup dark rum
⅓ cup good brandy

Mix everything in a large bowl, but hold back a quarter of the rum and brandy. Pack the mixture to ½ inch short of the top in some large sterilized jam jars with lids. Pour the remaining alcohol over the top, seal and store in a cool, dark place for 4 to 6 weeks.

Dark rich mincemeat

This is a very quick, suet-free mincemeat that can be ready in less than an hour for any last-minute mince pie making. Two different apples are used: dessert apples, which keep their shape when cooked, and a cooking apple like a Granny Smith, which falls apart when heated to create a rich thick sauce. The flavor is simple but you can intensify the spices by adding ¼ teaspoon each of ground mace, cinnamon and clove.

2 small dessert apples, peeled, cored and finely diced

1⅓ cups raisins

4 ounces soft prunes, chopped

4 ounces dried sour cherries

1⅔ cups currants

1 cup stout or ale

1 medium cooking apple, peeled, cored and grated

1½ cups brown sugar

grated zest and juice of 1 small lemon

1 tablespoon mixed spice (cinnamon, nutmeg, ginger and cloves)

4 tablespoons unsalted butter

3 tablespoons brandy or rum

Have the dessert apples and all of the dried fruit in a bowl, prepared and ready. In a large saucepan whisk the stout with the grated cooking apple, brown sugar, lemon zest and juice. Bring to a boil, stirring often, and simmer for about 5 minutes until the apple falls apart. Add the apple and dried fruit mixture, mixed spice and butter, and simmer until thick. Remove from the heat, leave until warm, then stir in the brandy. Leave to cool before using.

Double chocolate fudge sauce

The trick here is to give the impression that the sauce is simply hot molten fudge. The cocoa helps to thicken the mixture as it boils, giving the sauce a luxurious consistency and intense flavor. But you can overdo it with your choice of the chocolate you beat into it, so go for a bar that isn't too high in cocoa solids. For me, a good-quality milk chocolate is perfect.

½ cup cocoa powder	4 tablespoons unsalted butter
2¼ cups dark brown sugar	2 ounces milk chocolate
¾ cup heavy cream	2 teaspoons vanilla extract

Whisk the cocoa, sugar and cream together in a saucepan and bring to a boil, stirring all the time. Simmer for 1 to 2 minutes until very glossy and dark, then remove from the heat and beat in the butter, chocolate and vanilla. Either use immediately while still warm or leave it to go cold and reheat it gently to serve, thinning with a little boiling water to bring it back to a thick pouring consistency, if necessary.

Hot berry butter sauce

Though you can make a simple sauce by puréeing berries with sugar, there are times when you want to serve something warm and reassuring. Some berries need more sweetness than others, but you can easily add more sugar to taste once the sauce is made.

about 2⅓ cups washed ripe berries	¼ cup cold water
1 teaspoon cornstarch	1 tablespoon unsalted butter
¼ cup super-fine sugar	2 tablespoons brandy or orange juice

Pick out any stems or big seeds from the berries if you see them, likewise the stalks on strawberries or bits that aren't edible. If the berries are large, halve or chop them, then place in a clean bowl and crush about a third of them with the back of a fork.

Beat the cornstarch, sugar and water in a saucepan until smooth, then add the butter and bring to a boil, stirring all the time. Add the brandy and berries, stir until piping hot, then remove from the heat and leave to stand for 10 minutes so that the berries release more of their flavor.

BIG FLAVOR

I like to add a dollop of "matching" fruit preserve to the sauce, for example strawberry conserve if fresh strawberries are used, as this intensifies the flavor. If you need to store the mixture for longer, you can freeze it until it's required.

Classic caramel sauce

Possibly one of my favorite sweet sauces. To give this sauce the dark, rich color and flavor it should have requires a trip to the dark side of caramel making: cooking the sugar until it's very nearly burnt, and dark brown. What might help is knowing that even if you take the caramel slightly too far, it can usually be returned to the right balance with extra sugar and cream, if the burnt flavor is too overpowering.

¾ cup super-fine sugar, plus a little extra to finish
2 tablespoons water
1 cup heavy cream
2 teaspoons vanilla extract, or the seeds from a vanilla bean pod
a pinch of salt

Place the sugar and water in a deep heavy saucepan and bring to a boil, then cook for 6 to 7 minutes until the mixture turns a very dark reddish caramel color (see pages 299 to 302 for instructions). The caramel will start to smoke slightly and be just short of the point of burning black. Remove the pan from the heat and quickly pour the cream into the caramel. Be extra careful not to get hit by the spluttering.

Return the pan to low heat and cook gently until the caramel dissolves into the cream and the mixture is slightly thick. Then stir in an extra 1 to 2 teaspoons of super-fine sugar to sweeten the caramel to your taste, and add the vanilla and salt. Leave until warm before serving.

Vanilla custard sauce

I must be honest here; there's a degree of fear involved the first few times you make this sauce, as it is easy to overcook it so that little "scrambled egg" pieces appear. Made perfectly, it should be utterly smooth with only a very slight "body" to the custard, so that even when cold it only gently coats the surface of your spoon when poured, with little seeds from the vanilla pod suspended through it. This is essentially what chefs call a crème anglaise, a French term meaning a custard in the "English" style, which years ago meant a simplicity and leanness of ingredients.

For this recipe I've gone back to a French chef's dessert textbook from the 1930s written by Henri-Paul Pellaprat. Though the custard should be quite liquid, the recipe suggested using a little arrowroot to help avoid the yolks overcooking and curdling. Once you've got the knack of making it, you can leave the arrowroot out and replace it with an extra yolk.

¼ cup super-fine sugar
3 egg yolks
¾ teaspoon arrowroot

¾ cup whole milk
the seeds from a vanilla bean pod

Have a dish of ice water ready near the stove, to sit your bowl of custard in when it's cooked, and check that your heat-proof bowl is a good fit for your saucepan.

In a sturdy 1-pint bowl, stir the sugar, egg yolks and arrowroot together with a spoon until they are evenly mixed, but don't whisk them as the foam makes judging the cooking harder. Heat the milk and vanilla seeds in a small saucepan until simmering, then remove from the heat and whisk this quickly into the egg yolk mixture. Mix until smooth, then fill the same saucepan with an inch or so of boiling water, return this to the heat, and sit the bowl with the custard in it above the water. Cook over a very gentle simmer, stirring all the time with a wooden spoon, until the custard holds in a thin layer over the spoon's surface when lifted out. Immediately lift the bowl of custard and sit it in the dish of ice water, and stir it a little for a minute or two to cool it quickly. Once cold, you can keep it covered in the fridge for a few days.

Rich custard sauce

Replace the milk with heavy cream. This richer mixture will coat the spoon almost immediately, so cook only until the mixture appears thicker, piping hot but not boiling, then cool immediately.

CUSTARD CONFIDENTIAL

I usually do without the bowl over a saucepan of boiling water and just cook the custard over a low heat; much quicker but more nerve-racking. You may read that a curdled crème anglaise can be rescued by mixing it in a blender at high speed. It does regain its smoothness this way, and you should be able to fool your guests, but the texture isn't right as the gel-like emulsion is lost and the custard will be thinner.

Ice cream

This is the recipe I learned from Alastair Little when I was the pastry chef at his restaurant. The relatively small amount of egg yolk in the mixture keeps the fresh flavor of the cream and milk to the fore, making it a good accompaniment to most baked desserts. I like to whisk a little nonfat dry milk in with the regular milk, which makes the ice cream denser and smoother, as it helps the butterfat in the cream to stay emulsified as it freezes. If you have the time, make it the day before, and chill it in the refrigerator overnight before freezing, as that gives the smoothest texture. This recipe makes a large batch, because I like to make two flavors at a time.

MAKES AROUND 4½ CUPS
OF "BASE"

4 egg yolks
⅔ cup super-fine sugar
1 vanilla bean pod
1¾ cups cold heavy cream

1½ cups 1% milk
¼ cup nonfat dry milk
(optional)

Beat the yolks and sugar with the seeds from the vanilla bean until smooth but not too frothy, as the foam makes it difficult to accurately judge when the custard is cooked. Measure the cream into another bowl, sit a fine sieve above it, and leave this to one side. Bring the milk (and milk powder, if using) to a boil in a saucepan, whisk it into the yolk mixture, pour this back into the saucepan, with the scraped vanilla bean and stir with a wooden spoon until it's near simmering and the mixture coats the back of a spoon with a thin custard. If you have a kitchen thermometer you want it around 158°F. Only cook the custard until it just begins to thicken, as this gives a smoother texture when frozen. Immediately pour the custard through the sieve into the cream, stir well, then chill for a minimum of 4 hours or ideally overnight.

Vanilla ice cream

Simply churn 2 cups of the chilled base in an ice-cream maker.

Pandan ice cream

Pandan is the leaf of an Asian plant, used in cooking for its sweet fragrance. Buy it at Chinese supermarkets and freeze any spare leaves. Excellent served with fresh fruit, meringues and chocolate desserts.

4 fresh pandan leaves   2 cups ice cream base

The day before making the ice cream, fold and knot the pandan leaves. Stir them into the base mixture while it is still warm, refrigerate overnight, then fish out the leaves before churning.

Chocolate ice cream

Using a cocoa syrup enables you to make chocolate ice cream from a vanilla base, instead of having to start from scratch. Useful when making two flavors from one batch of base mixture.

½ cup cocoa powder

1 cup water

about ½ cup dark brown sugar

1 tablespoon rum

2 ounces chopped dark chocolate

2 cups ice cream base

Whisk the cocoa and water well, add half the sugar and bring to a boil. Simmer for 5 minutes, stirring often, then remove from the heat and add the remaining sugar to taste. While warm, stir in the rum and chocolate until combined, then mix with the chilled base mixture and churn.

Caramel ice cream

¾ cup super-fine sugar

2 tablespoons cold water

⅓ cup milk

2 cups ice cream base

Heat the sugar and water in a saucepan and cook to a very dark, almost burnt, reddish caramel (see pages 299 to 302). Right at this point remove from the heat, add the milk carefully as it splutters, then return to a low heat, stirring until you have a smooth caramel sauce. Allow to cool a little, then stir this into the chilled base mixture and churn.

Desserts

Desserts

Desserts fall into two groups, with a fairly fuzzy dividing line between them. On one side is fine patisserie, from delicate layers of crisp puff pastry to tender pieces of choux paste, elegant, precise and defined. In a scrum down the other end are the puddings, the rugby players of sweet pastry, the place where stodge is a good thing. Here lie the syrup-soaked desserts, the crumbles, suet crusts and sponge puddings, usually served straight from the oven or simmering pan to the table.

Fine patisserie can be roughed up too, and sometimes when I'm rushing that's almost inevitable. But as long as the flavor is deep and rich, it only needs a dusting of confectioners' sugar or a helping of softly whipped cream to keep it looking polished, while a sturdy dessert can be given finesse by baking it in individual dishes or just by taking extra care with its appearance or in the preparation of the filling.

Desserts complete a meal for me, and I do get a little grumpy if I'm in a restaurant and the chef hasn't given some thought to them. And, somewhere at the back of my mind, I make a mental note not to return. Yes, I should send an email and try to point out what's missing, but I suspect they won't get it. Many chefs view food in an entirely different way from their customers, and I've met only a few who have time for desserts that involve baking.

Chefs sometimes say to me that they fear putting good bread on the table, as there's a risk that people will fill up on a baguette and have no room for dessert. But those of us who order desserts are a different breed entirely, and will no doubt be studied by geneticists some day. We sweet-eaters valiantly suppress any overindulged rumbles from our digestion in order to try a curious dessert or a perfectly made pastry. In fact, the rest of the meal was probably merely a prelude that we tolerated until the sweet pinnacle was reached.

So that's where homemade desserts come in. All the flavors and textures you want on the plate, with second or third helpings just waiting if you want them. The perfect time to make use of extra ingredients, when there seems to be a mountain of lemons in the kitchen, plums ripening too quickly on the tree, or when the rhubarb at the market looked too good to pass up. A slab of pastry, freshly made or still cold from the freezer, lets you take this glut and turn it into the most welcoming of things: dessert.

So what I've done here is give simple all-purpose flour recipes for different pastries and then followed them with puddings that make use of them. Just as places to start, of course. Once you're comfortable with the rolling and fiddly bits, you'll think of lots of uses and variations. Though store-bought pastry gets us out of fixes, homemade is filled with achievement, pride, and only the ingredients you choose and prefer. That's why it tastes so good.

Different types of pastry are for the most part interchangeable, so even if tradition says that one particular sort is used, you can usually find a way of making another work as well. Though you can't quite make a chocolate éclair with shortcrust pastry, you could bake two 3-inch disks of shortcrust, spoon a thick pastry cream in between them and glaze the top with dark chocolate icing. I could eat one of those right now. Having said that, there are definite characteristics to each pastry type, and knowing a little about them makes it easier to find the right match with filling or topping.

Shortcrust is a simple, flat pastry that can be crisp or soft in texture, partly depending on the finesse or homeliness you want it to have. And, I suppose, the sort of home you have in mind. Typically, a French dessert or something rather glamorous and refined will cook the pastry to a crisp "snap," whereas for the old-school British table it would probably be less rich and softly tender. Shortcrust is usually made with butter but it can be made entirely or partly with lard. It differs from other types of pastry because it contains a large proportion of fat, all mixed in smoothly in one action. Best when you want an unfussy shell for a pie or tart.

Rough puff pastry has cubes of fat mixed randomly through the dough from the start, whereas "true" puff starts with all the fat in a single layer. Making puff pastry has a certain fear welded to it, as if it's the baking equivalent of climbing a mountain, but the truth is that both sorts are rather similar and surprisingly easy to do. Usually butter is used but it can also be made entirely or partly with lard. Through folding and rerolling the dough several times, it forms layers that expand when baked (whereas shortcrust has a much flatter, denser consistency). Ideal when you want a flaky interesting crust over a simple filling.

Suet crust is a kind of rough puff pastry that isn't rolled, but the tiny pieces of suet fat act like the flecks of butter found in rolled puff pastry. If you try baking a sweet suet crust, rather than steaming or boiling it, you'll see that it flakes slightly and almost gets a honeycomb texture as the suet melts.

Choux paste is a kind of thick cooked flour-and-butter emulsion that has whole eggs beaten through it. The yolks help to bind the mixture and give it richness and color, while the whites add some elasticity. What makes choux paste puff up is the water in the dough rather than the eggs. When the water in the dough turns to steam in the hot oven, it gets trapped, turning the choux paste blobs into pastry balloons.

Equipment

A rolling pin, a round-tipped metal spatula, a flour shaker and a couple of 1¼- to 1½-inch-wide bristle paintbrushes to brush excess flour off pastry and work melted butter into pans and for choux paste and meringues, an electric hand-held or stand mixer. All useful, verging on essential, tools for pastry work. Large, loose-bottomed fluted metal tart pans have two uses in my kitchen. They make removing tarts from their pans so much easier, and the bases are really useful for lifting large sections of pastry free from the work surface, especially when it sticks a little.

Get yourself a heavy-duty baking sheet. Aluminum is best as it's light and conducts heat evenly. You want the sheet to cover no more than four-fifths of the area of an oven shelf; there must be room at the back, sides and front for air to circulate, otherwise you'll stop whatever's on the baking sheet from baking evenly. Sometimes when you think you need a new oven, you might really only need a smaller baking sheet.

I use parchment paper rather than nonstick baking sheets and pans. I'm a bit rough when I'm cleaning up and I find that once a little of the nonstick surface scratches off, before long it all starts to come off.

A set of stainless-steel pastry cutters and piping nozzles makes a good if slightly bizarre present if friends wonder what to get you and your cupboard is already full of power tools or Manolo Blahnik shoes. And they're rather expensive; I don't know why. But they should last a lifetime (that's possibly why) and the sharpness of the cutters and nozzles will give you a really clean result.

Butter and other fats

Choosing the right sort of butter for pastry making is about finding one that stays slightly firm at room temperature, though there are tricks you can use to make softer butters perform better.

Typically, many European butters, like Lurpak and Président, are made from butterfat strained from soured or cultured cream, which gives the butter a fresher, deeper flavor, and they tend to be higher in butterfat: around 82 to 85 percent. The higher butterfat content means less moisture, which means that when used in pastry, it will be firmer. The souring of the cream also helps to produce butter that is more pliable and has more plasticity, making it easier to roll when cold without breaking into small fragments.

English butter might only contain 80 percent butterfat and is often (though not always) produced without souring the cream. It has a sweeter and creamier flavor and tends to be softer at room temperature and better for spreading. When you're using unsalted English butter, just remember these characteristics and slightly alter the recipe to help it. If there is additional water in the pastry, like in shortcrust for example, reduce it or leave it out if you feel your butter isn't that firm at a cool room temperature.

Lard, the rendered fat from pigs, makes pastry very crispy and can be used in place of the butter in a recipe. It does have a distinctive savory flavor so if you're using it in a dessert, you might want to use half butter and half lard to make the flavor more suited to a sweet dish. Mind you, in many traditional British desserts and cakes, lard was used on its own, so it has authenticity.

Suet is curious. Made from the fat found wrapped around beef and other animal kidneys, it has a clean smell and appearance, even when fresh from the butcher's. It's very firm at room temperature, and this means it can be grated easily into a mixture and will hold its shape, whereas fat from elsewhere on an animal carcass would be relatively soft, yellow and oily. The type of suet one can buy in packages in the United Kingdom, formed into tiny pieces, may have other fats (and probably wheat flour) mixed with it, and when labeled "vegetarian" is often made from palm oil. I use packaged suet as I don't have an old-fashioned butcher nearby to supply the real thing. If you're making something vegetarian and can't find nonanimal suet, use rough puff pastry.

Sometimes oil can be used in place of butter or suet, but it will always give a softer result as it stays liquid at room temperature. In a suet crust this might even be a good thing.

Flour

Choosing the right flour for shortcrust pastry is usually easy: just go for an everyday all-purpose flour. You can use bread flour if that's all you have, or mix in some whole-wheat or rye flour if you prefer a stronger grain flavor.

All wheat flour contains a compound protein called gluten, and generally for pastry making you want flour that has less gluten than bread flour. Short-crust pastry and choux paste also have ingredients and methods that play down the effects of the gluten. In shortcrust, the butter rubbed into the flour stops much of the gluten from forming in the first place, while with choux (and hot water crust), cooking the flour in boiling water inhibits the gluten's formation.

Puff pastry is a little more of a challenge. All-purpose flour will give you tenderness, whereas bread flour will be easier to roll but a little tougher. I think you have to be a slave to your pastry and choose the ingredients that give the best flavor and texture. Just use bread flour to start with, then try using half all-purpose flour and half bread flour for a more tender crumb, when you feel more confident.

Strictly speaking there's no need to use bread flour for choux paste: it won't give you a better rise, even though it contains more gluten. Yep, I used to think it did, but the gluten is made inactive at the initial stage of cooking in a saucepan. However, bread flour will absorb more moisture and make a firmer dough, which in turn will help the pastries rise better. But all-purpose flour is perfectly good for choux paste.

Suet crusts and crumbles can be made with almost any flour so long as the flavor suits what you're making. You could make a rye flour suet crust to line a dish holding a dark heady mixture of ale, beef, bacon and mushrooms, or add a little whole-wheat flour to a nutty crumble to make it darker with a distinct wheaten flavor.

Sugar

Though you can use any sugar to make pastry, your choice will slightly affect the results you get. Confectioners' sugar is the finest, dissolves instantly, and when used in pastry produces a very smooth rolling texture from the start. It makes pastry that bakes to a slightly firmer consistency than super-fine or granulated but if it's rolled thinly and baked well, it produces a very crisp result.

Super-fine sugar is the best all-rounder for pastries and desserts. It dissolves relatively quickly but can still provide a little crunch when sprinkled on pastry as it comes out of the oven. With shortcrust, it gives a slightly lighter result if the pastry is used soon after mixing, though if the dough is left for a few hours, the result is almost the same as confectioners' sugar.

Granulated sugar, the coarse everyday sort, is quite interesting. As it takes longer to fully dissolve, it can give you shortcrust pastry with a very light texture if rolled and baked soon after mixing, so don't disregard it as a lowlier sort than the others. When sprinkled on pastry, it gives a much heavier crunch when you bite into the crust.

Brown sugars can be used but you need to bake the pastry well, or strangely enough, it can come out looking a little gray instead of golden. Do consider Demerara sugar, or even larger crystal types, for sprinkling on fruit pies or into crumble toppings.

Cold hands and working with pastry

I have what you might call hot hands. When the room temperature is about 75°F, the temperature of the skin on my clenched palm is about 93°F, and it's rare for doctors to find patients with a skin temperature of 97°F or above unless they're doing heavy laboring in the bright sun. Typically our skin measures about 91°F in a neutral indoor environment. Yet I can still make and roll pastry with ease. But I meet people just like me, who say they can't make pastry because they've been told they have hot hands. That's just not true. The truth is: it's not about cold hands; you don't need to be constantly fingering your pastry, and reducing the physical contact while keeping your ingredients and equipment cool is what matters.

Cold eggs, cold water, even a cold mixing bowl and flour help, though they are perhaps a bit of an indulgence. You want the butter cool yet still pliable: not oily or spreadable, but not an ice block from the freezer either. When people say that marble is good to roll pastry on, they're talking about its coolness. But if you're quick and light, any surface is fine: wood, laminate or steel.

Cool mixing

No matter what temperature your hands are, simply aim to touch the pastry as little as possible. If you're rubbing in butter, stop as soon as the last few lumps vanish, using a rubbing action that lifts the butter and flour out of the bowl and sprinkles it back in. Be as quick as you can, with the lightest of actions. When you bring the buttery mixture together, be quick again and stop as soon as it's virtually combined, and don't overwork it.

The moisture contained in butter is suspended in an emulsion, and mixing shortcrust pastry as cold as possible effectively holds the moisture there and won't allow too much stretchy gluten to form, so you get the most tender crumb. However, you can also heat the butter with water, as in hot water crust pastry, and mix this with the flour when hot. This will make a more elastic and slightly tougher dough, but the quantity of fat will still ensure it has a delicious shortness if rolled thinly and baked well. But, typically, cold mixing is the way to go.

Resting, rolling and freezing pastry

You may wonder what all the calls for resting the pastry in the refrigerator are about. They're about making your life easier. If you roll shortcrust pastry out, poke it into the pan, line the inside with paper weighed down with beans and bake it in one swift transition without resting or chilling, then, with a bit of luck, all will be well. But for the times when you can't chance it, and it really must come right, the times when you don't want guests thinking, "Well, that tart was a bit crap," resting the pastry and keeping it cool will help you look good. Without the need for luck.

Dough is easier to roll, shape and fold when it's firm, cool but flexible than when it's warm and soft. Keeping shortcrust and puff pastry cold makes it easier to handle, your fingers won't poke through it like a spoon through a soufflé, and with puff pastry, keeping the butter and dough cold and ideally at the same consistency means that you should be able to fold and reroll it evenly. If the butter is too soft it has the tendency to squeeze out at the edges and through the dough as you roll it. And when you're rolling rough or "proper" puff pastry, you'll get a better lift if the pastry stays cold up until baking, plus sharper edges and neater scoring when cut. Really, the secret is cool working.

Rely more on tools like the rolling pin and spatula to move and lift the pastry, and once you've moved the rolled pastry to its final place, touch it as briefly as possible, and only with your fingertips. There is something pleasant about the feel of smoothly rolled pastry, but cut off a piece to fondle, if you need to do that. The pastry will be better off with as little touching as possible.

Freezing is also helpful. It's said that pastry shells shrink less when baked if frozen first. I haven't found this but certainly with shortcrust the dough seems to hold its shape better and is less inclined to slide down the sides of the pan. Back in my restaurant years, we always used to freeze shortcrust pastry shells, a few at a time, so that you could quickly whip up a tart if you ran out. A useful tip if you have spare tart pans is to keep one lined with pastry in the freezer.

Blocks of shortcrust, puff and rough puff pastry keep well for a few months if tightly wrapped and frozen. Frozen crumble mix is a great standby: I keep it in a bag in the freezer so if I have any fruit that is getting a bit soft, it can be stewed gently and turned into a beautiful crumble without any fuss.

Baking pastry

The basic rule for pastry is to give it a longer bake at a lower temperature to turn it a rich golden brown throughout. However, there are some exceptions.

I find that individual pies that have a semi- or fully-liquid filling that will boil out of the pastry are best baked at a higher temperature for a shorter time, because surprisingly it seems to be the longer baking that makes the filling bubble out. So if you need the pastry cooked more than that, you're best to blind-bake it first so that it gets a head start.

Puff pastry is best started at a high temperature for 20 minutes or until it has puffed well and started to turn brown, then you can lower the temperature and cook until the pastry is dry and evenly colored all over.

Equally for choux pastry, you get the best results by placing the choux pastry in a hot oven for the first 20 minutes. However, it then needs to stay in for a long time at a lower temperature until thoroughly dried out if it is to be filled, as the filling will make the pastry soft. Leave éclairs, profiteroles and choux buns in the oven until so hard that they don't sink at all when taken out. You'll think at first you've overbaked them, but within 10 minutes of the filling being piped inside and the icing layered on top, they will soften. Don't make slits in the choux pastry to release the steam, it doesn't help much as the moisture will still be in the crust. Better to reduce the heat after the crust has set and bake them until dry.

Blind baking

Blind baking means that a pastry shell is lined and baked or partially baked without its filling, so that the finished dish will have a flatter base and crisper pastry. Freezing the pastry shell first makes this easier.

With shortcrust pastry, if the butter has been mixed evenly through the dough, the only puffing that should occur is where it "domes" from the steam created where the pastry touches the metal baking pan. In this case, blind baking until the pastry sets on the bottom will stop this from happening.

When rough or puff pastry is used to line a tart pan, it is often blind baked to stop it puffing up all over. Though blind baking holds the pastry underneath flat until it is set, it doesn't remove the flakiness completely, so you should still get a beautifully crisp layered crust as long as the filling isn't too wet. Though puff pastry is rich with butter, I still often brush the inside of the pan with a little melted butter before adding the pastry, as this will slightly fry the crust's outer surface and make it easier to remove from the pan. Suet crust can be used in a similar way for baking, but will need the pan to be greased first.

Reusing pastry trimmings

If you're cutting shortcrust pastry and are left with scraps, you can just knead them together and reroll them, or wrap them well and freeze them. However, if you have just a few scraps, you might want to rub them with more flour and sugar to make a rough crumble mixture and freeze that instead, as I find there's more chance I'll use that than tiny pieces of raw pastry.

Puff pastry trimmings need a little more thought. Lay the scraps in a stack on a floured part of the countertop, flour the top as well, then gently roll the pieces together, flat. From here you can either wrap the block well and freeze for another time or roll it out thinly and use.

Steaming and baking

Steaming is more about trapping the moisture inside a covered mold to keep the pudding extra moist and tender without too much of a crust, than about surrounding the mold with hot water in a pan. So if your oven goes low enough, you could just cook the pudding in a dish tightly covered with foil, or wrapped in foil like an oversized sausage, on a baking sheet in the oven. The important thing is to keep the steam trapped inside and to keep the temperature quite low, no more than 300°F. Genuinely "baked" puddings are, however, about developing the crust and seeing it as a vital part of the dessert, either to set the shape or to produce a crisp or crunchy topping.

Meringues

Whisking egg whites into a thick meringue should be easy to do if you have an electric mixer. If it's a stand type, use the whisk attachments. You can make a meringue with a hand whisk but be ready for an outrageous amount of whisking that will tire you out.

Make sure the bowl and whisks are absolutely clean by washing them in hot soapy water, then rinse well and leave to dry. Any grease might stop the meringue from forming.

Whites separated from fresh eggs, without any of the yolk, are perfect and even better if left to slightly evaporate in a loosely covered bowl for a few hours or overnight, as this concentrates the protein slightly and will make a stronger meringue that's easier to use. A pinch of cream of tartar or a few drops of lemon juice will also help make the whisking easier.

Low temperature baking and cheesecakes

There is almost only one secret to a smooth uncracked cheesecake and that's long slow baking. I don't mind a cracked top so long as the flavor and texture are good, but if having no cracks is essential, try dropping the oven temperature really low to 300°F and bake it just until the middle rises a little. Then remove it from the oven and let it cool slowly.

Sweet shortcrust pastry

There's a delicate snap to this pastry once it's blind baked until golden, so when you use it to line tart pans and fill them after baking with custard, chocolate or fresh fruit, you're left with really good contrasting textures. But you can also fill this pastry before baking, say if you're making mince pies at Christmas or an open-topped fresh apple tart, and it then bakes to a tender softness with just a hint of crispness on the outer surface.

A lot of recipes for this kind of rich, slightly sweet pastry are much heavier on the butter. But I find that makes the shell very difficult to roll, and often just too greasy if you then want to use a rich or buttery filling, as the pastry draws fat from the filling during baking. So this recipe uses less butter, making it much, much easier to rub in quickly and lightly by hand. Egg yolks add a little richness and color, while the ice-cold water has the effect of making the dough very slightly elastic. While the crumb of the pastry may be a little tougher, it can be rolled thinner, and that in itself makes the pastry a joy to eat. I hope you'll find this helps to increase your confidence in your pastry making.

MAKES JUST OVER 1 POUND
  (enough for two 8-inch tarts,
  or 10 to 12 mince pies)
2 cups all-purpose flour
½ cup confectioners' sugar
a pinch of salt

10 tablespoons unsalted butter,
  cold but pliable
2 egg yolks
about 1 tablespoon ice-cold water

Spoon the flour, sugar and salt into a bowl. Break the butter into small pieces and rub this through the flour until it vanishes. Stir the egg yolks with the water, and mix this into the flour to form a very soft and smooth paste. Pat into a flat block, wrap well and chill for at least 30 minutes before using as it needs time to firm up.

Almond pastry

Stir ½ cup ground almonds into the mixture before the egg yolks and water are added.

Vanilla pastry

Add the seeds from a vanilla bean pod to the mixture with the egg yolks and water.

Chocolate pastry

To make just enough chocolate pastry for one tart, try the recipe on page 450.

USING SWEET SHORTCRUST PASTRY

1. Get your pan or baking sheet ready for the pastry. Shortcrust pastry is usually rich with butter so this should mean you don't need to butter the pan or baking sheet first. But if you're in any doubt then a light brushing with melted butter won't hurt. Have a thin metal spatula ready, or one of those removable bottoms from a fluted tart pan, to slip under the pastry when you lift it from the countertop.

2. Take the pastry out of the fridge and let it soften slightly. Try pressing your finger into the dough: it should feel cold, and indent when a little pressure is applied. If you have several pans to line, cut off just enough pastry from the block for one pan, wrap the remainder well and keep it chilled. It's easier to take more out when you need it than find it's gone too soft and have to chill it again.

3. Flour the countertop first. Get a fine-mesh sieve, or a small tea-strainer with some flour in it, so that you coat the countertop and pastry with only a light, even dusting. If you sprinkle the flour on by hand, aim to get it evenly spread, and when you sprinkle it on the pastry, smooth it out with your fingers.

4. Roll the dough out quickly and neatly while it is still cold. I press the dough out at first with the rolling pin, flipping it a few times and smoothing flour on each side. Then start rolling the dough out quickly. It will crack but these breaks will either disappear with more rolling or can be pressed together with your fingers.

5. Check the pastry isn't sticking as you roll it thinner by slipping the spatula under it. If the pastry is sticking, slide the spatula under it flat against the countertop, then roll the pastry up onto the rolling pin, sprinkle more flour on the countertop, then roll the pastry back down onto it.

6. Work quickly. The thinner you roll the pastry, the faster it will soften, so as soon as you get the pastry rolled, be ready to move it to the pan. If the pastry has started to warm up, you can move it onto a baking sheet and chill it, or just work even quicker.

7. Any pastry not immediately needed can be wrapped and frozen.

TO LINE A LARGE TART PAN

When the pastry is thin but still cool, about ⅓ inch thick for your first few attempts but ¼ inch or less with practice, roll it onto the rolling pin then unroll it over the tart pan. Now gently lift the edges of the pastry and ease it down into the shape of the pan while using your thumb (or a floured ball of dough if your nails are long) to press it firmly against the pan. Alternatively, if your pastry looks like it's tearing, you can cut it into pieces on the countertop, then patch them back together when they're in the pan, being careful to make sure you're not left with any cracks.

If you don't immediately get the hang of it, you can roll the dough between two sheets of parchment paper. Rolling between sheets of plastic wrap isn't advisable, as it's possible that chemicals called plasticizers can transfer from the plastic to the fat in the pastry. For the same reason, plastic wrap is not recommended for blind baking.

TO LINE SMALL TART PANS

Cut circles from the dough large enough to neatly cover the inside of each tart pan or muffin cup with just a little pressure from your fingers. Some cooks like to cut the disks first, chill them on a baking sheet lined with parchment paper in the fridge for 5 to 10 minutes, then line the pans once the pastry has firmed slightly. If I have the time, I freeze the tart shells for 10 minutes or even up to a few days before baking, as this seems to make the pastry less likely to slip down in the pans when baked.

TO BLIND BAKE A LARGE TART SHELL

Freeze the pastry shell first and heat the oven to 350°F. Line the pastry with a sheet of parchment paper or kitchen foil, going right into the corners, edges and up the sides, and half fill it with dried beans, uncooked rice or specially made pastry weights so the bottom is held flat and the sides are propped up. You don't have to get an utterly even layer of beans; as long as the pastry is pretty well supported that should be enough to stop it from slipping down. Bake for about 25 minutes, then remove from the oven and carefully lift out the paper liner, saving the beans to be used again. Return the pastry shell to the oven, lower the temperature to 325°F and bake for another 10 minutes or until barely cooked on the bottom if you plan to fill and rebake it, or longer if you want it extra crisp or plan to use a filling that needs no further baking.

TO BLIND BAKE SMALLER TART SHELLS

Freeze the pastry cases to firm the pastry, then line with paper muffin, cupcake or minicake liners according to the size of your pastries, and weigh them down with beans or rice. Heat the oven to 350°F and bake for about 15 minutes, then gently ease the paper liners and beans out of the pastry shells and bake for another 5 minutes if you plan to fill and bake the pastries more, or 10 minutes if that's all the baking they'll have.

Sweet gluten-free shortcrust pastry

A little cornstarch helps the pastry take on a rich color, and the egg whites slightly imitate the stretch you get with wheat flour.

ENOUGH TO LINE TWO
8-INCH TART PANS

1⅔ cups gluten-free pastry flour

½ cup cornstarch

1 tablespoon confectioners' sugar

½ teaspoon baking powder

10 tablespoons unsalted butter, cold but pliable

2 egg whites

a little cold water, if needed

Sift the flour, cornstarch, sugar and baking powder into a bowl. Cut the butter into small bits then rub it through the dry ingredients. Add the egg whites, plus a drop of water if needed, and work everything into a smooth dough. Wrap the dough and chill for at least 30 minutes before using.

HANDLING GLUTEN-FREE PASTRY

Gluten-free pastry does go a little crumbly when baked, so it's best used with fillings that have a little body to them and ideally ones that aren't too wet.

When you come to roll the pastry out, remember to use gluten-free flour or cornstarch to dust the work surface.

Malted chocolate and caramel tart

Dulce de leche, the sugar junkie's methadone, is whipped with cream cheese and swirled through a fudgy malted chocolate filling. You can also make little tarts, like chocolate Bakewells, tucking a spoonful of dulce de leche under the chocolate mixture instead of swirling it through. This is delicious with some really good homemade ice cream.

MAKES ONE 5-BY-13-INCH
RECTANGULAR TART

about 14 ounces Sweet
    Shortcrust Pastry (page 371)
flour for rolling
4 tablespoons unsalted butter,
    softened
4 ounces dark chocolate
¼ cup sunflower oil
1 cup super-fine sugar
¾ cup malted milk powder

1 tablespoon vanilla extract
2 tablespoons milk
3 eggs, with 1 separated
⅓ cup all-purpose flour
2 tablespoons cocoa powder
2 ounces cream cheese or
    fromage frais
¼ cup dulce de leche

Roll the pastry thinly, and line a rectangular 5-by-13-inch tart pan or similar. Heat the oven to 350°F. Line the pan with parchment paper and beans and blind bake for 25 minutes, then remove the paper and dried beans and bake until a pale golden brown.

In a saucepan, melt the butter with the chocolate and sunflower oil. Off the heat, beat in the sugar, malted milk powder, vanilla, milk and two eggs plus a yolk. Mix and sift the flour with the cocoa and fold through the malted chocolate mixture. Spoon this into the baked tart shell, then beat the cream cheese, dulce de leche and the egg white evenly together, and swirl this through the filling. Turn the oven up to 400°F and bake for 30 to 40 minutes, until risen and firm to the touch. Serve at room temperature, or barely warm.

Rice pudding tart

The starch from the cooked rice helps prevent the custard from curdling when you heat it. Do use whatever type of jam you fancy, and serve while still warm.

MAKES ONE 8-INCH TART

about 8 ounces Sweet Shortcrust Pastry (page 371)
flour for rolling
1 egg, plus 1 egg white
1 teaspoon vanilla extract
2 tablespoons super-fine sugar
⅔ cup heavy cream

⅔ cup boiled rice, cooked till soft and drained
3 to 4 tablespoons good soft apricot jam (or your favorite)
a handful of lightly toasted sliced almonds

Roll out the pastry on a lightly floured surface until it's 12 inches across, then use this to line a deep 8-inch fluted tart pan with a removable bottom. Trim the edges and pop it in the freezer while you heat the oven to 350°F. Remove the tart pastry from the freezer. Line the pan with parchment paper and dried beans. Blind bake for 20 minutes, then remove the paper and beans and bake for another 10 minutes until the pastry is firm.

For the filling, beat everything except the jam and almonds together in a small saucepan. Spread the jam over the bottom of the tart shell. Heat the rice filling mixture until just thickened, then spread this over the jam and sprinkle with the almonds. Turn the oven up to 400°F and bake for 10 minutes.

Raspberry ripple tarts

These are a great favorite in our house: white vanilla custard stirred with whipped cream, spooned into crisp fine shortcrust pastry shells and swirled with crushed raspberries.

MAKES 12

1 quantity Sweet Shortcrust
   Pastry (page 371)
flour for rolling
1⅓ cups milk
½ vanilla bean pod,
   split lengthwise
⅓ cup super-fine sugar

3 tablespoons all-purpose flour
2 egg whites
1¼ cups heavy cream
1⅔ cups raspberries
   crushed with ½ cup
   super-fine sugar

Heat the oven to 325°F. Roll the pastry out thinly and line the 12 cups of a muffin tray with circles of dough. Press a clean paper muffin liner into each cup to keep the pastry upright, half fill with dried beans or rice and bake for 20 to 25 minutes until dry and golden. Leave to cool in the pan, then remove the paper liners and dried beans.

Heat the milk with the vanilla bean. Meanwhile, whisk the sugar, flour and egg whites until smooth, then slowly beat in the hot milk, return to the pan and whisk until boiling. Remove from the heat, sieve out the vanilla bean, cover with a plate to stop a thick skin from forming and leave until cold. Whip the cream to soft peaks, fold through the custard and spoon into the pastry shells. Spoon teaspoons of crushed raspberries with a little juice over the tops and swirl to combine.

CHALAZA

After you cook any egg custard, it's a good idea to strain it as there's always a little thread-like part of the egg called the chalaza (it holds the yolk to the white) that has an odd texture when you find it in something sweet.

Bay custard tarts

Custard tarts are one of the true loves of my life, and always better when made at home. This recipe leaves you with plenty of egg whites, just perfect for making a Pavlova later (see pages 454 and 456).

MAKES ABOUT 8

½ recipe Sweet Shortcrust
  Pastry (page 371), made
  with lemon zest
flour for rolling
1¼ cups whole milk

1½ tablespoons cornstarch
¼ cup super-fine sugar
3 crushed bay leaves
1 egg, plus 4 egg yolks
a nutmeg, for grating

When making the shortcrust pastry, stir the finely grated zest of half an unwaxed lemon into the mixture before adding the egg yolks and water, then chill for 20 minutes.

Roll the pastry out until about ⅛ inch thick on a floured surface and cut out eight 4-inch rounds, saving a pinch of the dough to mend cracks in the baked shells. Press these gently into the cups of a deep muffin pan, then gently press a clean paper muffin liner into each pastry "cup," weighing each down with dried beans. Blind bake at 350°F for 15 minutes, then carefully remove the papers and beans and patch any cracks with the saved uncooked pastry.

Whisk the milk, cornstarch and super-fine sugar in a saucepan. Add the crushed bay leaves, bring to a boil, then leave to infuse for 15 minutes. Turn the oven down to 325°F. Beat the milk mixture with the whole egg and four yolks, strain out the bay leaves and fill the pastry cups. Dust with a little freshly grated nutmeg and bake for 10 to 15 minutes till barely set.

MAKE IT STICK

In this recipe, the pastry is deliberately baked a little less before filling, so that the custard slightly sticks to it. If the pastry is fully cooked, the set custard peels away from it on cooling.

Apple berry almond tart

The diced apple really helps to keep the filling of this tart wonderfully moist. If you have any fresh berries in season, scatter some over the jam in the bottom of the tart shell for a brighter flavor.

MAKES ONE 8-INCH TART

½ recipe almond pastry
   (see page 372)
flour for rolling
4 tablespoons unsalted butter,
   softened
⅓ cup super-fine sugar
1 cup ground almonds

1 egg
1 tablespoon brandy
1 large dessert apple
⅓ cup any sort of dark
   berry preserve
sliced almonds to decorate

Chill the pastry for 30 minutes, then roll it out and line the bottom and sides of an 8-inch fluted tart pan. Chill the pastry shell, then line it with parchment paper and dried beans and blind bake at 350°F for 25 minutes. Remove the paper and beans and bake at 325°F for another 10 minutes.

Beat the butter, sugar and ground almonds with the egg and brandy till smooth. Peel, core and finely dice the apple and stir this in. Spread the jam over the bottom of the tart shell, cover with the almond cream and sprinkle with sliced almonds. Bake at 350°F for 40 minutes until the filling is puffed and golden.

Strawberry tart

Each summer I long for the aroma of ripe freshly sliced strawberries as much as for their delicate flavor. Chez Savy, a very good tiny bistro in Paris's 8th, sometimes puts an uncovered strawberry tart like this one just near the door, and for me it signifies the uncluttered style of the food far more than any words on the menu could.

MAKES ONE 9½-INCH TART

½ recipe Sweet Shortcrust Pastry (page 371) or almond pastry (see page 372)
flour for rolling
½ cup milk
2 tablespoons cornstarch
1 egg white
¼ cup super-fine sugar
1 teaspoon vanilla extract
¾ cup crème fraîche
3¼ cup strawberries

Chill the pastry for 30 minutes, then roll it out and line a shallow 9½-inch tart pan. Line the pan with parchment paper and dried beans and blind bake at 325°F for about 30 minutes until a really golden color all over, removing the parchment paper and beans halfway through.

Whisk the milk with the cornstarch, egg white, sugar and vanilla in a saucepan till smooth, then heat, whisking constantly, till boiling. Remove from the heat, spoon into a bowl and cover with a plate to stop a thick skin from forming as it cools. When cold, beat in the crème fraîche and spoon this into the pastry shell. Hull the strawberries, slice them in half, and fan them over the top, cut-side and thick end down.

BEST RESULTS

Mixing the thick custard with the soft crème fraîche can be done by hand if you rebeat the custard first in a large deep bowl, but this is one case where I am wedded to my electric hand mixer, which makes it so much easier.

For a little extra buzz when you're making the pastry, you can use brandy instead of the water, if you prefer.

Extra rich mince pies

Adding cream cheese and ground almonds to a sweet shortcrust pastry, lightened with a little baking powder, gives a very moist rich crumb and a slightly sturdy feel to these pies. You hold one in your hand and it feels substantial and no-nonsense, and tastes heady and luxurious.

The secret to deep-filled mince pies is to bake them at a high temperature and stop once the pastry is brown and the filling hot. Leave them to cool in the pan and they should twist out when barely warm. Fiddle with them while they're hot and they'll fall apart.

MAKES ABOUT 9 OR 10

1½ cups all-purpose flour, plus extra for rolling

½ teaspoon baking powder

⅓ cup super-fine sugar

½ cup (1 stick) unsalted butter, cold but pliable, plus extra for the pan

3 to 4 ounces full-fat cream cheese

½ cup ground almonds

1 egg yolk

a little milk, if needed

2¼ cups mincemeat (see pages 343 and 345)

Measure the flour, baking powder and sugar into a bowl. Add the butter, cut into small bits, and rub it in with your fingers until no more lumps are seen, then do the same with the cream cheese, ground almonds and egg yolk until you have a smooth dough. Only add a little milk if it's needed to make a soft smooth dough.

Chill the dough for 30 minutes, then roll it out until about ¼ inch thick, before cutting disks of pastry 4 inches and 3¼ inches across, rerolling the scraps of pastry and cutting again. Lightly butter the cups of a muffin pan and line them with the 4-inch disks, pressing evenly into place. Fill each one about three-quarters full with mincemeat. Brush the rims with a little water, press the 3¼-inch disks into place as the tops, and pinch at the edges to seal. Cut a decent-sized hole in the center of each pie for steam to escape. Bake at 400°F for about 25 minutes until golden brown, then remove from the oven and leave to cool before easing the pies carefully from the pan.

For a gluten-free mince pie, use the Sweet Gluten-Free Shortcrust Pastry recipe (page 375).

For vegan mince pies, replace the butter in the Dark Rich Mincemeat recipe (page 345) with walnut oil. Layer four to five small squares of phyllo pastry for each pie, brushing between layers with a little sunflower oil and sprinkling with a little brown sugar, and press each stack into the cup of a muffin pan. Spoon some mincemeat into each pie, add slivers of candied cherries and almonds, bake, then dust with a little confectioners' sugar when cold.

Brandy and walnut mince pies with vanilla pastry

If time is really short and you need to use store-bought mincemeat, you can still make something, as this recipe gives the filling a bit of extra oomph.

MAKES ABOUT 10 to 12

2¼ cups mincemeat

¼ cup brandy

1 cup chopped walnuts

zest of 2 to 3 unwaxed oranges, finely grated

1 recipe vanilla pastry (see page 372)

flour for rolling, butter for the pan and a little milk and super-fine sugar to finish

Spoon the mincemeat into a bowl, stir in the brandy, chopped walnuts and orange zest, mix well, cover and leave for a few hours for the flavors to soak in.

Chill the pastry for at least 30 minutes, then roll it out till about ¼ inch thick. Cut disks of pastry 4 inches and 3¼ inches across, rerolling the scraps of pastry and cutting again. Lightly butter the cups of a muffin pan and line them with the 4-inch disks, pressing evenly into place. Fill each one about three-quarters full with mincemeat. Brush the rims with a little water, press the 3¼-inch disks into place as the tops, and pinch at the edges to seal.

Cut a decent-sized hole in the center of each pie for steam to escape, brush with a little milk and sprinkle with super-fine sugar. Heat the oven to 400°F and bake for 25 minutes or until a rich golden brown, then remove from the oven and leave to cool before easing the pies carefully from the pan.

Pear and ginger tart

Here's a great way to cut the pastry down a bit when you use mincemeat, at Christmas or any time of the year. Make the pastry and line the tart pan well ahead of time and keep it in the freezer, then simply bake it blind from frozen when you need it. Perfect with crème fraîche.

MAKES ONE 8- TO 10-INCH TART

about 8 ounces Sweet Shortcrust Pastry (page 371) or almond pastry (see page 372)
flour for rolling
1¾ cups mincemeat (see pages 343 and 345)
½ to 1 cup fresh white breadcrumbs
3 ounces crystallized ginger, sliced
1 large firm pear
juice of ½ lemon
a little super-fine sugar to finish

Chill the pastry for 30 minutes then roll it out thinly on a floured surface and use it to line a shallow 8- to 10-inch tart pan with a removable bottom. Line the inside of the pastry shell with parchment paper weighed down with beans and blind bake at 350°F for 25 minutes, then remove from the oven and carefully lift out the paper and beans. Return the tart shell to the oven, lower the temperature to 325°F and bake for another 10 minutes.

Remove from the oven, mix the mincemeat, breadcrumbs and sliced crystallized ginger together, then spoon this into the pastry shell. Halve, core and thinly slice the pear with the skin on and fan the slices over the top. Brush with lemon juice, sprinkle with super-fine sugar and bake at 400°F for 25 minutes. Remove from the oven.

Lemon tart

The intense lemon flavor of this tart is the perfect end to most meals, and if there was ever a desert island dessert, this would probably be it.

MAKES ONE 7-INCH TART

8 ounces Sweet Shortcrust
  Pastry (page 371)
flour for rolling
4 eggs
1 cup super-fine sugar

¾ cup lemon juice, plus the
  zest of 3 unwaxed lemons
1 cup heavy cream or crème
  fraîche
a little confectioners' sugar to serve

Chill the pastry for 30 minutes, then roll it out thinly and line a 7-inch tart pan with it, leaving just a few scraps over. Line the pan with parchment paper and dried beans. Blind bake for 25 minutes at 350°F, then carefully remove the lining paper and beans and bake the empty shell a little more at 325°F until the bottom turns a crisp golden brown (pale is a crime).

Whisk the eggs, sugar, lemon juice and zest and cream together, leave for 30 minutes, then skim off any froth. Heat the filling in a saucepan over low heat until very warm but not thickened, stirring constantly with a wooden spoon, then strain into a pitcher. Remove the pastry from the oven; use leftover raw pastry to fill any holes or cracks. Pour the warm filling into the tart shell and bake on a baking sheet at 325°F for 15 to 20 minutes until barely set (it continues to cook as it cools). Serve cold with a dusting of confectioners' sugar.

PALE AND INTERESTING

The whole eggs in the filling give it more of a "glassy" consistency, whereas egg yolks alone would give you something more opaque and creamy — still good, but not what I'm after.

Banana caramel cream pie

This is a lighter alternative to banoffee pie. There are loads of ways to make it your own. You can stir 2 tablespoons rum into the filling before it goes into the pastry shell, or if you're planning to demolish it as soon as it's made, toss some extra slices of banana in lemon juice and add them with the whipped cream before serving. If you want to go really bananas, try replacing the cornstarch with cocoa and beat in 3 ounces chopped dark chocolate with the mascarpone.

MAKES ONE 7-INCH PIE

½ recipe Sweet Shortcrust
    Pastry (page 371)
flour for rolling
½ cup super-fine sugar
2 tablespoons water
3 bananas, peeled and
    chopped into pieces

2 tablespoons unsalted butter
¼ cup milk
1 tablespoon cornstarch
¾ cup mascarpone or
    extra thick cream
¾ cup heavy cream
2 tablespoons rum

Roll the pastry out thinly and line a 7-inch round tart pan. Heat the oven to 325°F, line the pastry shell with parchment paper and dried beans and blind bake for 20 minutes, then remove the paper and beans and cook until a pale golden brown.

Heat a third of the sugar in a saucepan with the water and boil over high heat until the sugar turns to a dark reddish caramel. Add the banana pieces and butter and simmer gently until the banana is soft. In a bowl, beat the milk and cornstarch until smooth, then away from the heat beat this into the banana mixture with the mascarpone. Return to the heat, cook until boiling and spoon into the pastry shell. Bake at 350°F for 10 to 15 minutes until golden. Remove from the oven and allow to cool, then whip the cream with the rum and remaining sugar and spoon over the top to finish.

Soft crust apple pie

This pastry has a tender, almost pudding-like texture, and is really good warm with a spoonful of cold thick cream or fresh custard. Any tart dessert apple will do. I find the bright flavor of a Granny Smith works best.

MAKES ONE 8-INCH PIE

FOR THE PASTRY

1¼ cups all-purpose flour,
   plus extra for rolling

⅓ cup cornstarch

¾ teaspoon baking powder

¾ cup confectioners' sugar

9 tablespoons unsalted butter,
   cold but pliable

1 egg, beaten

FOR THE FILLING

5 or 6 Granny Smith apples

finely grated zest of 1 lemon

2 tablespoons lemon juice

2 tablespoons water

2 tablespoons super-fine sugar
   for finishing

To make the pastry, put the flour, cornstarch, baking powder and confectioners' sugar into a bowl. Cut the butter into small pieces and rub this through, then mix in the beaten egg, work to a soft dough and leave to chill for 10 minutes.

To make the filling, peel, core and dice the apples and place with the lemon zest and juice in a saucepan with the water and super-fine sugar and simmer until barely tender.

Roll two-thirds of the pastry out until about ¼ inch thick to line the bottom of a deep 8-inch pie dish, with a little pastry hanging over the edge. Spoon in the apple mixture, then roll out the remaining pastry and lay it over the top. Trim and pinch the edges, sprinkle with the super-fine sugar and bake at 325°F for 30 to 40 minutes.

Uppercrust apples

Perhaps the smart tarte Tatin started life a bit like this – as apples awash with buttery caramel, covered in a simple pastry. Don't invert it; serve it instead as a pie together with a tub of clotted cream. Quick, easy and delicious.

MAKES ONE 8-INCH PIE

½ cup (1 stick) unsalted butter, cold but pliable

⅔ cup light brown sugar

1¼ cups all-purpose flour, plus extra for rolling

¼ cup calvados or brandy

5 sweet eating apples, like Gala or Jonathan

¼ cup water

Take half the butter, cut into small cubes, and ⅓ cup of the sugar and rub this roughly into the flour. The odd lump of butter will make the pastry that bakes around it a little flaky, which is fine. Stir in the calvados, squeeze the mixture to a soft dough, then cover until the apples are ready. Heat the oven to 350°F, and get an 8-inch round pie dish out of the cupboard.

Peel the apples, halve them from top to bottom and cut out the cores. Place the remaining 4 tablespoons butter and ⅓ cup sugar together with the water in a large heavy-bottomed frying pan and heat slowly so that the sugar dissolves. Then boil until the sugar just begins to turn a dark golden brown and thickens to a slow bubbling caramel: about 3 minutes on high heat. Add the halved apples, remove at once from the heat, and carefully – using a long pair of tongs, and without burning yourself with the viciously hot sugar – turn the apples about until they are coated. Return the pan to the heat and let it bubble for a minute, then carefully tip the caramel and apples into the pie dish and arrange randomly. Roll the pastry out on a floured surface to about 10 inches in diameter, then lay this over the apples, tucking it in around the edge. Place on a baking sheet to catch the drips and bake for 40 minutes. Let it cool a bit before serving.

Chocolate crumble pear tart

Pears sautéed in caramel and brandy, baked in a crisp butter shortcrust shell and covered with a dark chocolate crumble. Serve with ice-cold crème fraîche.

MAKES ONE 8-INCH TART

¾ cup (1½ sticks) unsalted butter, cold but pliable

2 cups all-purpose flour, plus extra for rolling

¾ cup super-fine sugar

1 egg yolk

2 tablespoons cold water

¼ cup cocoa powder

6 firm pears, about 2 pounds, peeled and cored

2 tablespoons brandy or rum

Cut 10 tablespoons of the butter into small bits and rub it into the flour and ½ cup of the super-fine sugar. Weigh out 10 ounces of this mixture for the pastry, adding the egg yolk and 1 tablespoon of the cold water and working it to a soft dough, then chill for 30 minutes. Add the cocoa to the remaining mixture and rub it in well to make the chocolate crumble.

Heat the oven to 325°F. Roll out the pastry to line a deep 8-inch tart pan and blind bake it for 35 minutes, removing the paper and beans for the last 15 minutes.

Slice the peeled and cored pears into eighths from top to bottom. Heat the remaining sugar in a frying pan with the remaining water and cook until it turns a dark caramel. Add the butter, swirl it about, then add the pears and cook gently until they are tender, adding the brandy toward the end. Drain well and reserve any juice, then spoon the pears into the pastry shell. Spread the chocolate crumble over the top and bake at 350°F for 25 minutes. Spoon the pear cooking juice in fine drops over the crumble to serve.

DESSERTS

Hazelnut and plum tart

You'll have to shell the hazelnuts before toasting them for 10 to 15 minutes at 375°F.

SERVES 6

FOR THE CRUMBLE PASTRY
½ cup (1 stick) unsalted butter,
  cold but pliable, cut into
  cubes, plus more for the pan
1⅓ cups all-purpose flour
⅓ cup chopped
  toasted hazelnuts
¼ cup dark brown sugar
½ teaspoon baking powder
1 tablespoon milk

FOR THE FILLING
ripe soft red plums, pitted and
  cut into small pieces, making
  roughly 11 ounces
1 tablespoon cornstarch
¼ cup dark brown sugar
juice of ½ lemon

To make the pastry, lightly butter a 7-inch tart pan (with a removable bottom) and heat the oven to 375°F. Combine the butter, flour, hazelnuts, brown sugar, baking powder and milk in a food processor, or by rubbing the butter and dry ingredients quickly together with nimble fingers before mixing in the milk and nuts. Divide this mixture in half – cover and chill one portion, and use the other to line the bottom and sides of your tart pan by pressing the mixture into place.

To make the filling, in a bowl, stir the plums, cornstarch, brown sugar and lemon juice together. Spread the filling evenly over the pastry. Finally, crumble the remaining pastry mix evenly over the top of the fruit and bake for about 50 minutes, or until the fruit is bubbling and the top lightly browned. Remove from the oven and leave to cool before slicing.

MAKE LIFE EASIER

Use a tart pan with a removable bottom as the tart is still quite soft when freshly baked and you'll be able to serve it more easily this way.

Gâteau Basque

Sometimes all you want is a clean and straightforward flavor. The sweet short pastry breaks when rolled but can be patched back together in the pan.

MAKES ONE 8-INCH GÂTEAU

FOR THE PASTRY

1¼ cups all-purpose flour,
    plus extra for rolling
¼ cup super-fine sugar
¼ cup ground almonds
¼ teaspoon fine salt
¼ teaspoon baking powder
5 tablespoons unsalted butter,
    cold but pliable,
    plus extra for the pan
1 teaspoon vanilla extract
a pinch of finely grated
    lemon zest
2 egg yolks
2 teaspoons cold water

FOR THE FILLING

1 egg, plus 1 egg yolk
¾ cup milk
¼ cup all-purpose flour
½ cup super-fine sugar
1¾ cups ground almonds
5 tablespoons unsalted butter
1 teaspoon vanilla extract
2 tablespoons dark rum

To make the pastry, place the flour, sugar, almonds, salt and baking powder in a bowl. Add the butter, cut into small cubes, vanilla and zest and rub the mixture between your fingers until it resembles breadcrumbs. Add the egg yolks and water, work to a smooth dough, then wrap and chill for 30 minutes.

To make the filling, beat the egg and egg yolk together, save a tablespoon of this in a cup, then tip the rest into a saucepan with the milk, flour, sugar and almonds. Whisk everything together and bring to a boil then, off the heat, beat in the butter, vanilla and rum.

Heat the oven to 350°F. Butter an 8-inch tart pan, then take two-thirds of the pastry, roll out to ¼ inch thick, and use it to line the pan. Spoon in the filling, roll out the remaining pastry to make a top and lay this over the tart shell. Trim the edges, brush with the saved beaten egg and drag the prongs of a fork over the pastry in a "tartan" pattern. Bake for 50 minutes.

SHORT & SWEET

All-butter English puff pastry

If ever there was a show-stopping pastry, one that turned the simplest ingredients into something spectacular, it would be this. The same recipe works equally well with desserts and savory dishes, and seems to change character to suit the things paired with it. Roll a sheet thinly and cover it with a simple almond cream (see Apple Berry Almond Tart, page 381) and it tastes sweet and nutty. Cover a dish of chicken and wild mushrooms with it and it absorbs the flavor of the meat cooking under it.

This is the puffiest, lightest puff pastry I know, and not that hard to make. The recipe is based on an old English method from the late 1800s that varies slightly from the French puff pastry recipes from that era, in that it adds more of the butter when mixing the dough and, in turn, less during the folding and rolling. This makes the rolling much easier and produces a very delicate and tender pastry once baked, and one that I prefer eating.

If it seems like a lot of pastry, that's because it is, but it's much easier to roll a large piece than a small one and since it freezes really well, it can be made whenever you have a quiet patch at home and stored for use later on and you'll have the comfort of knowing that there's the making of a great dish, tucked away in the freezer.

MAKES ABOUT 2¾ POUNDS

4⅓ cups flour, half bread
    and half all-purpose,
    plus extra for rolling
1 teaspoon fine salt
2½ cups (1¼ pounds) unsalted
    butter, cold but pliable

2 teaspoons lemon juice, or
    ¾ teaspoon cream of tartar
    in 2 teaspoons water
1 egg yolk
¾ cup cold water

Place the flour and salt in a large mixing bowl, cut 9 tablespoons of the butter into small pieces and rub this through until the butter vanishes. Beat the lemon juice, egg yolk and water until combined, and add this to the flour (if using cream of tartar in place of lemon juice, add it first, followed by the beaten egg yolk and water.) Lightly knead to form a consistent dough, adding a little more water if the dough seems very dry (but aim to keep it firm). Wrap well and chill for 30 minutes.

Roll the pastry out on a lightly floured work surface to about 20 by 12 inches. Slice the remaining butter and lay this over two-thirds of the dough. Fold the unbuttered third of the dough over half the buttered area, then flip that over the remaining buttered third, so that the butter is wrapped inside the dough. Take a rolling pin and lightly roll the upper surface of the dough to press out any air bubbles. Seal the edges with a sharp thwack of the pin, then wrap the dough parcel well and chill for 30 minutes.

Lightly flour the dough and the work surface, roll the pastry out until it measures roughly 23½ by 8 inches, then fold the pastry in by thirds (like the blanket fold, see page 14) to give you a roughly 8-inch square parcel. This is called giving the dough a single turn. Place the pastry on a plate, cover, and chill for 30 minutes. Then give the dough a second turn by flouring the dough and work surface again, but this time roll the dough in the direction of the "unfolded" sides into a rectangle roughly 23½ by 8 inches, fold it in by thirds then cover and chill the dough once more for 30 minutes.

Give the pastry two more turns, each time rolling the dough in the direction of the "unfolded" sides, with a 30-minute chilled rest in between them. Then cover and chill again for one hour. Then give the pastry two more turns, giving the dough at least a 30-minute chilled rest after each rolling, before using or freezing.

PERFECTING YOUR PUFF

Like most things, it's in the details. There are a few tips that will make rolling much easier and help you to get a really good result.

1. You get the lightest pastry using a butter with a low moisture content, like Lurpak or Président. However, you still should be able to get a very good result with any high-quality butter that stays fairly firm at room temperature. You can use salted butter but the result will, of course, be salty. Try to get the dough and butter to roughly the same consistency as this makes rolling easier.

2. Ideally, use a fine-mesh sieve to dust the work surface and dough with flour, and have a pastry brush handy to brush off any excess. You want the surface of the dough you're rolling and the work surface underneath always covered

with a fine dusting of flour, without any lumps or heavy patches. Then when you fold the dough, brush away any excess flour, so the layers seal properly.

3. You want the dough cold when you roll, but with the butter soft enough to stretch without "breaking." This is hard to get right, and I find sometimes, on about the fourth or fifth roll, that the butter "breaks" and you can see it like stretch marks through a fine layer of dough. Not a huge problem but let the dough come back to room temperature slightly more next time.

4. Don't rush it: you can leave the dough longer between turns, even as much as overnight, so long as it's wrapped well to avoid a skin forming in the refrigerator. I usually regret it when I try to rush making puff pastry. Stretch the process out, and fit it in among other tasks in the day. And if you're really in a rush, make Sweet Rough Puff Pastry (page 409) or Light Spelt Rough Puff Pastry (page 497).

5. Sometimes the dough tears and the butter becomes exposed. This is either when the dough hasn't rested enough or when the dough becomes too warm. Best thing here is to dust a little flour over the broken patch, fold the worst of the break in upon itself, and chill the dough longer before continuing.

6. Always keep the edges straight and the corners squared, simply by tapping the sides with the edge of the rolling pin. That way the folds will be even and you'll get a better rise from your puff pastry.

USING PUFF PASTRY

Keep puff pastry in a block when chilled or frozen, and keep it cool when rolling as this will help the layers stay separate. For a really fine result, roll the pastry larger than you need it, then lay the sheet of pastry on a baking sheet covered with parchment paper and freeze it until firm but not rock hard. Then when you're ready to cut it to the right size and shape, take a small knife and cut progressively from one end to the other. Don't "guillotine" it with a large knife, as this will fuse the cut edge of the pastry together and it won't puff well.

MAKING IT SHINE

There is a trick to getting puff pastry to shine when baked, and it involves brushing a little egg wash over the top and letting it dry before it goes in the oven. I prefer using one egg yolk beaten with 2 to 3 teaspoons water and a pinch of salt, then left to stand for 5 minutes. The salt helps the egg to break down so it's easier to brush onto the pastry, and just using the yolk rather than the whole egg gives a much more intense and contrasting appearance to the wash.

If you intend to score a pattern into the top of the pastry, brush the egg wash over the chilled pastry first, then return it to the freezer for 10 minutes to set and dry out, then score it with a very sharp blade. That way, the cuts will puff and bake with beautiful crisp edges. If you score the pastry first and then egg wash it, the egg will clog up the scored lines.

USING UP PUFF PASTRY TRIMMINGS

The best way to rework puff pastry trimmings is to stack them, with the smaller pieces sandwiched between the larger ones, then reroll everything. Give the pastry a single turn before using or freezing. That way the pastry will be kept in layers and will puff well.

A REMINDER

Without going on too much about it, I would repeat: this pastry works brilliantly with savory recipes. The Supper chapter (see page 471) is full of fillings and toppings you can use; simply try pairing them with a puff pastry lid or base.

Apple turnovers

Brushing the tops of the turnovers with a mixture of egg white and confectioners' sugar forms a kind of simple royal icing that bakes to a pale tawny sugar crust.

MAKES ABOUT 8 to 10

6 medium-sized dessert apples,
   Braeburn or similar
6 whole cloves
¼ teaspoon ground cinnamon
juice of ½ lemon
2 tablespoons unsalted butter

1 teaspoon vanilla extract
2 tablespoons super-fine sugar
½ recipe All-Butter English
   Puff Pastry (page 399)
flour for rolling
1 egg white
1 cup confectioners' sugar

Peel, core and dice the apples into ½-inch pieces. Place them in a saucepan with the cloves, cinnamon, lemon juice, butter and vanilla. Stick the lid on and cook over medium heat until the butter melts and the apples have softened, without sticking or burning. Remove the lid, add the super-fine sugar and cook gently, uncovered, for another 5 minutes until the apple pieces dry a little. Then leave to cool before removing the whole cloves.

Next, roll the pastry out until a little under ¼ inch thick and cut out eight to ten squares. Lightly brush the edges with water and spoon on enough apple to cover the center of one half of the pastry, leaving a clear border. Fold the pastry over and press the edges together with the tines of a fork to seal. Finish the other pastries, then chill them on a baking sheet lined with parchment paper for 20 minutes while you heat the oven to 400°F. Beat the egg white and confectioners' sugar together, brush this over the tops, make one or two cuts to let steam release, and bake for about 35 minutes.

Use dessert apples as they will keep their shape much better than cooking apples in this recipe, or a mixture of Granny Smith and dessert apples. At the point where you would chill the apple turnovers, you can instead freeze them so that you have a dessert ready to bake for another occasion. Simply wrap each one in parchment paper once frozen, before bagging them for easier storage, and bake from frozen on a baking sheet at 375°F for 45 to 50 minutes or until the filling is piping hot.

Orange gâteau Pithiviers

This filling is based on a cake, flavored and sweetened with a cooked whole orange, which owed its first appearance in print to food writer Claudia Roden. The technique she used came from a handwritten recipe belonging to a Spanish Sephardic lady who lived near Claudia in Syria. I'd like to credit both women for my inspiration here.

1 small unwaxed orange
1¼ cups ground almonds
½ cup super-fine sugar
½ cup (1 stick) unsalted butter, softened

1 tablespoon all-purpose flour, plus more for rolling
3 egg yolks
1 pound All-Butter English Puff Pastry (page 399)
a little cold water

Boil the orange in water for 45 minutes, then drain and leave to cool. Chop the cold orange into pieces, then purée it in a food processor with the almonds, sugar, butter, flour and two of the egg yolks. Spoon into a small round bowl, then freeze for 2 hours.

Roll 8 ounces of the pastry out into a circle ⅛ inch thick, placing this on a baking sheet lined with parchment paper. Ease the filling out of its bowl (you may need to run the bottom of the bowl under hot water to loosen it) and center it on the pastry base. Beat the remaining egg yolk with the water and brush a little onto the edges of the pastry, but not onto the filling.

Roll the remaining pastry into a circle ¼ inch thick and just a little bigger than the base, place over the filling and press and smooth it into place, sealing it firmly around the edge with the tines of a fork.

Refrigerate the Pithiviers for one hour. Heat the oven to 400°F. Brush the top with the remaining beaten egg yolk, trim the edges of the pastry leaving a sealed 1¼-inch border around the filling, cut a penny-sized hole into the top and lightly score the pastry with a curvy sunburst pattern. Bake for 20 minutes, drop the temperature to 300°F and bake for another 35 to 40 minutes. Cool on a wire rack until cold.

WHAT IS A GÂTEAU?

This is usually referred to as a gâteau, even though to British eyes it may look more like a pie or covered tart than the traditional idea of a gâteau. However a gâteau was originally just a dessert where a basic dough or sponge was embellished with fruit, cream or another filling, in this case, oranges, almonds, sugar, butter and egg yolks.

Chocolate Napoleon

Once the pastry and custard are ready, you can be as simple or adventurous as you like with this dessert. You do need good all-butter puff pastry and a rich cream-laden pastry custard, but beyond that, you can keep it plain or enrich the custard with Marsala or brandy. The top layer of pastry can be covered with chocolate water icing or caramelized with super-fine sugar and a blowtorch, or dusted with confectioners' sugar and topped with berries. This is really a cousin of the vanilla slice, but here I've chosen to use circles of pastry.

1 pound All-Butter English
   Puff Pastry (page 399)
flour for rolling
1 recipe chocolate cream
   custard (see page 337)

chocolate water icing
   (see page 336)

Heat the oven to 400°F and line two baking sheets with parchment paper. Roll the pastry out until about ¼ inch thick and cut out disks, the size you want the Napoleon to be (small for afternoon tea, larger for desserts), allowing for a little shrinkage during baking. Place on the baking sheets, prick all over with a fork and bake for about 25 minutes until puffed and golden. Remove from the oven and cool on a wire rack.

Pipe blobs of custard onto half the disks, then top with the remaining pieces of pastry, pressed gently into place. Chill, then spread water icing over the tops to serve.

Custard sandwiches

You can simply cut the pastry into equal-sized rectangles, say about 2 by 4 inches, or 3-inch squares, and sandwich them together when baked and completely cold with a dollop of custard.

Sweet rough puff pastry

Rough puff pastry or simple flaky pastry is the easiest sort to make and gets its "rough" name from both the gung-ho way you drop pieces of cold butter in and then roll and fold it without worrying too much, and, subsequently, the rough way the pastry puffs and rises when baked.

But forgetting all that, most of the time rough puff can be used in place of classic puff pastry for a quick but excellent result. Though it can be made without the sugar and egg yolk, and using water in place of milk, I find that the recipe here produces a very delicate rich pastry that is good enough to be eaten on its own.

MAKES ABOUT 1¼ POUNDS

2 cups all-purpose flour,
    plus extra for rolling
¾ teaspoon fine salt
2 tablespoons super-fine sugar

1 cup (2 sticks) unsalted butter, cold
    but pliable, cut into ½-inch cubes
1 egg yolk
½ cup cold milk

Place the flour, salt and sugar in a mixing bowl and rub in about 2 tablespoons of the butter. Toss in the remaining butter cubes then mix the egg yolk with the milk and mix everything to a soft sticky dough while trying not to break up the butter cubes. Chill the mixture for 30 minutes.

Lightly dust the work surface with flour, then scoop the dough out of the bowl and onto it. Roll the dough out to an 8-by-14-inch rectangle. Fold it in by thirds (like the blanket fold, see page 14) so you have a piece of pastry about 8 by 5 inches, roll it out and fold it in once more, then return the pastry to the fridge for 30 minutes. Repeat this rolling and 30-minute chilling twice more.

Make sure the pastry is chilled before using it, or store it well-wrapped in the freezer and thaw it until soft enough to roll before using.

KEEP IT COOL

Though most of the tips about puff pastry making (see pages 399 to 401) apply in some form to rough puff, you can be a little bit more carefree when you make this. The important thing you have to watch is keeping the dough cool but rollable so the butter doesn't melt (too warm) or become brittle (too cold).

Sugar-crusted pear turnovers

An excellent way to capture the subtle sweet flavor of pears under a cinnamon-sugar crust. This recipe makes quite a stack, so maybe let some freeze completely and then increase the oven time by 5 minutes when you bake them.

3 very ripe pears, peeled, cored and finely diced
juice of ½ lemon
1 recipe Sweet Rough Puff Pastry (page 409)

flour for rolling
¼ cup super-fine sugar
beaten egg, Demerara sugar and ground cinnamon to finish

Stir the pears with the lemon juice then place in a sieve to drain. Roll the chilled pastry out until ¼ inch thick and cut into 6-inch disks.

Place a scant 2 tablespoons of the pears and a sprinkling of super-fine sugar in the center of each disk, keeping the filling ¾ inch away from the edges. Dampen the edges with a little water, then fold each piece of pastry over to form a half-moon and firmly crimp the edges together. Transfer to a large baking sheet lined with parchment paper, and freeze for 30 minutes. Heat the oven to 400°F. Brush the tops of the turnovers with beaten egg, dredge with Demerara and a little cinnamon, make cuts to let the steam escape and bake for about 30 minutes until puffed and golden. Serve warm.

CANNED FRUIT

Mixing the pears with lemon juice draws the excess liquid out of the fruit, which means that you won't end up with a filling that is too wet. Substituting drained canned fruit for fresh means you don't have to peel and core the pears, and you also get the right contrast between the crisp pastry and tender fruit.

Apple and mincemeat pasties

The combination of spiced pastry, apples and mincemeat makes these sweet pasties really delicious. Think of them as a brilliant alternative to mince pies. You can freeze the second batch, to finish and bake later; just increase the oven time by a few minutes when cooking from frozen.

MAKES 12

2⅔ cups all-purpose flour, plus extra for rolling

⅓ cup light brown sugar

1 teaspoon baking powder

½ teaspoon fine salt

2 teaspoons ground ginger

1¼ cups (2½ sticks) cold unsalted butter, cut into small cubes

1 cup cold milk

14 ounces mincemeat (see pages 343 to 345)

2 Granny Smith or Bramley apples, peeled, cored and finely diced

Demerara sugar, to finish

Put the flour, brown sugar, baking powder, salt and ground ginger in a mixing bowl, toss in the butter and stir in the milk. Mix until it just comes together, then chill for 30 minutes. Using lots of flour, roll the dough out until ½ inch thick, fold it in by thirds, then roll and fold again. Repeat this sequence twice more, chilling the dough for 30 minutes at the end of each set.

Line a baking sheet with parchment paper and heat the oven to 400°F. Roll half the pastry out to a 12-inch square. Cut this into six squares, brush lightly with water and put 2 teaspoons mincemeat in the center of each piece, along with some apple. Fold the pastry in half to form a triangle, twist the edges together to form a "pasty" and place on the baking sheet. Brush with water, cut two notches in the top of each pasty, sprinkle with Demerara and bake for 25 minutes. Repeat with the second block of dough and the remaining mincemeat and apple filling.

Little prune and cognac pies

Freezing the filling makes it less likely to bubble out during the longer cooking time given to this rough puff pastry.

MAKES 12

8 ounces pitted prunes, chopped into ¼-inch bits

a little boiling water

3 tablespoons super-fine sugar

2 tablespoons melted butter

1 teaspoon all-purpose flour, plus more for rolling

¼ cup cognac or brandy

1 recipe Sweet Rough Puff Pastry (page 409)

beaten egg and sugar to finish

Cover the prunes with boiling water for 10 minutes to soften, then drain well and mix with the sugar, butter, flour and brandy. Place the mixture in the freezer for at least 1 hour. Roll the chilled pastry to roughly 12 by 16 inches (1¼ to 1½ inches thick), cut out twelve 4-inch circles and press them into the cups of a deep muffin pan. Stack the pastry scraps with the smaller pieces sandwiched between the larger ones and carefully roll the pastry out, fold it in and, if possible, chill again before rerolling.

Divide the filling between the pastry shells, then top each one with a loose-fitting 1¼- to 1½-inch pastry disk, cut from the rerolled pastry. Brush with a little beaten egg and sprinkle with sugar. Chill while you heat the oven to 400°F, and bake for 20 to 25 minutes till golden. Lift the little pies out carefully and serve warm.

Sweet choux paste

It's probably fair to define pastry as any kneaded flour dough that is used to cover or wrap food before baking, while a paste is simply a soft, smooth, malleable mixture of ingredients, so I've come to think of choux dough as a paste rather than a pastry. *Choux* is French for "cabbages" and perhaps someone long ago thought that round baked puffs made from the paste looked like little cabbages. When I first started working in kitchens in the early 1990s, choux paste was deeply unfashionable and I was banned from making it. Well, the anarchist in me was aroused and I guess from that point on, I was hooked, making everything from the roundest cream puffs to profiterole mountains.

4 tablespoons unsalted butter	½ teaspoon fine salt
¼ cup milk	1 tablespoon super-fine sugar
⅓ cup water	1 cup all-purpose white flour
	3 eggs

Heat the oven to 400°F and cut a sheet of parchment paper or foil for lining a baking sheet.

Place the butter, milk, water, salt and sugar in a large heavy saucepan and bring quickly to a boil. While it's heating, sift the flour. As soon as the liquid reaches boiling point and the butter has melted, tip in the flour and beat well with a wooden spoon until a ball of dough forms that leaves the sides of the saucepan clean. Lower the heat and beat for about 30 seconds to let the mixture dry a little. Then remove the pan from the heat and leave to cool for 3 to 4 minutes. Next, beat in the eggs, one at a time, mixing each one thoroughly into the dough before adding another.

Line the baking sheet and while the mixture is still warm, spoon or pipe it onto the baking sheet in the shape(s) you want and bake for 20 minutes. Then without opening the door reduce the heat to 350°F and bake for another 15 to 20 minutes or until crisp and utterly dry.

HOW TO PIPE CHOUX PASTE

Piping choux paste requires a little knack, and this is what I do. Though you can pipe onto a buttered baking sheet, I find that parchment paper or aluminum foil cuts the fat down and gives a cleaner result.

1. Sit a metal baking sheet on top of a folded tea towel to keep it steady, and have a sheet of parchment paper ready to cover it. When the choux paste is made, dab spots of it directly onto the baking sheet in the corners and middle like glue, then lay the paper on top and press it down flat. Alternatively, you can cover the baking sheet with foil and wrap it tightly around the edges for the same effect. The idea is to make sure that both the baking sheet and the covering will stay utterly firm when you pipe the mixture.

2. Use a large pastry bag with a plain round or star-shaped nozzle firmly in place, and position it, nozzle downward, in a good sturdy pitcher to keep it steady, folding the open "sleeve" of the bag outward upon itself (as if you were rolling up the sleeve of a shirt) to keep it clean and out of the way. Spoon the warm paste into the bag, to roughly half fill it, then twist the open sleeve tightly shut above the paste, without trapping very much air inside.

3. Be sure in your mind where you are going to pipe. If you need to be really exact, just make little marks on the parchment paper with a pencil, or if you're using foil make tiny dabs with butter, using your finger. Otherwise just plan it in your head.

4. Pick up the filled pastry bag with one hand, gripping the twisted section firmly in a circle formed by your thumb and forefinger, so that you can exert a little pressure on the bag with the other fingers of that hand. With your other hand, steady the point of the nozzle and direct where the piping goes. If it goes wrong, drop the bag, nozzle first, back into the pitcher and start again.

5. Then I pipe the paste steadily onto the baking sheet, applying pressure from above and behind rather than from around the center. When the bag starts to empty and sag a little, I point it upward off the tray, tighten the twisted end, then turn the bag nozzle downward and continue piping.

6. There is a tricky bit. When you finish piping the éclair or bun, you need to quickly flick the nozzle upward, so that it cuts off the paste, before you move it to the next section, drop the nozzle down and pipe again. If the shape looks messy, you can smooth any jagged points down, using a small knife with a rounded end to the blade, dipped in water. Some cooks score the length of the éclair lightly with the tines of a fork to encourage the dough to crack evenly, but I don't usually do this, as I don't mind a slight roughness to the appearance.

7. Bake it past the point where it's golden, trying to open the oven door only a fraction to peek on its progress. Then lower the temperature to stop it burning, and continue the baking until it's thoroughly dry and hard. Remember, it will soften again once the filling is added.

CHOUX SHAPES

You can spoon or pipe choux paste for desserts into balls and fingers, large or small. Or even spread the choux paste thinly into 4-inch circles on a baking sheet, using a palette knife, so they bake into flattish pastry disks. Then sandwich them with thick whipped cream or custard, and fruit or chopped toasted nuts, maybe topped off with a simple water icing or just a dusting of confectioners' sugar.

Mini coffee Paris-Brest

These rings of choux paste have a crust filled with rich coffee-flavored pastry cream, and a crisp drizzle of hard toffee topped with toasted sliced almonds. Made at home they look so fine, and are really rather easy to make well.

MAKES ABOUT 6

1 recipe Sweet Choux Paste
  (page 415)
a handful of sliced almonds
1 recipe coffee cream custard
  (see page 337)

¾ cup super-fine sugar
2 tablespoons water

Heat the oven to 400°F and have parchment paper or foil ready for lining one or two baking sheets. Spoon the choux paste into a pastry bag fitted with a round or star nozzle that has a ¾-inch opening.

Line the baking sheets and pipe the mixture into wheel shapes 3½ inches in diameter. Sprinkle sliced almonds over them and bake for 20 minutes then, without opening the door, reduce the heat to 350°F and bake for another 15 to 20 minutes until firm and golden. Remove from the oven and leave to cool.

Cut the choux rings in half horizontally and pipe or spoon the custard generously into the bottoms. Pop the tops back on, then boil the super-fine sugar and water for 5 minutes or until a clear golden toffee forms. Drizzle this over the top of each Paris-Brest, let it set hard, then serve.

WHY PARIS-BREST?

This dessert was first made in the 1890s to celebrate a bicycle race from Paris to Brest and back, the first event of its kind, and the hollow shape is meant to suggest the wheel of a cycle. In this smaller size, you shouldn't have to pedal quite so many miles to work off the calories.

Black Forest éclairs

Cherries, chocolate and choux paste: the perfect threesome.

1 recipe Sweet Choux Paste
  (page 415)
14- to 15-ounce can pitted black
  cherries, drained well
1 recipe chocolate cream
  custard (see page 337)

1 recipe chocolate water
  icing (see page 336)
½ cup toasted sliced almonds

Heat the oven to 400°F. Fix a sheet of parchment paper onto a baking sheet then, using a pastry bag and a plain round nozzle with a ¾-inch opening, pipe the choux paste into 5- to 5½-inch strips, spaced about 1½ inches apart. Bake for 20 minutes then, without opening the door, reduce the heat to 350°F and bake for another 15 to 20 minutes until firm and golden. Repeat with the rest of the choux paste as necessary.

Remove from the oven and leave to cool, then split the éclairs horizontally. Halve the cherries and pat them dry on paper towels, then mix them with a little of the custard until lightly coated, and spoon some of this mixture along the bottom half of each éclair. Spoon more custard generously over the cherries, then replace the top halves of the éclairs.

Glaze the éclairs with the water icing and sprinkle with sliced almonds to serve. Best eaten within a few hours of filling, as this way the choux paste will stay crisp.

Rhubarb and custard buns

Drizzle the tops with a little plain water icing (page 335) if you like. The contrast with the rhubarb reminds me of giant white and pink profiteroles.

MAKES 8

1 recipe Sweet Choux
   Paste (page 415)
3 egg yolks
2½ tablespoons
   all-purpose flour
⅓ cup super-fine sugar

1 vanilla bean pod, split and
   scraped, with its seeds
1¼ cups heavy cream
8 ounces poached, sweetened
   and drained rhubarb

Heat the oven to 375°F and line two baking sheets with parchment paper, fixed into place.

Spoon or pipe four blobs of choux paste, each the size of a large egg, onto each baking sheet, evenly spaced, and bake for 15 minutes. Then, without opening the door, reduce the heat to 325°F and bake for another 25 minutes until the buns are brown and crisp. Remove from the oven and leave to cool on a rack before carefully cutting the buns in half horizontally.

Beat the egg yolks, flour and sugar with the vanilla bean pod scrapings and half the cream until smooth. Slowly heat the remaining cream in a saucepan with the vanilla bean until boiling. Remove from the heat, fish out the vanilla bean, beat in the egg yolk mixture, return to the heat and whisk till boiling and thick. Allow to cool, then spoon into the bottom halves of the buns together with an equal dollop of rhubarb, and replace the tops.

Hazelnut and coffee profiteroles

Everything can be made a few days ahead. Just freeze the unfilled balls and keep the custard and sauce in the fridge.

MAKES 26 to 28

FOR THE CHOUX PASTE
½ cup water
4 tablespoons unsalted butter
½ cup hazelnuts, toasted,
    skinned and finely chopped
1 cup all-purpose flour
¼ teaspoon fine salt
1 tablespoon super-fine sugar
3 eggs

FOR THE COFFEE CUSTARD
    AND CHOCOLATE SAUCE
¾ cup super-fine sugar
2 tablespoons cornstarch
1 tablespoon instant coffee
2 egg yolks
1½ cups milk
1¼ cups heavy cream, whipped
    to soft peaks
⅔ cup cocoa powder
4 ounces milk or dark chocolate,
    chopped
4 tablespoons unsalted butter

To make the choux paste, pour the water into a saucepan and bring to a boil with the butter and hazelnuts. Add the flour, salt and sugar, beat until the mixture forms a ball, remove from the heat and leave a few minutes. Beat in the eggs one at a time till smooth and glossy. Heat the oven to 400°F and fix parchment paper or foil to a baking sheet. Spoon teaspoon-sized blobs of paste onto the baking sheet and bake for 20 minutes, then drop the heat to 325°F and bake for 5 minutes more.

To make the coffee custard and chocolate sauce, mix ⅓ cup of the sugar with the cornstarch, coffee, egg yolks and ½ cup of the milk to make a smooth paste. Bring to a boil, whisking constantly, then leave until cold before whisking in the cream.

Cut and fill the choux balls with the custard. Whisk the cocoa, remaining sugar and milk together in a small saucepan, bring to a boil and simmer for about 5 minutes until it's the consistency of light cream. Stir in the chocolate and butter, leave until warm, then pour the chocolate sauce over.

Suet crust for puddings

This makes an exceptional pudding pastry. Corn syrup is used twice: first in the dough, then a little more is thinned with rum or whisky and poured over the pudding after cooking. Smashing stuff.

This is enough to line and make the top for a large traditional pudding mold (size 24, just over 7 cups), or a boiled pudding for 4 to 5 people.

2 cups all-purpose flour, plus
    extra for rolling
1 teaspoon baking powder
4 ounces suet

2½ tablespoons corn syrup,
    plus extra thinned with
    a little rum or whisky
2 egg yolks
½ cup milk

Place the flour and baking powder in a bowl and stir together. Add the suet, beat the corn syrup and egg yolks with the milk, then add to the dry ingredients and mix to a soft dough.

TO STEAM: Butter the pudding mold and place a disk of parchment paper in the bottom to stop the top of the pudding from sticking. Roll two-thirds of the pastry out until about ¼ inch thick and line the pudding mold, smoothing out any pleats before spooning in the filling. Brush cold water around the rim of the pastry, roll out the rest of the dough to make a top and lay this over the filling, pressing the edges together to seal.

Cut two large squares of parchment paper and one of foil, pleat them together in the center and secure them over the top of the basin with the foil on the outside. Wrap a few lengths of kitchen string tightly around and over to hold the covers in place and form a handle. Sit this on a trivet or old saucer in a large pan, pour in warm water to about 1¼ inches below the top of the mold, cover with a tight-fitting lid and simmer gently for 3 to 4 hours, checking to see that the pan doesn't boil dry. To serve, carefully lift the mold out of the saucepan and drain, then remove the covers, run a flat knife round the inside of the mold to release the pudding, and invert onto a large plate deep enough to catch the juices when you cut into it.

TO BOIL IN A CLOTH: This is a very old method for boiling a pudding. Take a large double layer of cheesecloth, run it under the tap to soak, then wring out dry. Open the cloth out onto the table and rub the upper surface generously with white flour. Lay the rolled pastry in the center of it, spoon on the filling, then lift the cloth up by the corners, pulling the edges of the pastry together and sealing them as you do so. All a bit tricky, I know, and another pair of hands will help. Pull the corners of the cloth together and tie them, and simmer in a pan of water for 3 hours. You may find that hanging the pudding from the handle of a sturdy wooden spoon placed across the width of the saucepan works best for you, so it is suspended in the water, and you may like to place the cooked, drained unwrapped pudding in a 400°F oven for 20 minutes to dry out slightly. Serve as directed.

TO BAKE: Roll two-thirds of the pastry out and line the bottom and sides of a large deep ovenproof dish, fill, then roll the remaining pastry out to cover the filling, pinching it snugly around the edge to seal. Brush with a little beaten egg and bake at 350°F for about 1 hour. Serve direct from the dish. To serve, pour the thinned corn syrup over the pudding once it's on the serving dish.

Steamed apple and currant
suet crust pudding

This is still one of my favorite ways of using suet crust, a wonderful way to finish a Sunday lunch during those cold winter months. I use a large traditional pudding mold (size 24, just over 7 cups).

2 tablespoons unsalted butter, plus extra for the mold
1 recipe Suet Crust for Puddings (page 424)
flour for rolling
7 or 8 large Granny Smith or Bramley cooking apples
1 tablespoon lemon juice
¾ cup super-fine sugar
3 to 4 tablespoons currants
corn syrup thinned with rum and lightly whipped cream to serve

Butter the pudding mold and place a disk of parchment paper in the bottom to stop the top of the pudding from sticking. Line with the rolled-out suet crust, reserving about a third for the top. Peel, core and dice the apples and place in a saucepan with the lemon juice, butter and sugar. Cover and cook over medium heat until the apples turn to a mush. Spoon the cooked apple into the suet crust in layers, each sprinkled with 1 tablespoon currants. Brush the rim of the suet pastry with a little water, roll out the remaining dough to form a top and cover the filling, sealing the edges of the pastry together.

Cover the pudding mold as described on page 424, and steam for about 3 hours. Invert onto a large serving plate with a rim to catch the juices. Spoon a little corn syrup thinned with rum over the pudding and serve with a bowl of lightly whipped cream.

Pond pudding

Sussex pond pudding with a lemon in the middle is better known. But the original just had a well of butter and brown sugar, sometimes with chopped apples or gooseberries added, trapped inside a crust dotted with currants. What I do is add a handful of currants to the flour when making the suet crust, then butter and line the mold as directed, and fill it with peeled and cored halves of tart dessert apples, ⅔ cup Demerara sugar and 9 tablespoons unsalted butter, and steam for about 3 hours.

Cherry dick

Make the suet crust and mix in 5 ounces dried sour cherries and 1 teaspoon ground cinnamon. Roll into a sausage, wrap tightly in a floured cloth and boil for about 3 hours.

Blackcurrant roly-poly

The roly-poly is a pudding style where the dough is rolled out flat to about ¾ inch thick, spread with a filling, and rolled up like a scroll. I spread the dough with a thick layer of blackcurrant jam, sprinkle a layer of currants over that, roll the dough up tightly then wrap it in a floured cloth and boil it for about 3 hours.

Marmalade and syrup
sponge puddings

Maybe you'll have some homemade marmalade in the cupboard, richly flavored after a few months of ripening. If not, buy a jar of something good that's rich in fruit, not just full of sugar. Serve piping hot with thick cream.

MAKES 7 OR 8

9 tablespoons unsalted butter, plus extra for the cups or molds

½ cup super-fine sugar

2 tablespoons corn syrup

zest of 1 unwaxed orange

2 eggs

1⅓ cups thick-cut marmalade

2 teaspoons baking powder

1½ cups all-purpose flour

½ cup heavy cream

Butter seven or eight old teacups or dariole molds and heat the oven to 350°F. Beat the butter, sugar, corn syrup and orange zest until light and fluffy. Beat in the eggs one at a time till combined, then beat in roughly a quarter of the marmalade. Sift the baking powder with the flour, then fold this into the butter mixture alternately with the cream. Divide the remaining marmalade between the cups, then three-quarters fill with the sponge mixture. Cover the cups with squares of foil scrunched down tightly in place, place in a roasting pan and bake for 25 minutes. Turn out onto individual plates or dishes to serve.

ONE BIG PUDDING

I like to bake these in old teacups in the oven, but a traditional big pudding does look impressive, and you get the wonderful sight of all that hot marmalade covering the sides of the pudding when you bring it to the table. Cover and steam in a pan as you would for a suet crust pudding (see page 424) but keep the cooking time down to more like 1½ hours.

Steamed chocolate pudding

An old-fashioned chocolate pudding simmered in a mold, best served with a hot chocolate sauce and very cold whipped cream.

4 tablespoons melted butter,
plus more for the mold
super-fine sugar for the mold
3 tablespoons cocoa powder
⅔ cup dark brown sugar

⅔ cup cold milk
2 ounces breadcrumbs
1 egg yolk
4 tablespoons all-purpose flour
½ teaspoon baking soda

Butter a 2½-cup pudding mold, put a small disk of parchment paper on the bottom and dust the inside with super-fine sugar. In a bowl whisk the cocoa and brown sugar with a dash of the milk till smooth, then stir in the remaining milk, breadcrumbs, egg yolk and melted butter, beating after each addition. Sift the flour and baking soda together, then fold this in. Scrape this batter into the mold.

Lay a square of foil on the work surface with a square of parchment paper on top, butter the paper, then pleat them together in the center. Secure them over the top of the mold with the foil on the outside, and a length of kitchen string tied under the rim of the mold and a second string looped over the top to form a handle. Place the mold on an old saucer inverted onto the bottom of a large deep saucepan with a lid. Half fill the pan with water, bring to a boil, then reduce the heat to a bare simmer. Put the lid on and cook for 1½ hours, checking the water every 30 minutes to make sure it doesn't boil dry. Carefully lift the mold out of the pan, remove the foil, run a knife around the inside of the mold and turn out onto a plate to serve.

SAUCY

The Double Chocolate Fudge Sauce (page 346) may be a bit rich for some with this pudding, so try the Classic Caramel Sauce (page 348), along with a bowl of thick whipped cream.

Pudding "pain d'épices"

Here, a French "pain d'épices" marries spotted dick and gets boiled in a mold in the British manner. Serve piping hot.

butter for the mold
3 or 4 cloves
3 or 4 juniper berries
½ teaspoon fennel seeds
1 teaspoon ground ginger
½ teaspoon each ground cloves,
    nutmeg and cinnamon
grated zest of 1 unwaxed orange
⅓ cup honey
5 tablespoons unsalted butter,
    softened

1 egg
2 tablespoons dark brown sugar
¾ cup rye flour
⅔ cup all-purpose flour
1 teaspoon baking powder
⅓ cup milk
½ cup currants
crème fraîche, or melted butter
    with a little brandy to serve

Butter the inside of a 4½-cup pudding mold and place a disk of parchment paper in the bottom. Crush the cloves, juniper and fennel to a powder with a mortar and pestle and stir with the spices. Beat with the zest, honey, butter, egg and sugar for 3 to 4 minutes using the whisk attachment on an electric mixer until light and fluffy. In a separate bowl combine both flours and the baking powder, then beat into the butter-spice mixture alternately with the milk. Finally, stir in the currants and spoon into the mold.

Lay a square of foil on the work surface with a square of parchment paper on top, butter the paper, then pleat them together in the center. Secure them over the top of the mold with the foil on the outside, with a length of kitchen string tied under the rim of the mold and a second string looped over the top to form a handle. Invert an old saucer onto the bottom of a deep saucepan, lower the mold in and two-thirds fill the pan with boiling water. Simmer for 1½ hours, checking the water every 30 minutes to make sure it doesn't boil dry. Carefully lift the mold out of the pan, remove the foil, run a knife around the inside of the mold and turn out onto a plate. Serve with crème fraîche, or melted butter and brandy.

SHORT & SWEET

Prune and Armagnac
sponge puddings

External heat creates steam inside the bowl of a steamed pudding and, when baked in a low oven, the results are impressive. You can prepare these puddings a few hours before you need to cook them.

MAKES 8

8 ounces soft prunes, pitted
   and quartered
⅓ cup Armagnac or brandy,
   plus extra to serve
9 tablespoons unsalted butter,
   softened, plus extra
   for the molds
½ cup super-fine sugar
¼ cup honey

2 eggs
1½ cups all-purpose flour
1 tablespoon cocoa powder
1 teaspoon mixed spice
   (cinnamon, nutmeg,
   ginger and cloves)
2 teaspoons baking powder
crème fraîche or thick cream
   to serve

The night before, put the prunes in the Armagnac, cover and leave to steep or microwave them for 1 to 2 minutes until hot. Next day, butter eight dariole molds and place a small square of parchment paper in the bottom of each to make the puddings easier to serve. Beat the butter and sugar until light and creamy. Beat in the honey, then the eggs one at a time, till smooth. Sift the flour, cocoa, mixed spice and baking powder together and stir this through alternately with the prunes and Armagnac. Heat the oven to 325°F, divide the mixture evenly between the molds, cover tightly with foil and, when you're ready for dinner, just put in a roasting pan and bake for 25 minutes. Keep warm till you need to serve them, with extra Armagnac poured over and a dollop of crème fraîche or heavy cream.

A simple Christmas pudding

This is a simple mixture from the 1930s, simmered to a cohesive richness. Go for the muscovado sugar and blackstrap molasses options if you want a dark pudding, or corn syrup and brown sugar for a lighter one. At the table, flame it with a little warm brandy, and hand round custard or cream sweetened with brandy.

SERVES 6 to 8

14 ounces mixed dried fruit such as raisins, prunes and currants

3 ounces suet

1 cup brown or dark muscovado sugar

⅓ cup corn syrup or blackstrap molasses

2 cups fresh brown or white breadcrumbs

⅓ cup all-purpose flour

½ teaspoon baking powder

2 teaspoons mixed spice (cinnamon, nutmeg, ginger and cloves)

1 teaspoon ground nutmeg or mace

2 eggs, beaten

½ cup grated carrot

½ cup blanched almonds or candied cherries

zest and juice of 1 unwaxed lemon or orange

½ cup dark ale

butter for the mold

Place all the ingredients in a mixing bowl and stir evenly together. Butter a 7-inch-diameter pudding mold and place a disk of parchment paper in the bottom. Scrape the mixture into the mold, cut a large square of parchment paper and one of foil, and pleat them together in the center. Secure them over the top of the mold (foil-side out) with kitchen string wrapped tightly around and over to secure the covering and form a handle. Sit this in a large pan on a trivet or inverted old saucer, pour water halfway up the sides and simmer for 3 hours, checking to see that the pan doesn't boil dry. Cool to room temperature, then store in a cool place until the big day — don't peek as this will invite bacteria — and simmer in the same way for another 3 hours before serving.

Plum plum pudding

So-called because most plum puddings don't, in fact, include plums. But this one does, twice over if you count the prunes (dried plums) as well.

9 tablespoons unsalted butter, plus more for the mold
¾ cup dark brown sugar
2½ tablespoons blackstrap molasses
2 teaspoons mixed spice (cinnamon, nutmeg, ginger and cloves)
a pinch of ground cloves
2 eggs

4 ounces chopped prunes
⅔ cup currants
⅔ cup raisins
the flesh of 2 large plums, roughly chopped
½ cup whole almonds or walnuts
1¼ cups all-purpose flour
¾ teaspoon baking powder

Melt the butter, then beat with the sugar, molasses, spices and eggs. Stir in the dried fruit, plums and nuts. Sift the flour and baking powder together then stir this through. Butter the inside of a 4½-cup pudding mold and place a disk of parchment paper in the bottom. Spoon the mixture into the mold, cut a square each of foil and parchment paper, pleat them together in the center and place paper-side down over the top. Tie it tightly in place with kitchen string under the rim of the mold, and tie another bit of string over to make a loop to lift it with. Sit it on a trivet or inverted old saucer in a deep pan, fill the pan with water to about 1 inch below the rim of the mold, bring to a boil and simmer for 3 hours, topping up with water as needed. Store it intact, without peeking, in a cool place until Christmas, then simmer again for 3 hours to serve.

CHRISTMAS CHEER

The fresh plums give this pudding a lovely flavor, but if you want to douse it in alcohol, go for something a little milder than "cooking" brandy — perhaps a few spoonfuls of calvados.

SHORT & SWEET

Figgy pudding

A kind of soft British panforte; serve piping hot with cream, then later, cold with a bit of cheese.

SERVES 4 to 6

4 tablespoons melted butter, plus more for the mold
super-fine sugar for the mold
8 ounces dried figs
boiling water
2 egg yolks
½ cup ruby port
⅓ cup dark muscovado sugar

2 teaspoons each mixed spice (cinnamon, nutmeg, ginger and cloves) and ground ginger
½ cup walnut halves
3 ounces crystallized ginger, chopped
1⅓ cups fresh breadcrumbs
cold whipped cream, to serve

Butter a 4½-cup pudding mold, place a small disk of parchment paper in the bottom, and dust the inside with super-fine sugar. Cover the whole figs with boiling water and leave for 10 minutes to soften, then drain, and chop them into quarters. In another bowl beat the egg yolks, port, muscovado sugar and spices, then add the figs, walnuts, ginger, melted butter and breadcrumbs. Mix well, then pack firmly into the pudding mold. Cut a square each of foil and parchment paper, pleat them in the center and place them paper-side down over the top. Tie down tightly with kitchen string, and place in a deep saucepan atop an inverted saucer. Pour boiling water into the pan halfway up the mold and simmer gently for 1½ hours, topping off the water as needed. Cook the pudding any time before the day and leave at room temperature once cooled so long as the foil top stays intact and undisturbed. On the day simply pop it back in the pot and simmer for another 1½ hours. Then remove the string and foil, run a knife around the inside of the mold, invert onto a plate and, holding it firmly in place with a cloth, shake it up and down to release it. Serve with whipped cream.

SHORT & SWEET

Sticky prune and orange pudding

A plummy baked sponge is covered with orange butterscotch sauce and popped back into a hot oven till the sauce bubbles like sugary lava. Serve with crème fraîche. You can always make the sponge and the sauce in advance, then combine and reheat them at the last moment.

FOR THE PUDDING
1½ cups chopped pitted prunes
1 cup boiling water
9 tablespoons unsalted butter, softened, plus extra for the baking dish
1¼ cups dark muscovado sugar
2 tablespoons blackstrap molasses
zest of 4 unwaxed oranges
1 egg
2 cups all-purpose flour
2 teaspoons baking powder
1 teaspoon cinnamon

FOR THE SAUCE
juice of 4 oranges
3 tablespoons all-purpose flour
1 cup light brown sugar
4 tablespoons unsalted butter
1 cup heavy cream
⅓ cup Cointreau

crème fraîche to serve

To make the pudding, put the prunes in a small bowl, cover with the boiling water, and leave until mushy (about 30 minutes). Cream the 9 tablespoons butter with the muscovado sugar, molasses and orange zest, then beat in the egg. Add the prunes and water with the flour, baking powder and cinnamon and fold into the butter mixture until evenly combined. Butter a 3- to 4-inch-deep, 9½-inch-diameter pudding dish, line the bottom with parchment paper, and spoon in the mixture. Heat the oven to 350°F and bake for 1 hour or until a skewer comes out with just the odd crumb attached.

To make the sauce, whisk the orange juice, flour and brown sugar together, then boil till reduced by a third. Add the butter, boil for another minute or so, then remove from the heat and stir in the cream and Cointreau.

Turn the sponge out of the dish, cut it into large chunks, discard the paper and arrange the pieces back in the pudding dish. Spoon most of the sauce over (serving any left over in a small pitcher) and bake for 15 to 20 minutes at 350°F.

Cherry and polenta pudding

This is like a crust-free tart, baked in a springform cake pan. Cooking the cherries first stops them from hardening when cooked with the jam, so you end up with a lush, soft filling. It does dry out quickly so, if you're not going to eat it all on the day, wrap it up well to keep it soft and moist.

½ cup (1 stick) unsalted butter, softened, plus more for the pan
¾ cup all-purpose flour, plus more for the pan
8 ounces pitted fresh cherries, or drained canned cherries
¼ cup water
¼ cup cherry jam (the good stuff)

1 cup super-fine sugar
2 eggs
⅓ cup polenta or cornmeal
½ teaspoon baking powder
1¼ cups ground almonds
½ cup milk
a handful pine nuts or sliced almonds
a little grappa to serve

Butter and flour the inside of a 9½-diameter springform cake pan. Place the cherries and water in a saucepan, bring to a boil, then simmer for about 5 minutes until the liquid has virtually evaporated. Add the jam, stir until it melts, then remove and leave to cool. In a bowl, cream the butter and sugar with the eggs until fluffy, then mix the polenta, flour, baking powder and almonds together and beat this through the butter mixture alternately with the milk. Spoon this into the pan, smoothing it up to the edges then, with a teaspoon, make swirling indentations or "rivers" through it. Fill these with the cherry compote, then scatter the nuts over the top. Heat the oven to 350°F and bake for 30 minutes or until just firm. Spoon a little grappa over when cool.

THE RIGHT PAN

A springform cake pan has a clip on the outside, fastened to hold the bottom tightly in place, then loosened to release the base. If you don't have one, line a regular cake pan with parchment paper.

Saucy monkey

What could be better than hot sugary buttered nutty bananas, topped with a banana chocolate sponge?

2 tablespoons unsalted butter,
   plus 5 tablespoons, softened
3 bananas; 1 banana, peeled
   and chopped, 2 bananas,
   peeled and mashed
¾ cup muscovado sugar
¼ cup super-fine sugar
⅓ cup brazil nuts,
   finely chopped

1 egg
¾ cup all-purpose flour
2 teaspoons baking powder
2 tablespoons cocoa powder
1 ounce rum
   (or milk, if you prefer)
⅔ cup boiling water
whipped cream to serve

Take a deep oval baking dish about 12 inches long and spread 2 tablespoons of the butter over the bottom, followed by the chopped banana. Mix together ¼ cup of the muscovado sugar, the super-fine sugar and brazil nuts, and sprinkle two-thirds over the bottom, saving the remainder for the top.

Heat the oven to 375°F. With an electric mixer, beat together the 5 tablespoons butter, ½ cup muscovado sugar and egg for 5 minutes until creamy and the sugar has dissolved. Beat in the mashed bananas. Sift the flour, baking powder and cocoa together and beat half through the mix. Stir in the rum, then stir in the remaining flour mixture until smooth. Spread the mashed banana mix over the nuts and sugar, leaving a gap between the mixture and the sides of the dish. Pour the boiling water into the gap around the mixture, then sprinkle the remaining sugar and nuts over the top. Bake for 35 to 40 minutes with the baking dish on a baking sheet to catch any bubbling over, until the pudding has risen and set. Serve with a little softly whipped cream.

Crumble mix

This might sound like traditional recipe heresy but I prefer a crumble mixture rubbed together with a spoonful of liquid in it, preferably heavy cream, but whole milk will do. And if I have a spare yolk in the fridge, I'll rub that in too. The reason I do this is that it stops the topping from being too powdery and makes it, well, more crumbly. Don't overdo it, though, or you'll have a ball of dough. So just a spoonful or two, rubbed in at the end to very slightly moisten the flour.

2 cups all-purpose flour
a pinch of salt
½ cup super-fine sugar

9 tablespoons unsalted butter, softened
1 to 2 tablespoons heavy cream or whole milk

Sift the flour and salt into a bowl. Add the sugar and rub in the butter until combined and the mixture resembles fine breadcrumbs. Spoon in the cream and rub this through well until the mixture is crumbly. Chill for 30 minutes.

Uses

Crumble the topping over the cooked warm fruit of your choice, and bake at 400°F for about 30 to 35 minutes until the fruit is bubbling and the topping golden brown. Or try scattering it over the top of a cake, cheesecake or muffins before baking, to give a crunchier finish. Or lightly egg-wash the pastry on something like an apple turnover and give it a sprinkle of crumble mix. The mixture may draw moisture from whatever's underneath it, so you may need to allow an extra spoonful of liquid in your basic recipe. Experiment with adding a little cinnamon or another spice to the mix, or by using brown sugar, or adding some chopped nuts or even chocolate chips.

You'll sometimes see the term "streusel topping," more common in American baking, which comes from the German word "streuen," to scatter or strew. And that's what crumble is, a streusel topping that is scattered rather than rolled out.

Damson cobbler with oat
and hazelnut crumble

Here's an idea to encourage you to experiment with a variation on the basic crumble mix recipe.

1¾ pounds damsons or other dark-skinned plums, pitted and chopped
½ cup super-fine sugar
1 cup hazelnuts
1¼ cups rolled oats
2 cups all-purpose flour
a pinch of salt
½ cup light brown sugar
9 tablespoons unsalted butter, softened
1 to 2 tablespoons heavy cream or whole milk

Place the fruit in a saucepan with the super-fine sugar and slowly heat until the mixture is hot and the plums have burst and are soft. Spoon the cooked fruit into an 8-inch round ovenproof dish, deep enough to leave about 1 inch of space above the cooked fruit. Set aside.

Roast the hazelnuts on a baking sheet in the oven at 400°F for 15 to 20 minutes until the skins darken. Remove, tip onto a tea towel and rub to flake off the skins. Pick out the toasted kernels and chop them roughly, then add the nuts and the rolled oats to the sifted flour and salt in a mixing bowl. Add the brown sugar and rub in the butter until combined and the mixture resembles fine breadcrumbs. Spoon in the cream and rub this through well until the mixture is crumbly. Chill for 30 minutes, then crumble the topping over the damsons, and bake at 400°F for 30 to 35 minutes until the fruit is bubbling and the topping golden brown.

Meringues

You could make a good meringue with a hand whisk, lots of elbow grease and effort. But if you really want it trouble-free, then buy an electric mixer, handheld or stand type. Even the cheapest machine will transform your meringues. Add the super-fine sugar gradually and whisk well after each lot is added, until the mixture is clearly much thicker than before. I warm the egg whites slightly, as this helps the protein inside to form a stronger structure when whisked. Finally, fold in the confectioners' sugar and any other ingredients as quickly and lightly as you can, and stop as soon it's barely mixed. The meringues will keep for several days in an airtight container and also freeze surprisingly well.

MAKES 6 to 8
3 egg whites
⅔ cup super-fine sugar

½ cup confectioners' sugar

Beat the egg whites to soft peaks then slowly add the super-fine sugar, about a quarter at a time, until the mixture is very thick, smooth and glossy. Sift the confectioners' sugar into the bowl and fold through gently. Spoon blobs onto a foil-lined baking sheet and bake at 250°F for 1½ to 2 hours.

Double chocolate

Barely melt 4 ounces of chocolate and gently fold this into the meringue mixture, so the mixture is streaked, then spoon onto the baking sheet and lightly dust each meringue on one side with cocoa powder.

Lemon sherbet

Finely grate the zest of a lemon, mix it with ¼ cup super-fine sugar and leave on a baking sheet, uncovered, overnight. Fold the finely grated zest of two more lemons into your meringues when you make them, then rub the sherbet mixture between your fingers and sprinkle a little over each meringue before baking.

Pistachio sundae

Make mock pistachio coloring by whizzing ½ ounce clean raw spinach, ½ teaspoon lemon juice and a drop of almond extract with 2 tablespoons water and 2 tablespoons super-fine sugar until utterly smooth. Strain and discard any coarse bits, then drizzle and swirl a little onto each meringue with a sprinkle of slivered pistachios before baking.

WHITE MAGIC

If you really want the meringue to whip easily, leave the egg whites out overnight at room temperature, loosely covered in a bowl. You'll get more volume this way.

Miniature rose meringues with strawberries and cream

You can make these meringues extra small and mix them with chopped-up strawberries and thick heavy cream or soft yogurt ice cream for a light summer sundae.

2 egg whites
⅓ cup super-fine sugar
2 teaspoons rosewater
a tiny drop of red food
    coloring (optional)

½ cup confectioners' sugar
fresh strawberries and cream
    or frozen yogurt to serve

Line one or two baking sheets with foil. Beat the egg whites to soft peaks with an electric mixer, then slowly beat in the super-fine sugar, about a quarter at a time, until the mixture is very thick, smooth and glossy. Then spoon a third into another bowl and beat the rosewater and food coloring into it.

Fold this very gently into the main batch, then sift and fold in the confectioners' sugar. Spoon rounded teaspoons of the meringue onto the foil-lined baking sheet and bake at 250°F for 1½ to 2 hours. Leave to cool on the baking sheet.

ROSEWATER

If you have a South Asian food shop near you, see if they have rosewater as I've found it has a much more pronounced flavor than the sort you can buy at most mainstream supermarkets.

Blueberry cocoa meringue pie

The custard turns a vivid purple-blue and has a slightly tart fruit flavor that goes well with the soft sweetness of the meringue. Best served when barely warm. For extra flavor make it with a chocolate pastry shell.

½ recipe Sweet Shortcrust
    Pastry (page 371)
flour for rolling

FOR THE CUSTARD
½ cup milk
3 egg yolks
2 tablespoons all-purpose flour
1 tablespoon cornstarch
3 tablespoons super-fine sugar
1½ cups crème fraîche
2⅓ cups fresh blueberries

FOR THE MERINGUE
3 egg whites
⅔ cup super-fine sugar
1 tablespoon cornstarch

a little cocoa

Roll the pastry out thinly and line a deep 8-inch round tart pan. Heat the oven to 350°F. Line the shell with parchment paper and beans and blind bake for 25 minutes, then remove the paper and cook until a pale golden brown. Allow to cool and leave in the pan.

To make the custard, whisk the milk, egg yolks, flour, cornstarch, sugar and crème fraîche in a saucepan until smooth, then bring to a boil. Add the blueberries and cook, stirring constantly and squashing the berries until they burst and the color turns deep purple. Then spoon the hot blueberry custard into the pastry shell.

To make the meringue, whisk the egg whites to a thick froth with an electric mixer, then gradually beat in the sugar until very thick and glossy. Sieve and fold in the cornstarch, then spoon and spread over the custard in soft peaks.

Lightly dust the meringue with cocoa and bake at 350°F for 20 minutes. Leave until cold before removing from the pan.

Chocolate pastry

Mix 1 cup all-purpose flour, ¼ cup cocoa powder and ¼ cup confectioners' sugar with a pinch of salt. Rub in ½ cup (1 stick) unsalted butter, softened, then mix with 1 egg yolk and 2 teaspoons cold water until you have a soft sticky paste. Cover and chill until firm, then line a tart pan with the pastry and blind bake before use. Replacing some of the flour with cocoa in this way makes a much softer mixture than regular pastry. But don't worry, it will firm up enough to be rolled if you chill it thoroughly.

Apricot meringue tart

In Britain's early spring, when the future promises so much but there is no fresh fruit to cook with, preserves are the traditional way to brighten up what we eat. Here, crisp pastry holds a layer of apricot conserve under a puddle of semolina pudding, covered with meringue.

FOR THE PASTRY
¾ cup all-purpose flour, plus
   extra for rolling
¼ teaspoon baking powder
1 tablespoon super-fine sugar
4 tablespoons unsalted butter,
   softened
1 egg yolk
2 teaspoons cold water

FOR THE FILLING AND
   MERINGUE
1 cup milk
¾ cup super-fine sugar
¼ cup semolina or rice
   ground in a spice grinder
½ cup heavy cream
2 eggs, separated, plus 1 egg white
1 teaspoon vanilla extract
½ teaspoon almond extract
½ cup good apricot jam

To make the pastry, sift the flour, baking powder and sugar together and rub the butter through evenly. Beat the egg yolk with the water, add to the bowl and work to a soft dough with a dash more water if needed. Wrap and chill the pastry for 30 minutes. Heat the oven to 325°F. Roll the pastry out thinly and use to line a deep 7-inch tart pan. Line the pan with parchment paper and dried beans. Blind bake for 30 minutes, then remove the lining paper and beans and cook until the pastry is golden.

To make the filling and meringue, combine the milk, ¼ cup of the sugar, the semolina and cream in a pan and whisk over heat until boiling, then beat in the egg yolks, vanilla and almond extract. Remove from the heat and leave for 10 to 15 minutes so that the semolina absorbs some of the moisture and the mixture thickens slightly.

Spread the jam over the bottom of the pastry shell and spoon in the semolina filling. Beat the egg whites to soft peaks with an electric mixer, then slowly beat in the remaining ½ cup sugar to make a stiff meringue, pile it high on the filling and bake again at 400°F for 7 to 10 minutes until barely colored.

Lemon meringue sundae

You can make your meringues and lemon curd the day before, and any unused meringues will keep in an airtight container or can be frozen. You could scrap the recipe and buy everything at the supermarket. But it won't taste of the glorious effort, or have that essential homemade quality.

5 egg whites
2 cups super-fine sugar
1 small tub vanilla ice cream
    (or see page 351 for home-
    made)

1¼ cups heavy cream
¼ cup milk
1 recipe Easy Lemon Curd
    (page 342)
toasted sliced almonds

Cover a baking sheet with foil. Heat the oven to 300°F. Heat the egg whites with the sugar in a saucepan and stir until the sugar is dissolved. Remove from the heat and whisk with an electric mixer until thick and cold. Spoon blobs onto the baking sheet, put in the oven, shut the door, turn the oven off and leave for 2 to 3 hours. Allow to cool before using.

To serve, remove the ice cream from the freezer and leave it to soften in the refrigerator for 30 minutes, then whip the cream with the milk until thick and serve scoops of the ice cream layered with lemon curd, whipped cream, broken chunks of meringue and sliced almonds in a parfait glass.

SUE'S STANDBY

Thanks to Sue Loewenbein for telling me another way to use some of these ingredients. She wrote that an old food magazine had suggested that "a rippled mixture of lemon curd and broken meringues stirred into crème fraîche can be frozen on a thin layer of sponge cake to make an ice cream gâteau – a useful standby dessert to have in the freezer – just allow to soften for 20 minutes before serving."

Classic strawberry Pavlova

A decade after ballerina Anna Pavlova's first tour of Australia and New Zealand, we were already unsure which of those two countries could claim the credit for having created a dessert in her honor — and the tussle had begun. Very easy to make, and an excellent standby dessert.

3 egg whites
¼ teaspoon cream of tartar
about 1 cup super-fine sugar
1 teaspoon white vinegar

1 tablespoon cornstarch, sifted
unsweetened whipped cream
fresh strawberries, sliced or
halved

Don't even attempt this without an electric mixer with a whisk attachment. Warm the egg whites slightly in a pan if they're fridge cold, then pour into a bowl with the cream of tartar. Beat until thick and fluffy, then gradually add the sugar and continue beating until all the sugar is mixed in, almost dissolved, and the meringue has turned very thick, glossy and absolutely holds its peaks firmly. (This might take 10 to 20 minutes of continuous beating.) Line a baking sheet with foil and heat the oven to 275°F. Fold the vinegar into the meringue, then the sifted cornstarch, and spoon the mixture onto the baking sheet in one dollop, or make individual ones. Bake for about 1½ hours, then remove from the oven and leave to cool. It will keep for a few days at room temperature unfilled; serve topped with the whipped cream and fresh strawberries.

Pandan pavlova

Another great Pavlova idea has become a Christmas favorite with us — Pavlova filled with homemade pandan ice cream (see page 351), whipped cream lightly flavored with coconut and lots of passion fruit pulp.

Almond maple Pavlova
with fresh cherries

Crisp meringue, a chewy middle and waves of soft whipped cream studded with fresh cherries and almonds made this my number one dessert last summer.

3 egg whites	½ teaspoon vinegar
¼ teaspoon cream of tartar	1 tablespoon cornstarch
¾ cup super-fine sugar	lightly toasted sliced almonds
2 tablespoons maple syrup,	heavy cream
plus more to serve	halved fresh sweet cherries

Heat the oven to 275°F and line a baking sheet with foil. Whisk the egg whites and cream of tartar with an electric mixer until the mixture is fluffy, white and holds its shape. Gradually beat in the sugar on high speed, a third at a time, until the mixture is even thicker and glossy, with the sugar almost dissolved.

Spoon a third of the mixture into another bowl and beat the maple syrup and vinegar in well. Return this to the main bowl and gently fold through lightly. Last of all, gently fold in the sifted cornstarch. Spoon the meringue onto the baking sheet, sprinkle with some of the sliced almonds and bake for 2½ hours. Leave until utterly cold before peeling off the foil and transferring to a serving dish.

To serve, whip some heavy cream with a little maple syrup, spoon over the Pavlova and spoon the cherries and the remaining almonds in the center.

Cream of tartar is an acid that helps egg whites hold their volume, so the meringue will be much lighter in texture than if you made it just with sugar. Technically, lemon juice does the same thing but, as it's a liquid, this would soften the meringue's thickness as well, which you don't want. Cream of tartar is the best acid to use here. Now, you might be wondering what mixing in vinegar — another acid — does. It's really to give a very slight flavor. Weird, perhaps, but utterly authentic, and essential to getting the true Pavlova experience.

Meringue-topped chestnut tarts

Though roasted or boiled chestnuts can have an almost crumbly, slightly dry texture, they turn to a silken smoothness when combined with super-fine sugar in a sweetened chestnut purée. If you can't find sweetened chestnut purée, use ½ cup unsweetened chestnut purée mixed with ⅔ cup super-fine or 1¼ cups confectioners' sugar. Here, it's mixed into a custard and spooned into shortcrust pastry shells, making a fine alternative Christmas dessert.

MAKES 12

1 pound Sweet Shortcrust
   Pastry (page 371)
flour for rolling
butter for the muffin pan

1 teaspoon vanilla extract
1 egg yolk
2 tablespoons unsalted butter
2 tablespoons brandy or rum

FOR THE FILLING
2 tablespoons all-purpose flour
¾ cup heavy cream
1 cup sweetened chestnut purée

FOR THE MERINGUE
2 egg whites
½ cup super-fine sugar

Heat the oven to just below 325°F. Roll the chilled pastry out to just under ¼ inch thick, cut circles 3 inches in diameter and press them into the lightly buttered cups of a muffin pan. Press an empty paper muffin liner inside each one and bake for 20 minutes, before carefully removing the paper liners and

DESSERTS   457 baking for another 5 minutes. Place the muffin pan on a wire rack and leave to cool before removing the pastry shells.

To make the filling, beat the flour with a quarter of the cream until smooth then, in a saucepan, whisk the rest of the cream with the chestnut purée, vanilla and egg yolk and heat until boiling, beating well to avoid it scorching. Remove from the heat, cool for 5 minutes then stir in the butter and brandy. Heat the oven to 400°F.

To make the meringue, using an electric whisk, beat the egg whites to soft peaks, then slowly beat in the sugar until firm meringue.

Sit the pastry shells on a baking sheet and spoon in the filling just short of the top. Spoon the meringue over the tarts, then bake for 8 to 10 minutes till the meringue is golden.

Classic cheesecake

Rich and simple. The classic texture full of cream cheese and little else.

8 ounces oatmeal cookies	1⅓ cups super-fine sugar
2 tablespoons unsalted butter, barely melted	2 tablespoons all-purpose flour
2 pounds full-fat cream cheese, softened	finely grated zest of 1 unwaxed orange or lemon
1¼ cups sour cream	2 teaspoons vanilla extract
	4 eggs, plus 2 yolks

Pound the cookies into fine crumbs, then mix them with the melted butter and pack them into the base of a deep 8-inch round cake pan with a tightly fitting removable bottom. Heat the oven to 350°F and bake the base for 10 to 15 minutes. Remove from the oven and leave to cool slightly.

Beat the cream cheese, sour cream, sugar, flour, zest and vanilla until smooth, then beat in the eggs, one at a time, and finally the egg yolks, until evenly mixed through. Spoon the mixture into the pan, tap it gently down on the countertop to remove any trapped air bubbles, and smooth the top. Reduce the oven temperature to 300°F and bake for 75 to 90 minutes until risen in the center and slightly golden around the edge. Remove from the oven, leave until cold, then chill in the fridge until firm before removing it from the pan by running a thin sharp knife around the edge.

As flour plays only a tiny part in creating a perfect cheesecake it's an ideal recipe to make gluten-free. If the base uses cookies, replace them with store-bought gluten-free cookies or make your own with suitable flour. Then, in the recipe, simply replace the all-purpose flour with either cornstarch or a gluten-free flour mix. If the recipe uses baking powder, make sure that's gluten-free too.

East End cheesecake

This recipe is as close as I can get to my memory of the glorious Grodzinski's cheesecake, late of London's Whitechapel. It gets a gentle bake that keeps the upper crust soft and blonde.

¾ cup all-purpose flour
¼ teaspoon baking powder
2 tablespoons super-fine sugar, plus ¾ cup
4 tablespoons unsalted butter, softened

½ cup heavy cream
1 pound full-fat cream cheese
2 eggs, separated
1 tablespoon cornstarch
zest of ¼ unwaxed lemon
1 teaspoon vanilla extract

Heat the oven to 325°F and line an 8-inch round springform cake pan with a single unbroken sheet of foil. Sift the flour and baking powder with the 2 tablespoons sugar, then rub in the 2 tablespoons of butter until the mixture turns to fine buttery crumbs. Mix in 3 tablespoons of the cream and combine into a dough. Roll this out to an 8-inch round, lay it on the bottom of the pan and press flat. Prick the surface with a fork, then bake for 25 minutes until golden brown.

Heat the remaining butter and cream in a saucepan till boiling, pour this over the cream cheese in a mixing bowl and beat until smooth. Add the egg yolks, cornstarch, lemon zest and vanilla and beat well once more. In a clean bowl, using an electric mixer, whisk the egg whites to soft peaks, then gradually beat in the remaining sugar until very thick and able to hold stiff peaks. Fold this into the cheese mixture until smooth. Scrape this into the pan, smooth the top and bake for 25 to 30 minutes until wobbly and barely set. Carefully remove from the oven and leave to cool at room temperature before chilling.

TEXTURE

If your perfect version of this style of cheesecake should have a grainier texture, there are two steps you can take. First, bake it for longer at a higher temperature (say 400°F for the first 20 minutes, then reduce the heat to 325°F for another 15 to 20 minutes). The mixture will separate very slightly and give a slightly grainy texture. Second, use a combination of half cottage cheese and half cream cheese. Drain the cottage cheese well, then put it in a food processor with the egg yolks, cornstarch, lemon zest and vanilla, and blend till smooth, then add the remaining ingredients. Cottage cheese will give the filling a slightly coarser texture.

Cherry crumble cheesecake

I worked as a grill chef in New York in the early 1990s, and lived on Flatbush Avenue in Brooklyn above a Nation of Islam office (having two men in suits outside your front door gave the street a little security). I'd go for coffee in the morning at a place called Junior's, and they had the best cheesecake I'd ever had. This is my attempt to re-create the dense creamy texture and I think it's damn good. The sponge base becomes gooey as it soaks up the juice from the cherries: messy to serve and eat but it tastes superb.

MAKES ONE 10-INCH CHEESECAKE

FOR THE SPONGE CAKE BASE
1 egg, warm or at room
    temperature
2 tablespoons super-fine sugar
1 tablespoon corn syrup
zest of ½ unwaxed lemon
¼ cup all-purpose flour

FOR THE CHERRY BASE
14- to 15-ounce can black
    cherries, drained
½ cup good cherry jam

FOR THE CRUMBLE TOPPING
    (or use half a recipe of
    Crumble Mix, page 443)
¾ cup all-purpose flour
½ cup light brown sugar
½ teaspoon ground cinnamon
4 tablespoons unsalted butter
1 tablespoon milk

FOR THE FILLING
1¾ pounds full-fat cream cheese
2 cups confectioners' sugar
¼ cup cornstarch, sifted
1 tablespoon almond extract
2 eggs
½ cup heavy cream

To make the sponge cake base, heat the oven to 350°F and line the inside of a 10-inch round springform cake pan with a single sheet of buttered foil. Beat the egg and super-fine sugar with an electric mixer until light and fluffy. Add the corn syrup and lemon zest and continue beating until very thick. Sift the flour, then fold this through the mixture until evenly combined. Spoon into

the pan, spreading it evenly and carefully to cover the bottom thinly, then bake for 10 to 12 minutes until golden and firm.

To make the cherry base, cut the canned cherries in half, press dry on paper towels and stir with the jam. Spread this mixture evenly over the sponge and set aside.

To make the crumble topping, put the flour, brown sugar and cinnamon into a bowl and rub the butter and milk through until the mixture resembles dry pastry crumbs. Leave at room temperature.

To make the filling, beat the cream cheese with the confectioners' sugar, cornstarch and almond extract until light and fluffy. Beat the eggs together in another bowl, then slowly beat the eggs into the cream cheese mixture. You don't want to aerate the mixture any more, so stop as soon as the eggs are barely combined. Stir in the cream until it disappears.

Spoon the cheese mixture into the pan over the cherries and bake for 20 minutes at 325°F. At this point, open the oven door, pull the cheesecake out a little bit and sprinkle the crumble topping evenly over the top, then shut the door and bake for another 25 to 30 minutes. At this point the cake should still be a bit wobbly. Lift the cheesecake out of the oven, cool at room temperature, then refrigerate for 3 to 4 hours until firm and chilled. Unfasten the "ring" of the cake pan and remove it, then very carefully invert the cheesecake onto a flat plate, remove the bottom of the pan and peel off the foil. Invert the cake onto a clean plate and serve.

GETTING YOU OUT OF A JAM

A cheesecake cracks if slightly overbaked, so the crumble topping hides this and makes the final cooking less fraught. Lining the pan with foil makes it easier to remove the cheesecake, as the jam bubbles out during cooking and literally jams up the springform pan.

Pear mousse cake

Mascarpone is a beautiful soft cream cheese, much richer than regular cream cheese, and it has only a slight acidity. Combined with pears and sparkling wine or champagne it makes the most delicate mousse. Though not really a "cheesecake," the cheese in this dessert leads me to place it here.

The genoise sponge is slightly tricky, I'll warn you, so you must fold the flour through extremely gently in order to keep the aeration. To really make it special, sprinkle a few drops of brandy on the sponge before filling, and dust with confectioners' sugar to serve.

MAKES ONE 9-INCH CAKE

5 egg yolks, plus 1 whole egg	1⅔ cups champagne, cava or
1⅓ cups super-fine sugar	white wine
⅔ cups all-purpose flour	1 tablespoon powdered gelatin
2 tablespoons cornstarch	¼ cup warm water
½ teaspoon baking powder	1¼ cups mascarpone
1½ pounds small Comice pears	⅔ cup heavy cream

Line the bottom of a 9-inch round springform cake pan with parchment paper and heat the oven to 350°F. Place the egg yolks, whole egg and 2 tablespoons of the sugar in a warmed bowl. Beat with an electric whisk until the mixture is thick and pale. Sift the flour, cornstarch and baking powder together, and fold them quickly but very, very gently through the eggs and sugar. Scrape the mixture into the cake pan and bake for about 20 minutes. Leave the sponge to cool in the pan. After the sponge has cooled, remove and wash the pan to be used again later.

Peel, core and quarter the pears (you want 1¼ pounds flesh) and simmer with the champagne and ⅓ cup of the sugar until tender. Strain, then return the liquid to the pan and simmer until reduced to just ½ cup. Purée the pears with the reduced liquid in a food processor and leave until barely warm.

Sprinkle the gelatin over the warm water to soften, then combine the gelatin and water with the pears and remaining sugar in the food processor and process until smooth. When cold and almost set, beat in the mascarpone and cream. Line the sides of the springform cake pan with a strip of parchment paper as this helps keep the edges looking clean. Slice the genoise sponge horizontally, lay half in the bottom of the pan, spoon in the pear mousse, place the rest of the sponge on top and chill for 4 to 6 hours until set.

PEAR TIPS

You can simply use 1¼ pounds of drained canned pears, and, for a non-alcoholic version, replace the champagne with either canned pear juice or white grape juice.

Tiramisu

There are simpler and quicker recipes but this is the one I turn to when I want the intense, rich dessert I think of as tiramisu. Back in 1995, I was working for Chef Giorgio Locatelli as the pastry chef in his London restaurant Zafferano and this was the recipe I constructed for the menu, no doubt tweaked by Giorgio who had a subtle sense of taste that awed me. I found it recently in a folder I'd kept from those days and when I made it again, the flavor was just as I'd remembered. I would have used intense shots of Illy coffee at the restaurant but now, at home, instant coffee takes its place and it's still good.

5 egg yolks
¾ cup super-fine sugar
¾ cup Marsala
¼ cup good instant
   coffee granules
2 tablespoons boiling water

¼ cup dark rum or brandy
2½ cups mascarpone
½ cup heavy cream
about 25 ladyfingers
cocoa powder or grated dark
   chocolate to finish

Find a saucepan that will hold a deep 4½-cup glass or metal bowl above it so that about three-quarters of the bowl is inside the pan. Then fill the pan with just enough water to avoid touching the bottom of the bowl, and set the pan on the stove to boil.

Whisk the egg yolks, ⅓ cup of the sugar and ½ cup of the Marsala together, then place the bowl over the pan on the stove, reduce the heat to a simmer and continue to whisk until the mixture is finger hot and almost doubled in volume, with a slightly thick foamy consistency. Remove from the heat and leave to get cold.

Meanwhile, dissolve the coffee in the boiling water, then mix with the rum and remaining sugar and Marsala. Beat the mascarpone and cream with the cold egg yolk mixture using an electric whisk until very smooth and thick. Now simply dunk the ladyfingers in the coffee liquid, and build alternate layers of them and the mascarpone cream in either one large or several individual bowls; just make sure the top layer is cream, then dust the top completely with sifted cocoa, or grated chocolate, and chill before serving.

Supper

Supper

INTRODUCTION

The shine on a top of rough puff pastry baked over a pie is a marvelous sight at the dinner table. Though the pastry is much less difficult to make than you might have been told, and easy both to decorate and bake, when taken from the oven and placed on the table the look is of something utterly complex and remarkable. The egg yolk and water mixture brushed over the cold pastry turns to a rich polished glow, the rough cut edges of the pastry flake and puff invitingly, and the aroma reminds me of sizzling butter and hot toast.

I've read that the sense of smell can bypass the logical parts of the brain and appeal directly to the emotions, hence the appeal of fresh-baked bread or cakes, but they really only work with me during the daytime. When the sun sets, it's as if a tiny switch has been flicked and I respond to a whole new set of stimuli. Cabbage cooking is probably the worst, roast chicken or some complex mixture of spices both rank among the best. And for me, right at the very top, is the aroma of a pastry crust baking in the oven.

The recipes in this chapter cover most needs, from little savory snacks that you can easily make and bake through to majestic pies that can take pride of place on the table. What they share is a certain casualness in the way they're eaten, so there are many recipes that can be diverted into dishes for picnics, lunch boxes or traveling. And lots of them can be frozen at some stage, and then finished so quickly that time isn't an issue.

Shortcrust pastry has the reputation of being the easiest, but getting it just right is much trickier than the ever-so-feared puff pastry. Good shortcrust is all about the crumbliness, the shortness, and that in turn is all about getting the maximum amount of butter into it while using the smallest amount of water and egg. Too much liquid turns the crust stodgy and heavy, and too much egg gives it a cake-like quality, but if you leave them out or use too little, then the pastry is almost impossible to roll. The secret is in letting the pastry get ice-cold first as this sets the consistency, then quickly rolling it when it's just on the point of softening.

Rough puff pastry, by contrast, is all in the rolling and folding, and very slight changes to the recipe won't drastically affect the result. I was taught to be terrified by pastry that involved rolling cold butter through the dough, usually by people who'd only make it with a grumble. I swear that success with rough puff can be achieved simply by applying a swashbuckling degree of confidence and a little arrogance. It requires some choreography, as you tap, roll and square the pastry with your rolling pin, but it's all fairly easy to learn.

Hot water crust is almost the easiest, as the hot water cooks the starch slightly and gives the dough an oily and flexible texture when rolled, a little like an edible clay that can be shaped into a sort of pot to hold the meat and its juices. Suet crust needs to be held in place, and forms a soft rich layer that blends into a reassuring stodge when it meets the juices from the pudding. Choux paste, on the other hand, needs to be baked to a shattering crispness, so that the moisture from whatever you fill it with softens it gently and makes it more tender.

Do read the Tips & Techniques section at the beginning of the Desserts chapter (page 355), as it explains in some detail a lot of things about ingredients, methods and techniques that are equally relevant to the savory recipes found in this chapter.

Adding a savory flavor to pastry

Usually if the filling is flavored strongly (and that's the best approach, as pastry seems to dilute the intensity of flavor in a kind of weird alchemical process), the pastry can be left plain and straightforward. But sometimes you want to create a harmony between two subtle flavors, and adding ingredients to pastry can help do this. Herbs, fresh or dried, can simply be added to the recipe without any other changes, as can things like powdered mustard or paprika, if added in 1 to 2 teaspoon measures. When you add more than that of any dry or liquid flavoring, it starts to change the consistency and fragility of the dough. Wherever possible, go for dry flavors and use them sparingly. All powdered flavorings soften the gluten in the flour, so be aware that the pastry will be more delicate to roll. If this is a problem, you can try replacing all-purpose flour with bread flour when you add dry flavorings and this will make rolling the dough easier.

Butter can be flavored and rolled through rough puff pastry. To do this, beat a small amount of ground dried herbs, puréed garlic or pepper, or another flavor you like with a similar consistency, through the softened butter, then shape it into a block and chill it until firm again. The key is only to use enough to give a hint of the flavor, and to avoid softening or changing the texture of the butter.

Egg wash and others

A wash made up of one egg yolk beaten with a pinch of salt and enough cold water to give it the consistency of thin cream gives a beautiful rich dark gloss when baked. But you can also use other ingredients to give a different result. Milk or cream alone gives a very subtle shine to the crust, whereas melted butter or olive oil can be brushed onto a hot bare crust after baking to add a gloss. Into this butter or oil, you can add herbs, or sautéed onions or garlic. You can even melt and brush a little dripping, saved from a roast, over the top of a pie and season it with a few twists of pepper: the effect is very rough and dirty but the flavor is intense.

Savory shortcrust pastry for "double crust" pies

These three recipes make a very spartan plain pastry, very lean and perfect for making an easy-to-hold case for individual hearty pies with pastry top and bottom, and work well with gutsy and well-flavored fillings. If you wanted something more elegant, you could use the Sweet Shortcrust recipe (page 371), leaving out the sugar, but it will be less robust, both to roll and to eat.

The combination of butter and lard makes for an extra crisp pastry, but you can use all butter if you prefer. Egg whites help to hold the gluten-free pastry together, but don't push it too far as it lacks the "elasticity" wheat flour gives and will be more inclined to crumble when cut.

HOW TO USE

You can use this pastry whenever you want a shell that holds its shape around a filling, or something you can hold in your hand and eat conveniently — for example, as a leaner crust for a pasty, or really minisized pies made in muffin pans, or as the durable base for a pie, paired with a fancier puff pastry top.

Though recipes will suggest cooking the filling first, that isn't strictly necessary as long as the pie is cooked until tender and piping hot (especially so for meat and fish), the crust is golden and allowance is made for the juice that will be released as the filling steams inside the crust. You need something to soak it up and usually dusting the filling ingredients with well-seasoned flour is enough. But very hard vegetables like carrots benefit from a little precooking and even softer ones like green beans or broccoli bake better if blanched in boiling water first.

Everyday shortcrust pastry

MAKES ABOUT 1¼ POUNDS

2¼ cups all-purpose flour

½ teaspoon fine salt

¼ teaspoon baking powder

5 tablespoons unsalted butter

⅓ cup lard

⅓ cup ice-cold water

Hot mustard shortcrust pastry

MAKES ABOUT 1¼ POUNDS

2¼ cup all-purpose flour

2 to 3 tablespoons English
   powdered mustard, sifted

½ teaspoon fine salt

¼ teaspoon baking powder

5 tablespoons unsalted butter

⅓ cup lard

⅓ cup ice-cold water

Gluten-free shortcrust pastry

MAKES ABOUT 1¼ POUNDS

2 cups gluten-free flour

½ teaspoon fine salt

¼ teaspoon baking powder

5 tablespoons unsalted butter

⅓ cup lard

2 egg whites

Mix the dry ingredients together in a bowl. Cut the butter and lard into small pieces, then rub these through the dry ingredients. Add the water (or egg whites for the gluten-free pastry, plus a drop of water if needed) and knead into a smooth dough. Wrap the dough well and chill for at least 30 minutes before using.

Gluten-free pastry doesn't keep well as an unrolled block in the fridge or freezer, and is at its best either used fresh on the day you make it, or rolled out to make pastry shells and then frozen unbaked to be pulled out and used later.

Remember, if you are using gluten-free pastry in any of the following recipes, use cornstarch or gluten-free flour to roll it out and to thicken the filling for the pie, not regular flour.

"Big match" beef pies

Inspired by the idea of that perfect pie you'd hope to find at a soccer match (but never do!), these pies are equally good for an informal supper or in front of the TV. If you don't have half a dozen individual ceramic pie dishes, buy some 5-inch round foil pie pans and use them instead.

MAKES 5 OR 6

1 pound boneless beef chuck, diced, or ground beef, not too lean
a little sunflower oil
1 medium onion, chopped
2 tablespoons all-purpose flour, plus extra for rolling
1 teaspoon ground white pepper
½ teaspoon fine salt

2 tablespoons Worcestershire sauce
2 tablespoons tomato paste
¾ cup dark ale or red wine
¾ cup strong beef stock
1 recipe hot mustard shortcrust pastry (see facing page)
1 egg, beaten with a pinch of salt and 1 tablespoon water

Fry the beef in a heavy saucepan with the sunflower oil until brown. Add the onion to the beef and cook until soft. Sprinkle in the flour and pepper, stir well, then add the salt, Worcestershire sauce, tomato paste, ale and stock and stir again. Cook over a high heat, stirring often, for 10 to 15 minutes until the liquid in the pan is thick but not evaporated, then remove and leave to cool before filling and baking your pies. The liquid is as much a part of the pie filling as the meat, so don't leave it out.

Heat the oven to 400°F. Roll two-thirds of the pastry out on a lightly floured surface until ¼ inch thick, and cut pieces to line the insides of five or six individual pie dishes or 5-inch-diameter foil pans. Pile in the filling to just short of the top, then roll the remaining pastry and cut disks slightly wider than the pies. Brush the underside edge of each disk with water, lay it over the filling and press the edges of the bottom and top together to seal. Brush the tops with the beaten egg and cut a hole in the middle to let the steam escape and bake for about 40 minutes until golden.

Chicken and leek pies

MAKES 5 OR 6

2 or 3 medium-sized leeks,
   thinly sliced
2 garlic cloves, crushed
a little sunflower oil
1 pound boneless skinless chicken
   breast or thighs, cubed
1 teaspoon fine salt
2½ cups sour cream
1 tablespoon cornstarch

a good handful of chopped
   parsley
ground black pepper
1 recipe everyday shortcrust
   pastry (see page 480)
flour for rolling
1 egg, beaten with a pinch of
   salt and 1 tablespoon water

Wash and drain the sliced leeks, then fry with the garlic in the oil until tender.
Stir in the chicken and salt and cook until the chicken begins to color, then
add the sour cream and cornstarch, stirring well. Simmer very gently over a
low heat until the chicken is barely cooked and the liquid reduced, then stir
in the parsley and season generously with pepper. Roll out the pastry and
continue in the same way as for the "Big match" beef pies.

Pollock, olive and caper pies

MAKES 5 OR 6

11 ounces pollock
2 or 3 medium onions, thinly
   sliced
4 tablespoons butter
⅓ cup flour, plus extra
   for rolling
⅔ cup milk
¼ cup heavy cream
2 tablespoons white vermouth
¾ teaspoon fine salt

1 to 2 tablespoons capers, washed
   and drained
2 tablespoons chopped pitted
   green olives, drained
1 tablespoon chives, roughly
   chopped
1 recipe everyday shortcrust
   pastry (see page 480)
1 egg, beaten with a pinch of
   salt and 1 tablespoon water

Skin the pollock and pull out any fish bones, then chop into ¾-inch chunks. Cook the onions in the butter until soft, then stir in the flour, followed by the milk, cream, vermouth and salt. Whisk over the heat until it boils, then simmer for a minute or two. Mix in the capers, olives and chives, and stir in the pollock. Roll out the pastry and continue in the same way as the "Big match" beef pies.

Spiced eggplant and lentil pies

MAKES 5 OR 6

1 large eggplant
olive oil
4 ounces dried red lentils
¾ teaspoon fine salt
3 tablespoons tahini
3 tablespoons yogurt
zest of 1 lemon, finely grated
2 garlic cloves, finely sliced

1 red chili, chopped
1 tablespoon cumin seeds
1 recipe everyday shortcrust
  pastry (see page 480)
flour for rolling
1 egg, beaten with a pinch of
  salt and 1 tablespoon water

Chop the eggplant into small cubes, leaving the skin on, and fry in olive oil until golden, then drain on paper towels to soak up some of the oiliness. Boil the red lentils in water for 10 minutes or until just beginning to soften, then rinse under cold water in a sieve and drain well. Mix the eggplant, lentils and salt with the tahini, yogurt and lemon zest. Fry the garlic, chili and cumin seeds in a little more oil until golden, spoon while sizzling onto the eggplant and stir well. Then roll out the pastry and continue in the same way as for the "Big match" beef pies.

Ham, egg and potato pie

The addition of some strong Cheddar to the dough gives it a bigger, savory flavor, and works well with the filling. For a pie man, not a quiche man.

FOR THE PASTRY
5 tablespoons unsalted butter
1½ cups all-purpose flour,
    plus extra for rolling
½ teaspoon baking soda
½ teaspoon fine salt
2 ounces sharp Cheddar,
    grated
3 to 4 tablespoons milk
1 egg yolk

FOR THE FILLING
⅔ cup heavy cream
3 eggs, plus 1 egg white
1 garlic clove, smashed
    and chopped
a small handful of chopped
    chives or parsley
salt and pepper
¾ cup sliced cooked potatoes
8-ounce piece of ham, diced

To make the pastry, cut the butter into small pieces and rub it into the flour, baking soda and salt, then stir in the Cheddar. Beat the milk and egg yolk together in a cup, then mix this evenly with the dry ingredients. Cover and chill the pastry for 30 minutes. Heat the oven to 350°F. Roll two-thirds of the pastry out on a lightly floured surface until ¼ inch thick and line a deep 8-inch long oval pie dish.

To make the filling, beat the cream, eggs and egg white, garlic and chives with a good pinch of salt and pepper. Layer the potatoes and ham in the pie dish and pour in the egg mixture.

Make a top crust by rolling out the remaining pastry to cover the filling and crimp the edges together, poking a hole in the middle to let the steam escape. Put the pie in the oven and bake for 40 to 50 minutes until the filling is set and the upper crust golden.

EGG MATTERS

If you want to be geeky about it and have a kitchen thermometer, it will read 163°F when the egg mixture is set.

486

Light cream cheese pastry

A pie is still a pie, even if the pastry only covers the top. This pastry is very quick to make and couldn't be easier to use. Not only do you put everything in the bowl or food processor, but it also rolls easily straight from the fridge. The texture after baking is tender and short, thanks to the acidity in the cream cheese, which helps break down the gluten in the flour.

MAKES ABOUT 1¾ POUNDS

3 cups all-purpose flour,
    plus extra for rolling
½ teaspoon baking powder
½ teaspoon fine salt

10 tablespoons unsalted butter,
    chilled and cut into cubes
5 ounces full-fat cream cheese
1 egg, beaten

Put all the ingredients except the egg into a food processor and combine, or sift the dry ingredients in a bowl, then work the butter and cream cheese through with your hands. Then, with either method, add the egg and knead to a smooth dough. Cover and chill for 10 minutes, then roll the pastry out until ¼ inch thick and cut into circles or ovals big enough to cover your pie dishes and tuck comfortably over the rim (about 5 ounces of pastry per top crust). Stack the pastry shapes with parchment paper between them, and either use straight away or pack into a ziplock bag to store in the freezer.

GRAVY

I wrote this recipe to make some simple pies that use a can of soup for the gravy, thickened with flour, and mixed with hunky bits of meat, fish or vegetables for a comforting but convenient dinner. Though gravy has fallen out of fashion, I prefer it to that nasty sticky brown stain mistakenly called "jus" that seems to coat everything in some restaurants. Flour-thickened gravy cooked slowly has a soft velvety consistency and mellowness that won't mask the natural flavors of the filling.

Chicken and mushroom pies

1¼ pounds boneless skinless
  chicken breast
2 tablespoons all-purpose flour
3 garlic cloves, finely sliced
2 medium onions, finely diced
4 tablespoons unsalted butter
1 chicken bouillon cube
¾ cup red wine
1 ounce dried porcini mushrooms
salt and ground black pepper

14-ounce can cream of mushroom
  soup
8 ounces button mushrooms
a little fresh thyme, finely
  chopped
1 recipe Light Cream Cheese
  Pastry (page 487),
  cut into 5 top crusts
1 egg, beaten with a pinch of
  salt, for brushing the tops

Cut the chicken into 1¼-inch pieces and toss in the flour. Fry the garlic and onion in half the butter until golden, crumble the bouillon cube in and add the red wine and porcini mushrooms. Bring to a boil then, after a minute, remove from the heat, cover and leave to stand for 15 minutes to soften. Add the chicken and any loose flour, with ½ teaspoon each salt and pepper and the mushroom soup. Stir well and simmer until the sauce is thick and the chicken cooked (about 15 minutes). Cut the button mushrooms into quarters and fry half of them in half of the remaining butter until golden, add these to the chicken filling, then fry the remaining mushrooms with the last of the butter and add these too, with the chopped thyme.

Heat the oven to 400°F. Spoon the filling into five individual 1¼-cup pie dishes, cover with the pastry tops, tucked a little way over the rim, brush with beaten egg and cut three peepholes in the top with a sharp knife. If you want to get fancy, you can score stripes ½ inch apart across the pastry once it has been brushed with egg wash. Bake for 30 minutes until the filling is hot, the crust crisp and the glaze crackled and golden.

Beef shank, chorizo and pinto bean pies

1 large onion, roughly chopped
3 tablespoons olive oil
½ teaspoon chili flakes
1 garlic clove, mashed
1½ pounds beef shanks
   or stew beef
2 tablespoons all-purpose flour
2 tablespoons paprika
¼ cup brandy
2 beef bouillon cubes

a little water
4 ounces chorizo, chopped into
   small pieces
14- to 15-ounce can pinto or borlotti
   beans, rinsed and drained
14-ounce can cream of tomato soup
1 recipe Light Cream Cheese
   Pastry (page 487),
     cut into 5 top crusts
1 egg, beaten with a pinch of
   salt, for brushing the tops

Heat the oven to 350°F. Fry the onion in the oil until soft and a little brown. Add the chili flakes and garlic and cook for a minute, then remove from the heat. Cut the beef into 1¼-inch pieces, then toss in the flour and add to the pan. Fry for 3 to 4 minutes until lightly colored then add the paprika and brandy, stir to dissolve any bits stuck to the pan, then transfer to an ovenproof pot with a snug-fitting lid. Crumble in the bouillon cube, add just enough water to half cover, put the lid on and bake in the oven for 1½ to 2 hours until the meat is tender. Check it occasionally to make sure it hasn't boiled dry, stir, and top up with water to keep it just moist (not swimming in liquid). When the meat is cooked add the chorizo, beans and tomato soup. Simmer for an hour with the lid on, then spoon the filling into five individual 1¼-cup pie dishes and continue with the pastry and beaten egg in the same way as for the Chicken and Mushroom Pies on the facing page.

Pork and parsnip pies

1½ pounds boneless pork
   shoulder chops
2 tablespoons all-purpose flour
2 tablespoons unsalted butter
8 shallots, peeled and cut
   in half
salt and ground black pepper
1 ham or chicken bouillon cube
⅔ cup dry cider

3 peeled parsnips, cut into
   1¼-inch chunks
14-ounce can pea and ham soup
5 tablespoons chopped fresh parsley
5 tablespoons sour cream
1 recipe Light Cream Cheese
   Pastry (page 487),
   cut into 5 top crusts
1 egg, beaten with a pinch of
   salt, for brushing the tops

Heat the oven to 350°F. Cut the pork into 1¼-inch pieces and toss in the flour, then fry in a pan with the butter until browned. Add the shallots, season with salt and pepper and cook a few minutes more. Transfer to an ovenproof pot with a snug-fitting lid, crumble in the bouillon cube, add the cider and bake in the oven for an hour. Then add the parsnips and soup, and cook for another hour with the lid on until the meat is tender. Divide between five individual 1¼-cup pie dishes, stir 1 tablespoon parsley and 1 tablespoon sour cream into each, and continue with the pastry and beaten egg in the same way as for the Chicken and Mushroom Pies on page 488.

Leek, smoked haddock and Lancashire cheese pies

4 large leeks, trimmed and cut
   into 1-inch pieces
a good handful of fresh parsley,
   chopped
½ cup heavy cream
8 ounces Lancashire or Cheddar
   cheese, cut into ½-inch chunks

8 ounces smoked haddock,
   skinned, boned and
   roughly flaked
14-ounce can leek and potato soup
1 recipe Light Cream Cheese
   Pastry (page 487),
   cut into 5 top crusts
1 egg, beaten with a pinch of
   salt, for brushing the tops

Wash the leeks well in cold water to remove any mud or grit, then simmer them in a pan, just covered with boiling water, until tender. Drain well and stir with the chopped parsley, cream, cheese and haddock, then mix in the soup. Heat the oven to 400°F, spoon the filling into five individual 1¼-cup pie dishes and continue in the same way with the pastry and beaten egg as for the Chicken and Mushroom Pies on page 488.

Broccoli, Stilton and potato pies

8 ounces broccoli florets, cut into
   bite-size pieces
1 pound waxy potatoes
2 14-ounce cans cream of broccoli
   soup
6 ounces blue Stilton cheese,
   crumbled into bits
1½ tablespoons chopped chives

5 tablespoons heavy cream
black pepper
1 recipe Light Cream Cheese
   Pastry (page 487),
   cut into 5 top crusts
1 egg, beaten with a pinch of
   salt, for brushing the tops

Blanch the broccoli in a large pot of salted boiling water for just 1 minute, then drain, and immediately plunge the pieces into ice-cold water. This will stop the broccoli from cooking fully before the pies are baked. Once cold, drain and keep in the fridge until needed. Place the potatoes in a pot of salted water, bring to a boil, then simmer until tender. Drain, cut into 1¼-inch pieces and heat with the soup. Heat the oven to 400°F, scoop the potatoes out of the soup and divide equally between five individual 1¼-cup pie dishes. Divide the broccoli, Stilton, chives and cream among the dishes, season with a few twists of black pepper, then top up with some of the soupy sauce, and continue in the same way with the pastry and beaten egg as for the Chicken and Mushroom Pies on page 488.

Lamb and parsley pie

This pie is topped with the real star of the show, a tender golden lattice of mustard shortcrust flecked with parsley: a good dish for Easter Sunday, or any other day of the year.

FOR THE PASTRY
1½ cups all-purpose flour
1 tablespoon powdered
    mustard
½ teaspoon baking powder
½ teaspoon salt
½ cup (1 stick) unsalted butter,
    cut into cubes
¼ cup finely chopped
    parsley
⅓ cup milk

FOR THE FILLING
2 large onions, finely chopped
8 garlic cloves, peeled and
    thinly sliced
5 tablespoons unsalted butter
2¾ pounds lean boneless
    lamb, diced
¼ cup all-purpose flour
⅔ cup milk, plus 1 tablespoon
    for brushing the top
1 cup water
salt and pepper
3 medium carrots, peeled
3 tablespoons finely chopped
    parsley

To make the pastry, place the flour, powdered mustard, baking powder and salt in a bowl. Rub in the butter, add the parsley and mix with the milk to form a soft dough. Cover and chill for 30 minutes.

To make the filling, cook the onions and garlic in a large pan with the butter for about 10 minutes until soft, then scoop from the pan, leaving the buttery juices. Add the lamb, cook for 20 minutes till the liquid almost evaporates, then stir in the flour and return the onions and garlic to the pan. Pour in the milk and water, stir well and season with salt and pepper, then simmer uncovered until the lamb is tender. Slice and boil the carrots, then drain and add to the lamb with the parsley. Spoon into a suitable ovenproof dish. Heat the oven to 350°F.

Roll the pastry thinly, cut into ¾-inch-wide strips and weave a lattice over the top of the pie. Brush with the 1 tablespoon of milk and bake for 30 to 40 minutes.

Sweet potato crescents

These are gorgeous when deep-fried but you can bake them (350°F for 20 minutes) for a healthier finish. A handful of chopped cilantro leaves can be added to the filling.

MAKES AT LEAST 15

2 cups all-purpose flour
1 teaspoon turmeric
1 teaspoon ground cumin
½ teaspoon baking powder
¾ teaspoon fine salt
¼ cup sunflower oil
½ cup cold water
1 or 2 small sweet potatoes,
    11 ounces peeled weight

1 small red pepper
sunflower oil for frying
2 garlic cloves, peeled and
    sliced
1 small bird's-eye chili,
    chopped
1½ teaspoons ground
    coriander
2 green onions, thinly sliced
½ teaspoon fine salt

Spoon the flour, turmeric, cumin, baking powder and salt into a bowl. Add the sunflower oil and rub it in with your fingers, then add the cold water and mix to a soft dough. Cover and leave to stand. Cut the sweet potatoes into ½-inch dice and steam till tender. (I give them 5 minutes in the microwave on high in a covered bowl with a dash of water.) Seed and chop the red pepper and fry with 2 tablespoons oil until soft. Add the garlic and chili, cook a few minutes more, then add the drained sweet potato and fry for 3 to 4 minutes until dry. Add the coriander, green onions and salt, stir well and leave to cool.

Roll the pastry out very thinly and cut into disks about 4 inches across, rerolling the trimmings as you go to make more. Place a heaped 1 teaspoon of the filling on each disk, moisten the edges, fold over and crimp together. Fry in hot oil for about 2 minutes until deep golden brown and drain on paper towels before serving.

Light spelt rough puff pastry

A small amount of spelt flour boosts the flavor of the pastry without affecting the texture, and the fiber content does your stomach heaps of good. A smidgeon of baking powder softens the pastry and helps to gently aerate the tender buttery flakes as they bake.

MAKES ABOUT 1½ POUNDS

2 cups bread flour, plus extra for rolling

½ cup spelt or whole-wheat flour

¼ teaspoon baking powder

½ teaspoon fine salt

1 tablespoon olive oil

¾ cup (1½ sticks) cold unsalted butter, cut into cubes

⅔ cup half milk and half water

Toss all the flour, baking powder and salt in a bowl, then rub the oil through till it disappears. Toss the butter cubes through the flour, then mix with the milk and water to make a soft lumpy dough without kneading. Cover the bowl and leave somewhere cool for 20 minutes. Dust the work surface lightly and evenly with flour, as the dough will stick to any bare bits, then scrape the dough out. Dust the top of the dough as well, then roll it out to about 8 by 16 inches. Fold it in by thirds (like the blanket fold, see page 14), then repeat this rolling and folding, and chill again. Repeat the rolling, folding and chilling twice more at 30-minute intervals before using the pastry.

HOW TO USE

Use this pastry as you would puff pastry, to make top crusts for pies and bases for tarts, to wrap around firm fillings like sausages, or simply to sprinkle with grated cheese and bake in tiny squares as a nibble to serve with drinks. See pages 498 to 502 for some ideas for individual savory tarts.

This pastry bakes to a perfect finish as long as you get your oven hot and keep the topping light. Plan how many tarts your oven will comfortably bake at a time, allowing space between the pieces of pastry on each baking sheet, as well as space around the edges of the baking sheets so that the heat moves freely in the oven. Imagine your oven is an aircraft on a long-haul flight; you want all the tarts to lie on spacious, first-class flat beds rather than sitting rammed shoulder to shoulder in economy. The more space they have, the better they'll "pop."

Chorizo and tomato tarts

This is a fancy version of bangers (sausages) and ketchup, albeit a little spicier. Best if you buy the chorizo whole and slice it yourself; the wafer-thin ready sliced sort will burn to a crisp.

MAKES 6 to 9

6 or 7 ripe plum tomatoes

2 tablespoons light olive oil

3 garlic cloves, peeled and
  thinly sliced

2 teaspoons cumin seeds

½ teaspoon cayenne pepper

1 tablespoon tomato paste

salt and pepper

1 recipe Light Spelt Rough
  Puff Pastry (page 497)

8 ounces thickly sliced chorizo

Halve the tomatoes, spoon out and discard the seeds and roughly chop the flesh into ½-inch chunks. Heat the oil in a small pan, add the garlic, cumin and cayenne and fry until golden, then tip in the tomato chunks and tomato paste and simmer for 5 to 10 minutes until reduced and thick. Season with salt and pepper.

Line baking sheets with aluminum foil or parchment paper and heat the oven to 425°F. Roll the pastry out until about ¼ inch thick, and cut into six to nine circles, squares or rectangles, according to how large you want the tarts to be. Spoon a little of the tomato sauce onto each piece of pastry and top

with the chorizo, leaving a ½-inch border of bare pastry. Bake for 20 minutes, then reduce the heat to 350°F and bake for another 5 minutes (small tarts) and up to 15 to 20 minutes (large tarts).

Tapenade and roasted pepper tarts

Spread the tapenade thinly to help keep the flavor delicate. Made with 2-inch disks of pastry, these also work well as hors d'oeuvres.

MAKES 6 to 9
3 large red bell peppers
1⅔ cups pited black olives
1 garlic clove, crushed
zest of ½ lemon

1 tablespoon capers, washed
free of salt (or use the ones
in brine)
1 or 2 anchovies, chopped
2 tablespoons olive oil
1 recipe Light Spelt Rough
Puff Pastry (page 497)

Roast the bell peppers in a hot oven until black and charred, then scrape off the skin; halve, remove the seeds (saving the juice) and cut into strips. Place the olives, garlic, zest, capers, anchovies and olive oil in a food processor and purée them roughly, adding a little of the pepper juices to thin it slightly.

Roll out the pastry and continue in the same way as the Chorizo and Tomato Tarts on page 498, spreading the tapenade on each tart and crisscrossing with the pepper strips before baking.

Chard, chèvre and walnut tarts

If you want a fancier look, soak the walnuts in boiling water for 10 minutes then slice them thinly with a very sharp knife.

MAKES 6 to 9

5 large stalks of chard
1 large onion, thinly sliced
4 tablespoons unsalted butter
1¼ cups walnuts,
   roughly chopped

1 recipe Light Spelt Rough
   Puff Pastry (page 497)
salt and pepper
11 ounces chèvre or other soft
   goat's cheese

Wash and chop the chard. Cook the onion with the butter until soft, then turn up the heat, add the chard and walnuts and cook until the chard wilts. Remove from the heat, tip into a colander and leave to drain.

Roll out the pastry and continue in the same way as for the Chorizo and Tomato Tarts on page 498, placing a layer of the chard mixture on each tart, seasoning with salt and pepper and crumbling the goat's cheese on generously before baking.

Butternut squash, bacon and sage tarts

You can substitute eggplant or sweet potato for the butternut squash if you would prefer.

MAKES 6 to 9

2-pound butternut squash
a handful of chopped sage
   leaves
½ teaspoon chili flakes
salt and pepper

1 recipe Light Spelt Rough
   Puff Pastry (page 497)
8 ounces dry-cured bacon
1 to 2 tablespoons sunflower oil
sour cream

Heat the oven to 350°F. Bake the squash whole in its skin until tender and a knife pierces the flesh easily (45 to 60 minutes), then peel, seed and cut into ½-inch chunks. Add the sage, chili flakes and a little salt and pepper, and stir gently.

Roll out the pastry and continue in the same way as for the Chorizo and Tomato Tarts on page 498, spooning the squash mixture onto each tart before baking. Meanwhile, chop the bacon into ½-inch squares and fry in the oil until crisp. Once the tarts are baked, drizzle with sour cream and sprinkle with crispy bacon to serve.

Mozzarella, broccoli and Parma ham tarts

Be a bit stingy with the mozzarella, as it spreads over the pastry during baking.

MAKES 6 to 9

2 to 3 balls of good fresh
    mozzarella, drained
1 small head of broccoli,
    boiled until tender, then
    drained
¼ cup pesto sauce
1 recipe Light Spelt Rough
    Puff Pastry (page 497)
6 slices Parma ham
2 or 3 sprigs fresh basil

Chop the mozzarella into ½-inch chunks and drain on paper towels for 30 minutes (or preferably overnight in the fridge). Cut the broccoli into small florets and toss with the mozzarella and the pesto.

Roll out the pastry and continue in the same way as the Chorizo and Tomato Tarts on page 498, spooning the mozzarella and broccoli mixture onto each tart before baking for 20 minutes. Remove from the oven, reduce the oven temperature, lay some Parma ham on each tart and bake for another 5 to 10 minutes. Tear the fresh basil leaves and sprinkle over the tarts before serving.

Goat's cheese and celeriac tart

Go for a mild and creamy goat's cheese in this recipe, as you're trying to hit a balance with the delicate flavor of the celeriac. You don't want sharpness or acidity. Serve with a watercress salad and good cider or perry.

FOR THE PASTRY

¾ cup all-purpose flour,
    plus extra for rolling
½ cup (1 stick) ice-cold
    unsalted butter,
    cut into ½-inch cubes
½ teaspoon fine salt
about ¼ cup cold milk

FOR THE FILLING

2 eggs
¾ cup heavy cream
1 teaspoon cornstarch
1 garlic clove, finely chopped
salt and pepper
5 ounces celeriac, peeled and sliced
    into very fine strips
a handful of chopped parsley
4 ounces goat's cheese, cut into
    small chunks

To make the pastry, put the flour, butter and salt in a bowl, pour in most of the milk and mix to a soft lumpy dough without kneading, adding more of the milk to reach the required consistency. Liberally flour the work surface and roll out the dough until about 10 inches square. Fold it in by thirds (like the blanket fold, see page 14), roll again, fold again and chill for 30 minutes. Repeat this rolling, folding and chilling twice more before rolling the pastry very thinly to line a deep round 8- to 10-inch pie or tart dish, and trim it, leaving ½ inch of pastry gently folded over the edge. Heat the oven to 350°F.

To make the filling, beat the eggs, cream, cornstarch and garlic together, season with salt and a good twist of pepper, then stir in the remaining ingredients.

Spoon into the pastry shell. Bake for 25 to 35 minutes until puffed and golden.

SOFT OR CRUNCHY?

Use the celeriac raw for a crisper al dente finish, but for something more tender and almost velvety, cut broad slices of celeriac and parboil them before cutting them into fine strips to use in the filling.

Hot crust sausage rolls

Turn a package of ordinary sausages into lip-tingling marvels.

2 cups all-purpose flour,
  plus more for rolling
1 teaspoon red chili flakes
1 tablespoon paprika (not the
  hot one)
1 teaspoon fine salt
½ teaspoon baking powder
1 cup (2 sticks) ice-cold unsalted
  butter, cut into ½-inch cubes

⅔ cup cold milk
1 pound uncooked sausages,
  any sort
1 medium onion, very finely
  chopped
a handful of chopped parsley
1 beaten egg

Place the flour, chili flakes, paprika, salt, baking powder and butter in a bowl, toss the butter through, then stir in the milk to make a lumpy dough without kneading. Using lots of flour, roll the dough out to 12 inches across. Fold it in by thirds (like the blanket fold, see page 14), roll again, fold again and chill for 30 minutes. Repeat this rolling, folding and chilling twice more before rolling the pastry out to about 12 by 18 inches and cutting it into three 12-by-6-inch strips.

Heat the oven to 400°F. Strip the sausages of their casings and mix the meat with the onion and parsley. Shape the meat into three equal-sized "sticks" about 12 inches long, place one in the center of each dough strip, fold the dough around, enclosing the filling, and seal the edges with a little water. Press each roll flattish, cut to the size you want, and place seam-side down on a baking sheet lined with parchment paper. Brush with beaten egg, slash the tops and bake for 40 minutes if they're large pieces, a little less if they're small.

Gruyère, saffron and onion tart

The flavor is slightly sweet, perfect with green beans tossed in strong mustard vinaigrette.

FOR THE PASTRY
¾ cup all-purpose flour,
  plus extra for rolling
½ cup (1 stick) ice-cold
  unsalted butter,
  cut into ½-inch cubes
½ teaspoon fine salt
about ¼ cup cold milk

FOR THE FILLING
2 large onions, peeled and
  sliced
a large pinch of saffron
2 tablespoons olive oil
2 teaspoons cornstarch
½ cup milk
salt and pepper
2 eggs
3 ounces Gruyère, cut into
  small cubes

To make the pastry, put the flour, butter and salt in a bowl, pour in most of the milk and mix to a soft lumpy dough without kneading, adding more of the milk to reach the required consistency. Liberally flour the work surface and roll out the dough to about 10 inches square. The blobs of butter make rolling a bit awkward, but don't worry about it. Fold it in by thirds (like the blanket fold, see page 14), roll again, fold again and chill for 30 minutes, then repeat this rolling, folding and chilling twice more before using the pastry.

To make the filling, cook the onions and saffron in the oil in a large covered skillet for about 10 minutes until really soft. Beat in the cornstarch then the milk and bring to a boil, stirring often. Take the pan off the heat, season with salt and pepper, then beat in the eggs. Heat the oven to 400°F. Roll the pastry out thinly to line a deep round 8- to 10-inch pie or tart dish and press it snugly into the bottom and sides, leaving a bit draped over the edge. Spoon the onion mixture in, stir in the Gruyère and bake for 25 to 30 minutes until puffed and golden.

Rough puff lard crust

It's reassuring that there is still room on the supermarket shelf for a traditional product like lard. Different fats produce different characteristics in baked or fried food, and hard fat — the stuff we're meant to shun — will produce a crisper texture than any other fat. I've added some bread flour, to make the dough a little more resilient, enough to make shaping easier without sacrificing too much tenderness. But you can use more all-purpose flour if that's all you have in the cupboard; just don't be too vigorous with the rolling.

MAKES ABOUT 1¾ POUNDS

2¼ cups all-purpose flour,
    plus extra for rolling
¾ cup bread flour
1 teaspoon fine salt

4 tablespoons unsalted butter,
    softened
5¼ ounces lard, at room
    temperature
⅔ cup lukewarm water

Place both flours and the salt in a mixing bowl. Cut the butter into ½-inch pieces and rub into the flour, then cut the lard into ½-inch pieces and toss it through. Stir the water in without kneading until the dough just combines, then leave for 10 minutes.

Generously flour the work surface to stop the dough from sticking, then roll out the dough to 20 by 8 inches. Fold the dough in by thirds (like the blanket fold, see page 14), then roll out again toward the "unfolded" ends and fold in once more. Cover the dough and let it rest somewhere cool (not as cold as the fridge) for 30 minutes, then repeat the rolling, folding and resting twice more. The pastry is then ready to be used. Or freeze it, sealed in a ziplock bag, and allow to thaw completely before using.

HOW TO USE

This is a lovely flaky pastry with a pronounced savory character, so use it for meat or to give a blander filling like potato and mushroom a bit more depth.

It stays slightly pliable even after baking so needs a firmer filling, rather than one with a lot of sauce or gravy. Use it for making pasties, "one crust" pies or draped over some boneless beef chuck in a large dish, supported by a "pastry bird" or pie funnel. And when you're reheating a pie, it microwaves to a less flabby finish than shortcrust or puff pastry.

Steak, rutabaga and mustard pasties

Make them, and find out what a great British tradition is all about.

MAKES 4 OR 5

8 ounces round steak
  or skirt steak
⅔ cup peeled and diced
  rutabaga
½ cup peeled and diced potato
1 teaspoon fine salt

¾ teaspoon ground white
  or black pepper
1 tablespoon all-purpose flour,
  plus extra for rolling
1 recipe Rough Puff Lard
  Crust (page 507)
2 to 3 teaspoons freshly made
  English powdered mustard

If you have time, put the steak in the freezer until almost frozen, as it's then easier to dice evenly. Cut the meat into ½-inch cubes, place in a bowl with the rutabaga and potato (ideally whittled into small curved chunks with a blunt knife, as that's the traditional way Cornish cooks used to prepare them). Add the salt, pepper and flour, toss the filling together and chill.

Roll the pastry out until about ¼ inch thick and cut out circles, using a small plate as your guide. Lightly coat the center of each piece with the mustard and brush the edges of the pastry with water, then place a generous spoonful of filling on one half of the pastry, leaving a clean ¼-inch border. Fold the pastry over the filling and press the edges together gently to seal. Repeat with the remaining pasties, then place on a baking sheet with a slight rim, to catch any oil that runs from the pastry during cooking. Chill them while you heat the oven to 400°F and bake for 45 minutes until the pastry is a rich golden color and the filling is hot.

The hoggan

MAKES 4 OR 5

8 ounces pork shoulder, diced

⅔ cup peeled and diced turnip

½ cup peeled and diced potato

1 teaspoon fine salt

¾ teaspoon ground white or black pepper

1 tablespoon all-purpose flour, plus extra for rolling

a good handful of chopped fresh herbs, such as chives

1 recipe Rough Puff Lard Crust (page 507)

2 to 3 teaspoons freshly made English powdered mustard

Put the pork in a bowl with the turnip and potato. Add the salt, pepper and flour, toss everything together with the herbs and chill. Roll out the pastry and continue in the same way as the Steak, Rutabaga and Mustard Pasties on page 508.

Duck, carrot and shallot pasties

MAKES 4 OR 5

3 or 4 duck legs

5 to 6 medium shallots, thinly sliced

1 cup peeled and diced carrot

½ cup peeled and diced potato

1 teaspoon fine salt

¾ teaspoon ground white or black pepper

1 tablespoon all-purpose flour, plus extra for rolling

1 recipe Rough Puff Lard Crust (page 507)

Roast the duck legs at 375°F until tender, reserving the fat that drains from them, then remove the meat from the bones and chop roughly into good-sized chunks. Fry the shallots in some of the duck fat until golden, then mix with the meat and the rest of the ingredients and chill. Roll out the pastry and continue in the same way as the Steak, Rutabaga and Mustard Pasties on page 508 (without using any mustard).

Mushy pea and pork pasties

You can always purée cooked fresh or frozen peas instead of canned. A simple feast for an autumn evening.

MAKES 4

FOR THE PASTRY

2¼ cups all-purpose flour,
    plus extra for rolling
½ teaspoon baking powder
2 teaspoons powdered mustard
½ teaspoon fine salt
1 tablespoon shortening
10 tablespoons cold unsalted
    butter, cut into ½-inch cubes
⅔ cup half milk and half water

FOR THE FILLING

1 large onion, diced
1 stick celery, diced
4 tablespoons butter
1 pound pork, diced
1 tablespoon Worcestershire
    sauce
salt and pepper
1 small can peas, drained
a little milk, to finish

To make the pastry, mix the flour, baking powder, powdered mustard and salt together in a large bowl. Rub the shortening into the flour, then toss in the cold butter cubes and mix to a soft dough with the milk and water. Don't knead it but simply pat it together, cover and chill for 30 minutes. Flour the work surface and roll the pastry out to roughly 8 by 16 inches. Fold it in by thirds (like the blanket fold, see page 14), then repeat the roll and fold, and chill again. Repeat this rolling, folding and chilling twice more before using the pastry.

To make the filling, gently fry the onion and celery in the butter until soft, then add the pork and Worcestershire sauce, season generously with salt and pepper and cook for about 25 minutes till the pork is tender and the pan almost dry. Leave to cool, then stir in the peas.

Roll the pastry out to a 16-inch square, cut into quarters, then spoon the pork mixture onto the middle of each square. Fold the pastry over to form a triangle, pinching and twisting the edges for a strong seal. Place on a baking sheet lined with parchment paper, brush the tops with milk and leave to rest. Heat the oven to 350°F and bake for 35 to 45 minutes until golden.

Hot water crust

This recipe bakes to a rich brown finish, perfect for holding the filling in snugly as it cooks and sets. Both the pastry and pie are much easier to make than many recipes suggest, and I suspect that there has been some protective ramping up of the difficulty. I mean, if you let on how manageable pie making is, people might try it. Pork pie cans are easier to find in cookware shops these days, but this method gives you a more traditional look.

Hot water crust pastry, to my mind, is always made with rendered animal fat, either lard (pig fat) or dripping (beef fat). I like to add a bit of butter to the dough, but you can use all lard. As I can't think of a vegetarian filling that would suit the long cooking time, this one is strictly for the meat-eaters.

MAKES ABOUT 2¼ POUNDS

½ cup (1 stick) unsalted butter, (or extra lard)

5 cups flour (half bread and half all-purpose), plus extra for rolling

½ cup lard

¾ cup water

2 teaspoons fine salt

Rub the butter into the flour until the mixture resembles breadcrumbs. Place the lard and water in a saucepan and heat gently until the lard has melted and the mixture is hot but not boiling. Add the salt, stir until it dissolves, then pour this over the flour and mix quickly into a dough. Work it with a knife to begin with, then as soon as it is cool enough to get your hands in, knead the dough well with your fingers until it is mixed evenly and formed into a ball. Press the dough out onto a plate, cover with plastic wrap and leave until barely warm (75 to 79°F).

Lightly flour the work surface and roll the dough out to about ¼ inch thick. Fold the dough in by thirds (like the blanket fold, see page 14), then repeat this roll and fold again. I prefer to leave the dough until it is room-temperature cold (about 70°F), as I find it produces a smoother finish. If the dough looks a bit lumpy, give it another roll and fold, then let it rest somewhere cool for 20 minutes before using.

How to use

This is the classic dough for the Great British pork pie and all its relatives. Where the filling has some of the characteristics of a coarse meat pâté or terrine, it needs to be packed in a stout pastry case so that, during cooking, juices can be released and then reabsorbed without the pastry crumbling.

Ham and pork pie

The cured ham will make the filling stay pink after cooking; if you can plan ahead, the mixture is best made the evening before and kept in the refrigerator overnight. If you have a good strong homemade stock, use that for the jelly and omit the gelatin if your stock was made with a pig's head or pig's feet.

MAKES 2 PIES

FOR THE FILLING
6 ounces ham
1 teaspoon dried sage
1 teaspoon white pepper
½ teaspoon ground mace
½ teaspoon ground ginger
⅓ cup cold water
1½ pounds boneless fatty
    pork chops

1 recipe Hot Water Crust
    Pastry (page 513)
flour for rolling and shaping
1 egg, beaten with a pinch of
    salt and 1 tablespoon water

FOR THE JELLY
1 pork or ham bouillon cube
⅔ cup boiling water
⅔ cup warm water
4 teaspoons powdered
    gelatin

Put 2 ounces of the ham, chopped into small pieces, into a food processor with the sage, pepper, mace and ginger. Add the cold water and blitz this to a smooth paste, then put in a bowl with the pork chops and remaining ham, both cut into ½-inch cubes, and stir well. Chill the filling for at least four hours and preferably overnight.

Use a large clean jar about 4 inches in diameter as the mold: a 750-ml canning jar is perfect. Roll out half the pastry to about ½ inch thick and cut out a circle 10 inches in diameter, saving the trimmings to make the top crust. Stand the jar upside down, dust the bottom with flour, then lay the pastry over it evenly, so the edges drape down the sides. Now press the dough against the sides of the jar with your fingers, working it to remove any pleats from the pastry and stretching it to 3 to 4 inches in depth. Repeat with another jar and the remaining pastry.

Place both pie molds in the fridge to set. Once the pastry is slightly firm (after about 5 minutes), remove from the fridge and carefully pry the dough away from the jars with a blunt butter knife, to leave you with two pastry shells.

Pack half the filling into each pie, then roll out the pastry trimmings to make top crusts. Brush a little water around the inside rim of one pastry shell, then lay the top in place. Press it down so that it sits tightly against the filling and up to the edge of the shell. Trim away any excess but leave a ¾-inch pastry join, and pinch this together firmly with your fingers. Wrap some 4-inch-high strips of parchment paper around the middle of the pie and tie snugly with string to stop the pie bulging. Brush the lid and edge with a little beaten egg and cut a hole in the center of the lid, fingertip-width, for steam to escape. Repeat with the other pie.

Chill the pies for an hour before baking, then heat the oven to 350°F and bake on a foil-lined baking sheet for 1½ hours or until the center of the pie reaches 167°F. Let the pies cool for 30 minutes.

To make the jelly, crumble the bouillon cube into the boiling water in a pitcher and stir well. Sprinkle the powdered gelatin into the warm water, stirring until dissolved. Stir this in with the bouillon and cool slightly. Pour enough jelly to fill each pie through the hole in the top and chill overnight before eating.

For these two pie fillings, use the recipe and method given for the Ham and Pork Pie (page 514), substituting either of these fillings before filling, chilling and baking the pies and finally adding the jelly.

Ruddy pork pie filling

1 cup red wine
2 slices Canadian bacon
¾ teaspoon ground ginger
¾ teaspoon mace

¾ teaspoon pepper
¼ teaspoon fine salt
1¾ pounds pork shoulder

Simmer the red wine until it reduces to ⅓ cup then allow to cool. Purée the bacon with the wine, spices and seasoning in a blender. Dice the pork into ¾-inch cubes, mix with the bacon and seasoning, and chill overnight before finishing.

Squab, pork and herb pie filling

1 pound boned squab breast
   (or dark turkey leg meat)
5 ounces slab bacon,
   cut into lardons
¼ cup sherry
½ teaspoon fine salt
8 ounces pork shoulder,
   coarsely ground

a handful of chopped
   fresh sage
a handful of chopped
   fresh parsley
1 teaspoon ground black
   pepper
¾ cup shelled and roughly
   chopped pistachios

Chop the squab breast into small cubes and mix with the lardons, sherry, salt and minced pork shoulder. Stir in the sage, parsley, pepper and pistachios and chill overnight before finishing.

Butter suet crust

A combination of butter and suet gives you a satisfying, soft and very mellow crust, so make sure the filling puts some perky flavors in there. This can be done by including mustard, or lots of onion or black pepper, or through a more complex, aromatic mixture of wine and vegetables. The best thing about a meat filling cooked in suet crust is the way it develops a smooth but intense flavor, quite different from the result you would get if you just heated the filling in a saucepan. Be generous with the seasoning, then let the long slow cooking encourage those rich flavors.

MAKES ABOUT 1 POUND

2 cups all-purpose flour
1 teaspoon baking powder
½ teaspoon fine salt
4 tablespoons butter

3 ounces suet, grated
2½ tablespoons minced onion
½ cup water

Place the flour, baking powder and salt in a bowl and rub in the butter until it vanishes. Add the suet, onion and water and mix to a soft dough. It's ready to use straight away. The longer cooking time provided by steaming or boiling suits a savory suet pudding more than baking.

TO STEAM A PUDDING

Butter the pudding mold on the inside and place a disk of parchment paper in the bottom to stop the top of the pudding from sticking. Roll two-thirds of the pastry out until about ¼ inch thick and line the pudding mold, smoothing out any pleats before spooning in the filling. Roll the remaining pastry out to form a top crust, brush cold water around the edge of the pastry in the mold, put the top in place and press the edges together to seal.

Cut two large squares of parchment paper and one of foil, pleat them together in the center and secure them over the top of the mold with the foil on top. Tie kitchen string tightly under the rim of the mold and over the top, to hold the cover in place and form a handle. Sit this on a trivet or old saucer in a large pan, in enough warm water to come halfway up the sides of the mold, cover with a tight-fitting lid and simmer gently for 3 to 4 hours, checking once or twice to make sure it does not boil dry. To serve, lift out, drain, remove the cover and run a knife around the inside of the mold, then either serve direct from the mold or invert onto a large plate deep enough to catch the juices when you cut into it.

TO BOIL A PUDDING

Take a large double layer of cheesecloth, run it under the cold tap until soaked, then wring it out. Spread the cloth on the work surface and rub the upper surface generously with white flour. Lay out the rolled-out pastry in the center of it, spoon on the filling, then lift the cloth up by the corners, pulling the edges of the pastry together and sealing them as you do so. You may find it easier if you have one person drawing the cloth up and another sealing the edges of the pastry. Pull the cloth around the pudding with the corners together and tie them, and simmer in a pan of water for 3 hours. You may find that hanging the pudding from the handle of a sturdy wooden spoon placed across the width of the saucepan works best for you, so it is suspended in the water. To serve, lift the pudding out of the water, empty the pan and allow the pudding to drain for a minute or two before carefully unwrapping it onto a rimmed serving plate.

Guinea fowl, onion and bacon filling

4 tablespoons unsalted butter
1 medium onion, finely
   chopped
⅓ cup all-purpose flour
1 tablespoon powdered mustard
1 cup cold milk
salt and freshly ground black
   pepper

1 guinea fowl
8 ounces slab bacon,
   cut into lardons
a handful of chopped parsley
1 recipe Butter Suet Crust
   (page 518)

Melt the butter in a pan with the onion, cook until soft and translucent, then add the flour, powdered mustard and milk. Season with ¼ teaspoon fine salt and some black pepper. Whisk everything together, return to the heat and continue to whisk until the mixture is very thick and boiling. Remove from the heat and leave covered with a lid until warm.

Portion the guinea fowl (cut the breast away from the bone and divide that, and cut the wings and legs away from the carcass, dividing the thighs from the drumsticks), and add the meat to the sauce, discarding the carcass. If you don't want any bones in the filling, trim the meat off and just use that, but I think the bones add a little more flavor. Stir in the bacon and parsley, spoon the filling into the crust, then finish and cook according to your chosen method (see pages 518 to 519) and serve.

Steak, wine and shallot filling

10 shallots

4 tablespoons unsalted butter

2 small sticks of celery, finely
diced

2 small carrots, finely diced

3 garlic cloves, peeled and
crushed to a paste

⅓ cup all-purpose flour

1 tablespoon powdered mustard

1 cup red wine

salt and pepper

1½ pounds boneless beef chuck,
cut into 1¼-inch chunks

8 ounces slab bacon,
cut into lardons

1 recipe Butter Suet Crust
(page 518)

Roast the shallots at 350°F in their skins until just tender, then leave to cool and skin with a small knife, doing your best to keep the flesh intact. Melt the butter in a pan and cook the celery, carrot and garlic until beginning to soften. Stir in the flour and powdered mustard, cook a minute more, then whisk in the wine and bring to a boil. Leave to cool, then season with a generous amount of pepper and ¼ teaspoon fine salt (don't worry if it tastes a little raw at this point). Gently stir in the shallots, steak and bacon, spoon the filling into the crust, then finish and cook according to your chosen method (see pages 518 to 519) and serve.

Mutton, caper and cream filling

4 tablespoons unsalted butter

2 medium onions, finely
chopped

⅓ cup all-purpose flour

1 tablespoon powdered mustard

½ cup white vermouth, or
white wine

¾ cup heavy cream

3 bay leaves

¼ cup washed capers, drained

salt and pepper

1½ pounds shoulder of mutton
or lamb, cut into 1¼-inch
chunks

1 recipe Butter Suet Crust
(page 518)

Place the butter and onion in a saucepan and cook until soft, then mix in the flour and powdered mustard and cook until it's sizzling. Whisk in the vermouth and cream, bring to a boil stirring all the time, then remove from the heat. Stir in the bay leaves and capers and season, then leave until cool. Stir in the mutton, spoon the filling into the crust, then finish and cook according to your chosen method (see pages 518 to 519) and serve.

(see pages 518 to 519)

CHOUX PASTE

Savory choux paste

There are lots of ways you can tweak this recipe – you could add chopped ham or olives or fresh herbs to the mixture, or sprinkle with sesame or black onion seeds just before baking.

⅔ cup all-purpose flour	1 tablespoon olive oil
1 teaspoon fine salt	½ cup water
a large pinch cayenne pepper	1 tablespoon white
1 shallot or small onion,	vermouth
finely chopped	2 tablespoons unsalted
1 garlic clove, finely	butter
chopped	2 eggs

Measure the flour, salt and cayenne pepper into a small bowl and place this by the stove somewhere handy. In a saucepan, cook the shallot and garlic in the oil with a splash of the water until soft and transparent. Add the rest of the water, vermouth and butter to the pan. As soon as it boils, add the flour mixture all at once and beat briskly with a wooden spoon until the mixture comes away from the side of the pan. Remove from the heat and leave to cool for 3 to 4 minutes, then add the eggs, one at a time, beating well after each addition until the mixture is smooth, glossy and lump-free. Use while still warm.

HOW TO USE

The Sweet Choux Paste recipe (page 415) explains the details of preparing your baking sheets and piping the paste, but you can just spoon it into blobs of the desired size. In all cases, the first 20 minutes of baking should be at 400°F to make the pastry puff up. That may be all that tiny choux balls need, but larger pieces will then need more baking at a lower temperature (350°F) until dry, crisp and golden.

Little choux amuse-gueules

Translates to something between "cocktail snacks" and more literally "mouth amusers." Split and filled with a little pâté or soft cheese, they're great to have with drinks.

Beat ¼ cup grated sharp Cheddar cheese into the mixture after the eggs, then pipe or spoon small blobs, about 1½ inches high and wide, onto a foil-lined baking sheet. Bake for 20 to 25 minutes until risen and golden brown. Remove from the oven, leave to cool, then split and fill with whatever you fancy.

Soup choux

Pipe tiny pea-size blobs of choux paste onto a baking sheet lined with parchment paper and bake until golden and crisp, then leave these to cool and sprinkle them on the top of soup or salad like croutons.

Fried choux

Heat a mixture of olive and sunflower oil to about 340°F in a pot just deep enough for the choux to be submerged as they fry and not touch the bottom of the pot. Using a star or plain nozzle, pipe the choux paste into the oil in small sausages or balls, then cook until golden all over. Keep in a warm oven on a baking sheet lined with paper towels while you cook the remainder, then sprinkle with salt and pepper and serve hot with a sauce to dip them in. Also very good with cheese, olives, herbs, ham or other flavors stirred through the paste before frying.

Choux pie crusts

I first saw these in a cake shop in Turin, but now I make them as free-form pie tops. Leave Savory Choux Paste plain, or grate cheese over it; or for a dessert, use the Sweet Choux Paste recipe (page 415) and dust the top with sugar and almonds.

Butter a baking sheet and spread a thin layer of the choux paste on it, just large enough to cover the pie (or pies). Drag your finger around the edges if you want them smooth, then bake until crisp.

Choux "Yorkies"

Bake scoops of choux paste the size of a golf ball on a baking sheet lined with parchment paper until golden and crisp, then, once cold, store them in the freezer. Reheat in the oven and serve with a roast dinner or casserole in place of traditional Yorkshire puddings.

Poached choux gnocchi

Drop spoonfuls of choux paste into boiling salted water and cook until they float to the surface. Remove with a slotted spoon, toss with melted butter, grated cheese and chopped fresh herbs, then place in an ovenproof dish and bake in a hot oven until sizzling and golden.

Baked brie in choux ramekins

Butter the insides of some individual ramekins and half fill with choux paste. Bake until puffed and crisp, then remove from the oven, cut off the tops, and fill with chopped up brie or camembert. Put the tops back on, bake until the cheese melts, and serve hot.

Black olive gougères

These little puffs are usually loaded with butter and cheese but here I've used olive oil, a little Parmesan, black olives and herbs. Serve the small ones as a nibble with drinks, and the larger ones as part of a supper dish – a bit like an olive-studded Yorkshire pudding.

1½ cups pitted and drained Kalamata olives
1 garlic clove, mashed to a paste
1 tablespoon chopped fresh thyme or rosemary
¼ cup olive oil
½ teaspoon fine salt
1 teaspoon ground black pepper
½ cup water
1¼ cups bread flour
3 eggs
½ cup grated Parmesan, plus extra to finish

Quarter the olives, then mix with the garlic, thyme, oil, salt and pepper in a saucepan, add the water and bring to a boil. As soon as it's boiling fiercely, tip in the flour and beat well until it forms a lump that comes away from the sides of the pan. Remove from the heat and allow to cool slightly, then add the eggs, beating each one in well before adding the next, then beat in the Parmesan.

Line a baking sheet with foil and heat the oven to 400°F. Then either scoop small balls of the mixture (roughly the size of a large olive) onto the tray, spaced about an inch apart, sprinkle a little extra Parmesan over the tops and bake for 18 to 20 minutes until puffed and golden, or use a bigger, heaped tablespoon size, sprinkle with Parmesan and bake for 25 to 30 minutes until golden and crisp.

OVEN CRISP

You can make these ahead and then warm them in the oven before serving, but be warned, the larger ones need to be good and crisp from their first bake to avoid collapsing. Small ones should come through unharmed.

SHORT & SWEET

Pizza dough

This is the basic pizza dough I use when I want a good thin crust. I add a little more water to make the dough extra soft and easy to shape and toss, but try this wetter approach later when you've got the knack of it.

MAKES AT LEAST 5 TO 6 PIZZAS

4⅔ cups Italian "oo" flour, or bread
   flour, plus extra for shaping
1 teaspoon instant yeast
1½ teaspoons fine salt

1⅔ cups warm water
2 tablespoons olive oil,
   plus extra for kneading

Put the flour, yeast and salt in a bowl, then pour in the water and oil. Mix everything together evenly, then cover the bowl and leave for 10 minutes. Lightly oil the work surface, knead the dough on it gently for just 10 seconds (see pages 13 to 14), then return the dough to the bowl and leave for 10 minutes. Repeat the light kneading and 10-minute rest twice more, then leave the dough until risen in volume by half: about an hour. From this point on it's ready to use, but if you need to leave it more than a couple of hours, it is best left in a covered container in the refrigerator.

TO SHAPE AND BAKE

Divide the dough into pieces (5 to 7 ounces for a large pizza), shape them into balls with flour and leave to rest for 20 minutes. This shape and rest method gets the dough into a round form and lets the gluten relax before you stretch it. Meanwhile, heat the oven to 475°F, or as hot as you can get it. If you have a pizza stone, place that in the oven before you turn it on. Roll or stretch the dough out, then pat around the edge firmly to create a rim, working on a flour-dusted baking sheet (or a floured board or peel if you're planning to shovel it onto the baking stone). Be sparing with the sauce and topping, then bake for 15 to 20 minutes until sizzling on top and golden at the edges.

Slow-rise pizza dough

Reduce the yeast to about ¼ teaspoon and the water to 1½ cups and mix the dough early in the day. Leave the dough covered in a bowl for 10 to 12 hours at room temperature, giving it just one quick knead 10 minutes after mixing, then another 30 minutes before you use it.

Sourdough pizza

Reduce the flour to 4 cups and the water to 1¼ cups, and replace the yeast with 8 ounces sourdough leaven (see page 101). Give the dough just one quick knead 10 minutes after mixing. It's ready to use when your dough has risen by half, which depending on the activity in your leaven, should take 4 to 5 hours. You can also leave the dough in the refrigerator after mixing and then use it 12 to 24 hours later, but let it come back up to room temperature before you attempt to shape it.

PERSONALIZED PIZZA

The choice of pizza toppings is so wide and so personal that I've left this part entirely up to you, but I hope you enjoy making a better class of pizza with this simple homemade dough.

Occasionally, I add a teaspoon of malt extract or brown sugar, or a little beer in place of some of the water, to make my pizza color extra fast in the oven. If you have any of the liquid that mozzarella cheese sits in, this can replace water in the recipe and this really boosts the dough flavor. A little hard fat like lard rubbed into the dough (about 1 ounce to the quantity of flour used here) makes the crust extra tender. And a tablespoon of polenta or cornmeal and a dash more water added during mixing gives a good golden color and crunch to the crust.

Double-corn bacon muffins

There's such a wallop of flavors here, put together mostly from pantry bits and bobs. If you add ½ teaspoon each of chili powder and cumin, you can spice it up even more.

MAKES 12

1½ cups all-purpose flour

⅓ cup polenta or cornmeal

1 tablespoon super-fine sugar

1 tablespoon baking powder

½ teaspoon salt

3 eggs

⅓ cup low-fat plain yogurt

⅓ cup sour cream or crème fraîche

2 teaspoons Tabasco sauce

½ red onion, finely diced

⅔ cup canned corn, drained

4 ounces zucchini, coarsely grated

5 ounces bacon

½ cup (1 stick) unsalted butter

paprika to finish

Line 12 pockets of a muffin pan with paper liners and heat the oven to 400°F. In a mixing bowl, stir the flour, polenta, sugar, baking powder and salt together. In another bowl, beat the eggs, yogurt, sour cream and Tabasco together, then stir in the red onion, corn and zucchini.

Fry the bacon until crispy, cut it into ½-inch pieces, then in the same pan, melt the butter and pour this with the bacon into the egg mixture. Stir well, then fold this evenly into the dry ingredients. Spoon the mixture into the muffin cups right up to the top, as it doesn't rise that much during baking, packing it in gently with the spoon, and sprinkle with paprika. Bake for 25 minutes until puffed and golden, then remove from the pan and leave to cool on a wire rack.

Garlic butter and Cheddar scones

These turn a bowl of soup into a feast. In 45 minutes you can have a baking sheet filled with crisp buttery garlic scones, marbled with melted cheese.

MAKES 6

¾ cup all-purpose flour, plus extra for shaping

¾ cup whole-wheat or rye flour

2 teaspoons powdered mustard

¼ teaspoon cayenne pepper

2 teaspoons baking powder

½ teaspoon fine salt

1 teaspoon brown sugar

1 garlic clove, finely mashed

4 tablespoons unsalted butter, in ½-inch cubes

8 ounces Cheddar cheese, diced

1 egg

about ¼ cup low-fat plain yogurt

Heat the oven to 400°F and line a baking sheet with parchment paper. Place the dry ingredients in a bowl and add the garlic and butter (or ready-made garlic butter if you have it). Rub everything together until the butter has almost disappeared, then toss the cheese through. Beat the egg with the yogurt and stir this in to make a soft dough. Pat this out on a floured surface until about 1½ inches thick. Either cut out six circles of dough 3 to 4 inches wide or tidy the edges and cut the dough into squares. Place them a wee bit apart on the baking sheet. Bake for 20 to 25 minutes until golden on top. Leave on the baking sheet to cool slightly before eating.

Walnut and Stilton scones

If you used some Stilton cheese in place of the Cheddar and added a few chopped walnuts, they would dress this recipe up. All you'd need to add for a quick supper would be a fine pork sausage and some fried mushrooms. Or maybe some frizzy salad leaves, if you wanted to keep it healthful.

SHORT & SWEET

Pumpkin and cider farls

The cider cuts the sweetness of the pumpkin in these satisfyingly stodgy griddle cakes, good served with a poached egg and some crispy bacon.

MAKES 8

1 medium onion, finely chopped
2 tablespoons unsalted butter
1⅓ cups cooked mashed
   pumpkin
¼ cup dry hard cider
2 cups all-purpose flour,
   plus extra for shaping

3 ounces Cheddar, grated
1 teaspoon fine salt
½ teaspoon ground black
   pepper
2 teaspoons baking powder
sunflower oil

Put the onion and butter in a saucepan over low heat with the lid on for 5 minutes until it sizzles wildly. Turn the heat off and leave it to steam for another 5 minutes. Then tip the onion and juices into a bowl and mix thoroughly with everything except the sunflower oil, to form a soft dough. Divide in two, flour and roll each piece until ½ inch thick and cut into quarters.

Heat 2 tablespoons oil in a large thick-bottomed frying pan (nonstick makes it easier) until it's hot but not smoking. With a spatula, slip three or four farls into the pan, leaving enough space for you to get the spatula under them later. Keep the heat low so that it takes about 4 minutes for one side to crisp and brown, as they're thick and need time to cook. When the underside is a good brown color, scrape underneath with a spatula to release the cheesy bits and carefully flip each farl over. Fry the other side until it's crisp and golden too, then cook the remaining quarters.

WHAT'S A FARL?

It's an old Scots word meaning "a quarter." The texture of these farls has a "gnocchi" quality, and they work equally well made with cooked mashed rutabaga or carrot.

Spinach and ricotta pasties

A lovely supper dish that also makes a hearty lunchbox "smart snack" to take to work. They have a tender golden tomato crust and a filling that tastes good cold or warm.

MAKES 4

2 teaspoons instant yeast

2 teaspoons tomato paste

⅔ cup milk, scalded and cooled, plus fresh milk to finish

4 tablespoons unsalted butter, cut into cubes

2 cups bread flour

2 tablespoons grated Parmesan

1¼ teaspoons fine salt

8 ounces mushrooms (button or wild), sliced

2 garlic cloves, sliced

½ teaspoon red chili flakes

½ teaspoon dried oregano

1 tablespoon sunflower oil

8 ounces ricotta

1 egg

1 pound fresh spinach, blanched, squeezed dry and chopped

Stir the yeast and tomato paste into the scalded milk. Rub the butter into the flour, Parmesan and ½ teaspoon of the salt, then mix in the yeast mixture. Cover the bowl for 10 minutes, then knead the dough gently for just 10 seconds. Repeat this gentle kneading twice more at 10-minute intervals then leave the dough for an hour.

Fry the mushrooms, garlic, chili flakes and oregano in the oil until colored and dry, and spoon onto a plate. Beat the ricotta, egg and remaining salt together, then add the spinach and the cooked mushrooms. Divide the dough into four pieces, rolling them out into circles about 8 inches across. Pile a quarter of the filling into the center of each piece, wet the edges of the dough, fold the pastry over and squeeze and twist to seal the edges together. Place on a baking sheet lined with parchment paper and leave for 30 minutes. Heat the oven to 400°F, brush the tops with milk, cut two deep diagonal slits in the top of each pasty and bake for 35 minutes.

Buckwheat onion kugel

Top these noodle pies with a layer of sour cream and smoked salmon, or rare roast beef with fresh horseradish cream. The noodles are easy to make, but if you haven't the time, buy an 8-ounce package of buckwheat soba noodles from a supermarket or health food store.

MAKES ABOUT 12 PIECES
(enough for 4 people)

about 4 tablespoons olive oil
1¼ cups matzo meal or
   cracker crumbs
¾ cup buckwheat flour
⅔ cup bread flour, plus
   extra for rolling
Fine salt

3 eggs
a little cold water
1 large onion, finely chopped
1 garlic clove, finely chopped
⅔ cup cottage cheese
¼ cup sour cream
a handful of chopped parsley
black pepper

Prepare a 12-cup muffin pan by lightly oiling each cup and sprinkling the insides with some of the matzo meal. Put the buckwheat flour, bread flour and ¼ teaspoon salt in a bowl, beat one of the eggs and add this to the flour with enough water to mix to a firm dough. Roll the dough out as thinly as you can on a well-floured surface, then roll this up tightly into a cylinder and slice from one end, to make thin, curled-up ribbons, and leave covered on a plate.

Heat the oven to 400°F. Cook the onion and garlic with a little oil until soft and slightly browned, then spoon into a bowl and beat with the two remaining eggs, cottage cheese, sour cream and parsley, and season with salt and pepper. Bring a big pan of water to a boil, cook the noodles for 1 minute, then drain well and mix in a bowl with the beaten egg mixture. Spoon the egg and noodle mixture into the muffin pan cups, drizzle with the remaining matzo meal and olive oil, and bake for 10 to 12 minutes until golden and set.

Pigs in blankets

The hefty dose of yeast in this quick brioche-like dough keeps it working fast despite all the butter.

MAKES 8

FOR THE ENRICHED DOUGH

5 teaspoons instant yeast
½ cup warm milk
    (at about 95°F)
½ teaspoon sugar
4¼ cups bread flour,
    plus extra for rolling
10 tablespoons melted butter
6 egg yolks
1½ teaspoons fine salt

FOR THE FILLING

1-pound package of 8 pork sausages
English or Dijon mustard
1 egg, beaten with a pinch of
    salt and 1 tablespoon water,
    to finish

To make the enriched dough, stir the yeast, warm milk, sugar and ⅓ cup of the flour together and leave for 30 minutes to bubble. Beat the butter and egg yolks into the mixture until smooth, tip the remaining flour and salt into a big warm bowl and work the yeasty mixture in to form a soft dough. Leave for 30 minutes, kneading the dough for 10 seconds every 10 minutes. Then cover and chill the dough for another 30 minutes to make it smoother to roll.

To make the filling, grill the sausages and, once cooked, keep them warm. Flour the work surface and roll the dough out to about 16 by 8 inches, then cut it into eight 4-inch squares. Spread a little mustard on each square, then roll a sausage in each piece, lengthwise not diagonally, and seal it tight. Place seam-side down on a baking sheet lined with parchment paper, cover with a cloth and leave for 45 minutes or until doubled in height. Heat the oven to 400°F. Brush the porky parcels with a little beaten egg and bake for 15 to 20 minutes until puffed and golden.

Mushrooms in blankets

If you want an alternative to mushrooms, try using strips of roasted vegetables, generously piled into the squares of dough before you seal them. Leave them to rise and then bake.

14 ounces portobello or large
    wild mushrooms
a little salt and pepper
1 to 2 tablespoons oil
2 medium onions

about 1 cup soft white
    breadcrumbs
1 or 2 beaten eggs
all-purpose flour for rolling
1 recipe enriched dough
    (facing page)

Finely chop the mushrooms and cook them in a large frying pan with a little salt and oil for 10 to 15 minutes until completely dry. Spoon into a bowl with a little pepper to season, then finely chop the onions and cook these in the same way with salt and oil until translucent and very soft. Mix these with the mushrooms, then add the breadcrumbs and enough of the beaten egg to make a fritter that holds together well when a teaspoon of the mixture is test-fried in the pan (that's the best way to test the texture and flavor before baking). Add more breadcrumbs if the mixture seems too soft, and check the seasoning. Shape like sausages and fry gently, then flour the work surface and roll out the dough, and continue in the same way as the Pigs in Blankets on the facing page, leaving the little piggies to play undisturbed.

Index

Steak, wine and shallot
filling 522
bagels: Simple bagels 61
**Baked brie in choux
ramekins 525**
baking powder
in cakes 111, 112, 164
gluten-free 112
baking soda 10
in cakes 112, 164
baking sheets 362
baking911.com 297
Banana blondie 204-5
Banana bran muffins 185
Banana caramel cream pie 391
Banana fudge cookies 250
**Banana maple pecan buns
83-84**
bananas
acidic/alkaline 111
Banana blondie 204-5
Banana bran muffins 185
Banana caramel cream pie
391
Banana fudge cookies 250
Banana maple pecan buns
83-84
Butterscotch banana cake
126-27
Saucy monkey 442
baps 11
Soft white baps 60
Basic butter caramels 303-4
batters 269, 273
adding extra sweetness and
flavors 273
Beer batter for fish 285
Betsy's Scotch pancakes 279
Chestnut blinis 277
Crêpes Suzette Tour
d'Argent 280
Onion rings 285-7
pancake 271
Parsley crumpet fry-up 284
tempura 271
Walnut and berry blintzes
283
yeasted beer 271
Bay custard tarts 380
beef
"Big match" beef pies 481
Beef shank, chorizo and
pinto bean pies 489
Steak, rutabaga and mustard
pasties 508

Steak, wine and shallot
filling 522
**Beef shank, chorizo and
pinto bean pies 489**
beer
in bread making 11
Personalized pizza 530
Beer batter for fish 285
beet: Cherry beet cake 122-23
Betsy's Scotch pancakes 279
"Big match" beef pies 481
Black bread 43
black cherries, *see also* cherries
Black Forest éclairs 421
Cherry crumble cheesecake
462-64
Black Christmas cake 169
Black Forest éclairs 421
**Black millionaire's
shortbread 209**
Black olive gougères 526
Black pepper rye 44
Black Russian caramels 310
blackstrap molasses
A simple Christmas
pudding 434
Basic butter caramels 303-4
Black bread 43
Black Christmas cake 169
Black millionaire's
shortbread 209
Caramel cashew popcorn
boulders 313
Caramel Christmas cake 172
Carrot, orange and pistachio
cake 120
Cinnamon honey fruitcake
167
Crème fraîche molasses
caramels 304
Dark aniseed cake 162-63
Dark blueberry bran
muffins 188
Ginger cake 129-31
Malt vinegar rye 48
Marmalade oat bars 212
Marrakesh Express loaf cake
170
Molasses chocolate fudge
frosting 332
Plum plum pudding 436
Sesame, date and ginger
cookies 255
Sprouted grain seed bread
38

Sticky prune and orange
pudding 439
blackberries
Blueberry almond bar 210
Cinnamon cake with
blackberries 127-29
blind baking 367-68, 373
blinis: Chestnut blinis 277
blintzes: Walnut and berry
blintzes 283
blueberries
Blueberry almond bar 210
Blueberry cocoa meringue
pie 448-50
Blueberry crème fraîche
cupcakes 191
Dark blueberry bran
muffins 188
Blueberry almond bar 210
**Blueberry cocoa meringue
pie 448-50**
**Blueberry crème fraîche
cupcakes 191**
**Blue cheese and oatmeal
crackers 256**
Borrowman, Gunn 123
Bourbon pecan brownies 206
bran 30, 111, 236
Banana bran muffins 185
Dark blueberry bran
muffins 188
brandy
Apple berry almond tart 381
Apple, walnut and custard
cake 124-26
Beef shank, chorizo and
pinto bean pies 489
Brandy and walnut mince
pies with vanilla pastry
386-87
Caramel apples 302-3
Chestnut chocolate cream
cookies 231
Chocolate crumble pear tart
394-5
Chocolate truffle cubes 324
Cinnamon honey fruitcake
167
Crêpes Suzette Tour
d'Argent 280
Dark rich mincemeat 345
Fresh cake syrup 339
Hot berry butter sauce 347-49
Little prune and cognac pies
414

SHORT & SWEET

SHORT & SWEET